WILD MEN and HOLY PLACES

Daphne Brooke

WILD MEN and HOLY PLACES

St Ninian, Whithorn and the Medieval Realm of Galloway

CANONGATE PRESS

To Tom

First published in Great Britain in 1994
by Canongate Books Ltd
14 High Street, Edinburgh EH1 1TE
© Daphne Brooke 1994
Reprinted 1998

The moral right of the author has been asserted

The publisher acknowledges subsidy by the Scottish Arts Council towards
publication

The publisher gratefully acknowledges grant-assistance from the Drummond
Trust 3 Pitt Terrace, Stirling

Title page illustration: Medieval illuminated manuscript depicting the sort of
atrocity with which the Gallovidian fighting men were habitually charged by
English monastic writers.
(Courtesy of the Dean and Chapter of Lincoln Cathedral)

Typeset by Servis Filmsetting Ltd, Manchester
Printed and bound in Great Britain by
Bookcraft (Bath) Ltd

British Library Cataloguing in Publication Data
A catalogue record for this book is available on request from the British
Library

ISBN 0 86241 479 2

CONTENTS

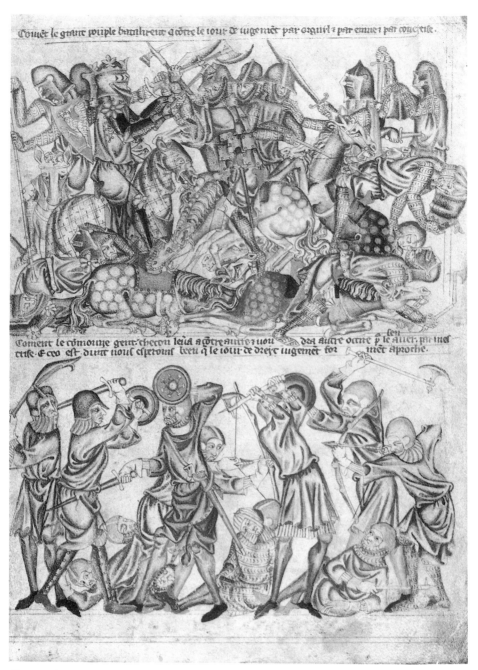

Fourteenth-century images of war: mounted knights in battle (top); archers and knights in hand-to-hand fighting with swords and battle-axes. (British Library)

ACKNOWLEDGEMENTS

Professor Geoffrey Barrow and Dr Richard Oram have read and commented on individual chapters, and Dr Peter Hill has read most of the book, and has shared unstintingly his knowledge and enthusiasm. Dave Pollock has allowed me to reproduce his elegant maps and drawings, and W F Cormack has assisted and advised me in many ways. These good friends have helped and encouraged me over years, and I am glad of this opportunity to thank them. My thanks are also due to my agent, Duncan McAra, for inspiration, much needed guidance, and steadfast concern for my interests; to Judy Moir of Canongate Press for sensitive, sympathetic editing and indispensable help; and to my children, who have all, according to their diverse talents, contributed significantly.

I acknowledge with gratitude permission to reproduce illustrations and maps from Professor Rosemary Cramp, Peter Hill, Dr John Jones, Dean of Balliol College, Oxford, Alistair Penman, Dave Pollock, Bodleian Library, Oxford (for 'The Romance of Alexander', MS. Bodl. 264. fol. 144r on the book's jacket; 'Man shearing a sheep', MS. Auct. D.2.6. f. 4r on p. 102 and for 'Man with a scythe', MS. Auct. D.2.6. f. 4v on p. 103 and MS. Rawl. D939 Section 3 on p. 105), British Library (for 'A storm at sea', Yates Thompson MS. 26. f. 26 on p. 64 and a page of the 'Lindisfarne Gospels', Cotton MS. Nero. D.IV.1. 139 on p. 66), Glasgow Museums, Burrell Collection, Dumfries & Galloway Natural History & Antiquarian Society (DGNHAS), Dumfries Museum, Dean and Chapter of Durham Cathedral, Ewart Library, Dumfries (EL), Historic Scotland, Dean and Chapter of Lincoln Cathedral, Trustees of the National Library of Scotland, Ordnance Survey, Royal Commission on the Ancient and Historic Monuments of Scotland (RCAHMS), Society of Antiquaries of Scotland, Trustees of the Royal Museum of Scotland, Wigtown and District Council Museum Service, Trinity College Library, Dublin, and University of Edinburgh Library.

Daphne Brooke
Auchencairn, 1994

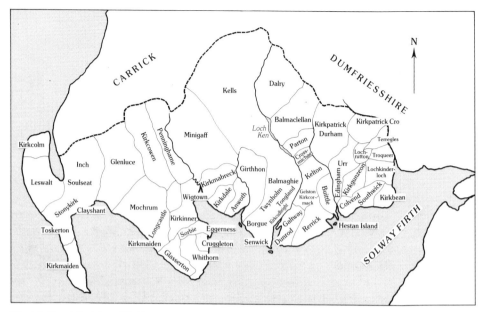

The Medieval Parishes of Galloway

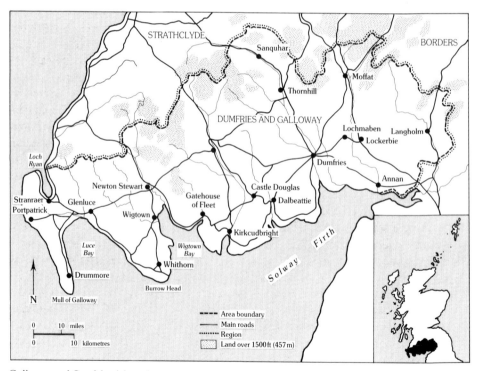

Galloway and Carrick with modern towns

PROLOGUE

Historically Galloway was known for its Christian church, more ancient than the churches of Iona or Canterbury, and for the ferocity of its people. That paradox reflected the love-hate existing between medieval Galloway and its neighbours to north and south. This story is therefore something more than a parish-pump history, for those neighbours were distinguished and formidable powers. Over the years, they included the Roman Province of Britannia, the post-Roman (British) kingdoms of the North, and the Anglian Kingdom of Northumbria. All three extended their territory into Galloway in their time. Then later, when the little Scots Kingdom of Dalriada had absorbed Pictland, and swallowed Lothian as well as the Kingdom of Strathclyde, Galloway found itself facing across an extended frontier an enlarged Kingdom of Scots, claiming overlordship. An even hungrier predator occupied the south — the Norman Kingdom of England — offering opportunities for a three-cornered diplomatic game. 'The little kid fought all night but in the morning the wolf ate him.' The night lasted nearly 400 years, and the metaphorical morning was as much feast-day as funeral.

The term Galloway, though originally more elastic, applies today to the extreme south-west of Scotland, west of the river Nith and south of the Ayrshire border. Its countryside is a system of promontories and river valleys sloping south from a rocky spine to the waters of Solway Firth. Its western peninsulas are washed by the Irish Sea. So it is encircled to the west and south by the sea, and to the north by the hills. To the east the corridors of Nithsdale and Annandale, running north and south, are slotted by Roman roads, and for centuries formed a defended boundary. Hence Galloway seemed to be set apart by its very geography to be a separate territorial entity. As such it was populated in Roman times by a tribe called the Novantae. The Novantae were Britons, Celtic people akin to the native population in the south already under Roman rule. In Galloway they were to have a long history. In the twelfth century a Scottish charter referred to them as 'Welsh'. Today the language they had spoken is sometimes called 'Cumbric'; but these terms are ambiguous. It will perhaps be least confusing consistently to call their descendants Britons and British, and their language and culture Brittonic. Over centuries their territory had been carved out of the great southern arm of the Caledonian Forest. It was the Coit Celidon of Arthurian tales, from which (it can be argued) the name Galloway derived.[1]

As territory it was desirable both economically and strategically. Only the strong could hold Galloway because acquisitive powers invariably wanted it. Its broken coastline and natural harbours had invited ships to its shores since the Bronze Age, when the trade routes between the Mediterranean and the western coasts of Britain were first developed. Galloway's centrality on the Irish Sea coasts made its people habitual sea-farers. Their destinations were not confined to the Isle of Man, Ireland, or the Scottish firths and Western Isles. They had regular commerce with Wales, Cornwall and Brittany, and even the Loire valley and Mediterranean ports.

Inland the countryside was rich. It is tempting to speak of milk and honey. Medieval food-rents were paid in cheese; and the wax from local bees lit the shrine of its holiest saint. The pastures not only fed cattle, sheep and goats, but made the country famous for horse-breeding. For home consumption the south-facing valleys produced cereals. There was timber in plenty, and an abundance of wildlife and fish. In the Middle Ages and probably before, salt was panned along the coast. Wool, hides, horses and hunting dogs, and crafted jewellery were exported; and Galloway had minerals — iron, copper, silver and a little gold. In exchange its people could afford to import wine, oil, fine glass, millefiori rods for jewellery making, and artefacts that lent prestige to the possessor.

The Roman Army reached Galloway in AD 82. The classical writer Tacitus describes how that summer the Romans crossed the river Annan and marched westward along the northern Solway coast until stopped by the western sea. From the Rhins of Galloway, where the double peninsula thrusts its hammer-head into the strait, their Commander-in-Chief Agricola, must have stood and gazed across the bright choppy water, his eyes narrowed in calculation. The hyacinth-blue outline of the shore and the floating mountains of Ireland tantalised and beckoned him. He would talk sometimes in later years of his hopes of conquering Ireland, the troops that would have been needed, and the relatively low cost of the operation. But his dream was not to be realised. His immediate duty was to subdue the land of the Novantae and order routine operations for its occupation.

These included a systematic survey of the newly acquired territory. It was to some extent on that military survey that the second-century geographer Ptolemy based part of his map of Britain. It is a rough sketch-map with the defect that the north of Britain is turned through an angle of 90 degrees. Instead of lying due west, the Rhins of Galloway stand perpendicular like an obelisk pointing due north. Once this is rectified by turning the map round, it has useful information to offer. It is the source for the name of the tribe Novantae, and shows the two native *oppida* or tribal centres — Rerigonium and Loucopibia.

The Roman occupation of southern Scotland was relatively short. By AD 200 the Romans had withdrawn their northern boundary to the line of Hadrian's Wall which they held until the early years of the fifth century. The place-names of Ptolemy's map however survived. The exact site of Rerigonion is not known, but it must have lain on the shores of Loch Ryan, that derived its name from that root, meaning 'very royal place'.[2] The *oppidum* may lie under the modern port of

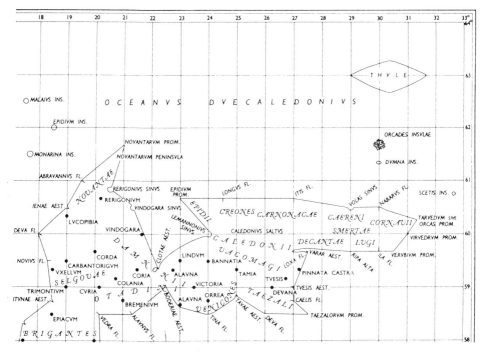

Ptolemy's map of North Britain. The peninsula of SW Scotland is pointing due north (Crown copyright, Ordnance Survey)

Stranraer, but an alternative and more likely site is Innermessan, which is now a village but was once a town with a grid of streets and a busy economic life.

The second *oppidum* of the Novantae, is marked on Ptolemy's map with the garbled name of Loucopibia. A seventh-century document — the Cosmography of Ravenna — called it Loucovia, and variants of this name suggest a Greek word 'Leukoikia' corresponding to the Latin 'Candida Casa' (meaning shining white house), the early name for Whithorn. That the Cosmographer may have had information identifying 'Loucopibia' with Candida Casa is an attractive thought, but for the present can be no more than a speculation. Alternatively the Roman fort at Glenlochar near Castle Douglas has been suggested as the site of Loucovia. It lies a short distance from the great medieval Castle of Threave, and Carlingwark Loch which the Romans may have called 'Loctrebe'.[3] After AD 200, when the northern frontier of the Roman Province was moved back to Hadrian's Wall, 'Loucopibia' was forgotten; but the prestige of Rerigonium was hazily remembered. The name was preserved in Welsh tradition as Penryn Rionyt, the Rerigonium peninsula.

A medieval Welsh Triad recalled the three thrones of Britain, which meant apparently the three centres of British power that survived the English settlement of Britain. One was Cornish, one Welsh, and one, the power centre of the Men of the North, was Penryn Rionyt. According to the Triad the ruler at Penryn

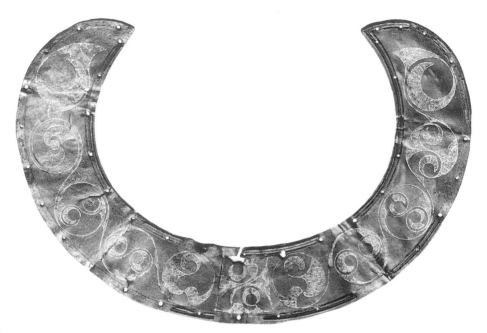

A Bronze-Age crescentic plate, an outstanding specimen of La Tène art (200–400 BC). It testifies to the wealth and culture of the British Celts in general and the Novantae in particular. Found in Balmaclellan with a mirror of the same period (Royal Scottish Museum)

A stretch of the military road at Skyreburn Glen, west of Gatehouse of Fleet. Although this road was built in the eighteenth century, it is believed to follow the course of a Roman road (Crown copyright, RCAHMS)

Aerial view of the Roman fort at Glenlochar, Castle Douglas. The military installations from Dalswinton in Dumfriesshire via Glenlochar to the fort at Gatehouse of Fleet were the chief legacy of the Roman occupation of Galloway (Crown copyright, RCAHMS)

Rionyt was the legendary Arthur, and the bishop Strathclyde's St Kentigern.[4] Kentigern was a stranger to Galloway, and his presence in the Triad marks transmission of the memory to Wales via the tenth-century Kingdom of Strathclyde. Although this tradition was imperfectly remembered, or more precisely suffered distortion in being handed down, the core of the message was authentic. For Galloway remained an enclave of Brittonic social organisation, law and language, after the kingdoms of the North in Lothian, northern England, and even Strathclyde itself, had passed away.

The name Rerigonium, 'the very royal place', still vibrates in the place-name Loch Ryan.[5] Yet a younger place-name became current in the post-Roman period,

Roman bronze patella *(skillet) discovered on the crannog in Dowalton Loch in the medieval parish of Longcastle, when the loch was drained in 1862. The* patella *was stamped with the founder's name P. Cipius Polibius. A similar* patella *with the same stamp was found at Pompeii, thus dating both to first century AD (Royal Scottish Museum)*

with an even more evocative quality. The Latin Candida Casa explicitly — proclaimed a humble and a holy place — the shining white house (or more precisely) cabin. In the seventh century the Northumbrian Angles translated it into Old English as 'aet Hwitan aerne', now Whithorn, and this has remained the name of the town. The symbolic implications of the Latin Candida Casa, radiating the light that shines in darkness, the light of Christ, ensured its use throughout the Middle Ages as applying to the bishopric, the monastery and the cathedral church.

In 1984 proposals to develop the Glebe field alongside the ruins of the medieval cathedral church of Whithorn led to a quick check on the archaeological potential

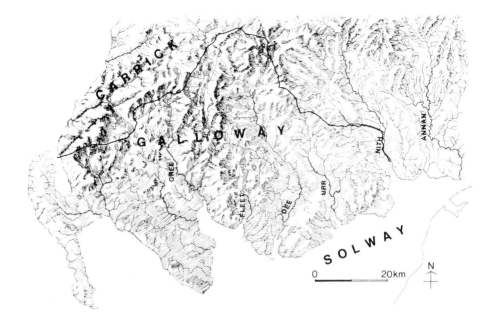

Relief and main rivers of Galloway and Carrick (Map by Dave Pollock, reproduced in PSAS)

of the site. A few trenches quickly revealed rich deposits. The development plans were found another site, and after consultation between church leaders and academics, the Whithorn Trust was set up to undertake a major archaeological excavation. The excitement of the Dig and its discoveries have brought both local people and visitors from around the world to Whithorn. In their interest and enthusiasm they want to know more about Candida Casa, and about the early Christian and medieval kingdom of Galloway, and they ask for a book. This one is a response.

Celtic dress ornament from the Longcastle crannog. (Collections of the Ayrshire and Galloway Archaeological Association, reproduced EL)

1

THE FIRST BISHOPRIC:

St Ninian of Candida Casa

I shall proceed then, to write the life of the holy man . . . during his episcopate, in spite of having been unable to ascertain all the facts . . . deeming it sufficient to record only what is outstanding. There was the reader to be considered, who might be wearied with an accumulated mass of material. But I do ask those who are intending to read, to give credence to what is said, and not to think that I have written anything not duly ascertained and tested. Rather than utter false-hoods, I would have chosen to say nothing at all.

Sulpicius Severus[1]

There stands today in a small museum in Whithorn in Wigtownshire a memor-ial stone dating from about AD 450, with the Latin inscription: 'We, Latinus aged thirty-five and his daughter aged four, praise thee, Lord. Barrovadus, a nephew [or grandson] set up this monument.'[2]

An alternative translation reads: 'We praise thee, Lord. Latinus (kinsman of Barravadus) aged 35 and his daughter aged 4, made a refuge here'. Despite the ambiguity the essential message is clear beyond doubt. 'We praise thee, Lord', proclaims the arrival of the Christian Gospel at Whithorn by the mid-fifth cen-tury. The archaeological excavation at Whithorn which began in 1984, has revealed a settlement roughly contemporaneous with the memorial to Latinus. In parallel with the archaeological evidence, literary sources name Nynia or Ninian as Bishop of Candida Casa.

Ninian's career must be viewed against the dissolution of Roman Britain and its impact on Britons living north of the limits of the Roman Empire. Before AD 410 Roman military forces had been evacuated from the Roman Province in the south. The plight of the Romanised 'citizens' of that Province, and their struggle to defend themselves and their 'romanitas' against barbarian attack is well-known. It is less often considered that the Britons to the north of the Wall (accustomed to autonomy over the preceding 200 years) proved better able to deal with the con-sequences of Roman collapse.

While the southern 'citizens' were yet paralysed with shock and fear at the departure of the Roman garrisons, the emerging British kingdoms of the North came into prominence. They had developed their political organisation in the course of a long struggle to protect their tribesfolk and territory against the Picts

The Latinus stone (Dumfries and Galloway Natural History and Antiquarian Society, reproduced EL)

from the far north and the Irish in the west. Out of the looser tribal societies of the Votadini, Selgovae, Damnonii, Novantae and (spanning the Roman Wall) the Brigantes, small states came into being ruled by princes with the support of a native military elite. Their territories lay beyond the boundaries of the Roman world; but constant Pictish attack had compelled their alliance with the Roman Province so long as it lasted. To that extent the kingdoms of the North were superficially Romanised. The 'Picts and the Scots' as later chroniclers called them, were sea-raiders as well as formidable land fighters, and had been a constant threat to the Britons north of Hadrian's Wall. The Novantae in the west had no common boundary with the Picts, but were vulnerable to raiding from the sea. Once the last of the legions had left southern Britain and it was clear that they would not return, the Picts and Irish increased their pressure, and the Britons of the north bore the brunt of the initial onslaught.

A British writer of the sixth century, looking back, expressed his countrymen's loathing and fear: 'from curroughs in which they had been carried across the valley of the sea, there eagerly emerged foul crowds of Scotti [Irish] and Picts, like dark hoards of maggots from the narrowest cracks of recesses when the sun is overhead and its rays grow warm.'[3]

The Picts from the north of the abandoned Antonine Wall, and the Irish along the western sea-lanes, launched constant assaults on the tribal *oppida* and isolated British settlements. There was merciless plundering and attacks on civilians; and the worst was the capture of young men and girls who were carried off as slaves. Patrick, a well-to-do Romano-Briton of Cumbria was a victim of just such a raid as a boy. The raiding gathered momentum into outright warfare. The Picts made deep inroads into the former Province and the Irish were eventually to seize territory in Cornwall and Wales. The terror lasted through the first half of the fifth century, by which time the Britons, impotent at first, had mobilised an effective defence. The Picts were driven back towards their traditional homelands, until their southernmost settlements lay in the basin of the Firth of Forth. The raiding gradually diminished, and there was peace. A period of exceptional prosperity followed. The most reliable chronology for these events puts the period of acutest crisis for the Britons of the north roughly between AD 450 and 455, after which they rapidly gained successive victories.[4] This deliverance was undoubtedly brought about by cooperation and effective military action, but a change of incalculable significance had meanwhile been wrought in the enemy themselves — the Picts and the Irish. They had become Christian.

The consequence was that slaving ceased. The Picts remained a formidable people, and a strong military and diplomatic force in the north; but the raids and slaving stopped. As Christians, both Picts and Irish turned much of the energy that had gone into warfare and piracy into the development of the creative skills that in both peoples amounted to genius. In the early Christian centuries their scholarship, their metalwork, sculpture and book illumination, and their religious commitment made an outstanding contribution to the culture of western Europe. This transformation by conversion to the Christian faith is traditionally ascribed to the work of two men above all others: to Patrick, missionary to the Irish; and to the bishop of Candida Casa, Nynia or Ninian, who took the Christian gospel to the southern Picts. The facts that can be established about either of these men are sparse, and the dates at which they lived controversial. Both are credited with a whole canon of miracles, but few of them compare with that metamorphosis.

MEMORIAL STONES

Tertullian, writing in the third century, referred to the 'parts of the island of Britain inaccessible to Rome, which were subject to Christ'. In other words there were Christians in districts north of Hadrian's Wall, almost certainly in the British kingdoms of the North, if not specifically in Galloway. Nevertheless the earliest datable evidence of a Christian congregation in the north is the memorial stone to Latinus and his infant daughter. This, and somewhat similar later stones at

The sixth-century Christian memorial stones at Kirkmadrine. The monument on the left commemorates the holy and distinguished priests, Ides, Viventius and Mavorius, and that on the right Florentius (Royal Scottish Museum)

Whithorn and Kirkmadrine indicate a prolonged contact between Galloway and a Christian centre in western Gaul. The formulae of these inscriptions closely resemble those of classical paganism, and so mark them as very early Christian; but the wording is distinctive and manifestly Christian in content. With one exception, nothing similar is known in Britain;[5] but counterparts are to be found between the river Loire and the Pyrenees and especially around Poitiers.[6]

LITERARY SOURCES: BEDE

The earliest surviving account of St Ninian is a brief passage by the venerable Bede.[7] It appears in the context of St Columba's conversion of the northern Picts in the sixth century. Bede describes how these people were divided from the southern Picts by steep and rugged mountain ridges, and explains that those southern Picts had 'long before, as the story goes' been converted to Christianity by the preaching of Nynia or Ninian. Ninian, says Bede, was 'a most reverend bishop and holy man of the nation of the Britons' who had been regularly trained in Rome. After converting the southern Picts, he returned to 'his episcopal see distinguished by the name and church of Martin the bishop, where he himself together with many other saints rests in the body'. The place was called in the vernacular 'at the White House' because 'he there built a church of stone in a manner to which the Britons were not accustomed'.

Bede implied that Ninian, in contrast to Columba, was trained in Catholic orthodoxy at the very source, in Rome itself, and that he was free from any Celtic 'deviations' such as existed in Bede's time in Wales, parts of Ireland, and in Iona. With characteristic respect for accuracy in matters of chronology, he would not set a date on Ninian's episcopate. All he would say was that it was said to take place 'long before' St Columba had founded his monastery on Iona, AD 565.

THE 'MIRACULA' AND THE 'LIFE OF ST NINIAN'

Apart from Bede's terse passage, the main literary sources relating to St Ninian and the church of Candida Casa consist of a Latin poem written by a monk in the eighth-century monastery of Whithorn: 'Miracula Nynie Episcopi' (the 'Miracles of Nynia the Bishop'),[8] and a prose Life of St Ninian by Ailred of Rievaulx.[9] The 'Life' was written a few years before 1167, by the abbot of Rievaulx Abbey in Yorkshire. He visited Galloway several times, and took a keen interest in its affairs.

Both sources have their value. The 'Miracula' has some good stories, and gives an attractive picture of the Northumbrian monastery at Whithorn in the writer's own time. Ailred's 'Life' claims to have drawn upon an old book in a barbarous tongue, and it can be shown to contain genuinely archaic material. It has been suggested that the old book was a prose Life written in Old English, which in turn drew upon an earlier Latin Life from a British milieu.[10]

Three hundred years separated St Ninian from Bede, the earliest of these writers. All three would have appeared to Ninian himself as aliens, potentially hostile to his people and culture. Bede was a Northumbrian Angle whose forbears had destroyed the kingdoms of the North, and so probably was the writer of the 'Miracula'. Ailred, many generations later, was of Northumbrian descent, although in education and sympathies he was a Normanised Englishman. These men inevitably wrote with the limited knowledge and prejudices of their own time. Bede's view of Ninian was coloured by the controversies of his own day, that championed Roman orthodoxy in the computation of Easter and the shaping of the tonsure against the irregularities of Iona. Hence he emphasised Ninian's training in Rome, and episcopal rank to Columba's disadvantage. Despite Bede's manifest integrity as a historian, this bias has caused modern scholars to question the trustworthiness of his account.

Both the other literary sources echo Bede's statement, starting with Ninian's journey to Rome, but they present the matter more pictorially. The 'Miracula' tells how:

> the holy man came to the shore of the wave-wandering sea and went aboard a ship with [a] broad hull. The sails, filled out by eager breezes, flew on, until the rough timbers completed the journey and the bark quit the sea and fastened its prow in the yellow sands. Then on foot he crossed the Alps.[11]

The 'Miracula' follows Ninian's return to his native land with the mission to the Picts. Ailred puts this later. Ailred also describes Ninian crossing the Alps on the way to Rome, and says on the return journey he visited St Martin at Tours. It is possible that Ninian's ship entered the Loire estuary on its outward journey, and took him some way up river, possibly even as far as Tours, and the return was made the same way. After a short stay with St Martin, says Ailred, Ninian left for home, taking with him a team of stone-masons supplied by St Martin, in order to build his church.

Apart from the visit to Tours, Ailred contributes two facts unique to his account. One appears in a miracle story in which Ninian is pictured making a journey with Plebia, 'one of his brethren'. While resting by the wayside Ninian pulls out a psalter and begins to read a psalm. Rain starts to fall. It wets everything, but leaves Ninian and his book untouched — until momentarily Ninian raises his eyes from the book, distracted by 'an unlawful thought'. 'Soon the rain, falling on the book revealed his secret'. Then Plebia recognised what was happening and gently reproached Ninian — 'reminded him of his Order and his age, and showed him how unbecoming such behaviour was' — and Ninian, blushing, 'put aside the thought and stopped the rain'.[12]

The name Plebia seems to be a latinisation of the Welsh Peibio who appears in Welsh medieval genealogy with Nyniau in the relation of nephew and uncle.[13] Plebia's existence was recorded in sources reaching back ultimately to British oral tradition, and reference to him vindicates the antiquity of the sources behind Ailred's ancient book. Here it seems, contact is being made with sources that predated Bede. Ailred's other contribution, which no other document offers, is a date. By relating that Ninian's church at Whithorn was in the process of being built when the news came of Martin's death, Ailred proposed the only available date for Ninian's episcopate. St Martin died in AD 397.

ST MARTIN

The 'Life of St Martin' was circulating very soon after St Martin's death. It is a splendidly readable account, written by Sulpicius Severus, a friend and disciple of his. In the urbane and polished milieu of the Roman church in Gaul, Martin was conspicuous as an eccentric and an innovator. His vision of the Christian life was both literal and austere. He was a Christian, and while serving as an officer in the Roman army, he came to see this commitment as compelling him to declare himself a pacifist. After a period of imprisonment, he left the army and spent some time with St Hilary at Poitiers, where he was ordained priest. Before long he was made bishop of Tours by popular acclaim. His fellow bishops looked askance at his asceticism and complained that his 'insignificant appearance, his sordid garment, and disgraceful hair' made him unfit for office. He nevertheless became exceptionally popular with the people of Tours.

Martin introduced into Gaul the ascetic monasticism of the Middle East and founded communities in Ligugé a few miles from Poitiers, and Marmoutier just outside Tours. His second most striking innovation was evangelising the countryside. Roman bishops had hitherto confined their pastoral care to the cities. Martin travelled over the countryside of Touraine, intent upon spreading the Gospel. His methods were drastic and direct. Wherever he found a pagan shrine, he destroyed it and built a church — his preaching and the physical courage he often showed in facing hostile crowds, won him adherents. This mission to the country folk would alone commend itself to Bishop Ninian. The population of most of his own diocese, and of his mission field in Pictish territory, were essentially rural, tribal societies, a pattern of villages and homesteads set among great tracts of forest.

It has been objected that Ninian's church would not have been dedicated as early as the fifth century to St Martin, or anybody other than a Gospel saint or a martyr; and that it is unheard of for a diocese to be dedicated to anyone.[14] That objection was based on misunderstanding. There was a difference between formal dedication (which involved an official church ceremony) and the growth of a local speech-habit calling the church 'St Martin's', perhaps because it possessed a copy of his 'Life' and possibly a relic, and did Martin special honour in its services. A similar place-name applied both to the church and diocese of St David's in Wales. A later Irish tradition called the monastery of Candida Casa 'Tig Mhartain' (Martin's House).[15]

The commemoration of St Martin has often been ascribed to a later date. But the similarity of the fifth-century memorial stones at Whithorn and those in south-western Gaul supports an early commemoration of St Martin at Candida Casa, and points to a further possibility. That is, that Ninian's church stood for

Christian memorial stone from Civaux, now in the Baptistery at Poitiers. It commemorates Aeternalis and Servilla, 'may they live in God'. The style of lettering, the use of the Chi-Rho and Alpha and Omega symbols, and the prayer (which is Christian but still not stereotyped) are reflected in the Latinus stone and those at Kirkmadrine (by courtesy of Professor Rosemary Cramp)

the innovations that had made St Martin famous — a monastic lifestyle based on solitary contemplation and prayer, and missionary outreach among pagan peoples.

THE EXCAVATION 1984–93

Several attempts to increase current knowledge of the church and bishopric of St Ninian have been made by archaeologists. The Marquess of Bute conducted an excavation in the 1880s as did Dr Raleigh Radford in 1949. Radford's discovery of a small white-plastered building near the ruins of the cathedral church caused excitement at the time, and it was hailed as the veritable white church. There was however, no secure dating evidence and the identification was treated with caution. The recent Dig has been by far the most extensive and has yielded fuller information than ever before. The site — the Glebe field — lies on the south side of a low gently rounded hill crowned by the cathedral. This hillock lies on the eastern edge of a poorly drained plateau overlooked by higher ground to east, west and south. The area is drained by the Ket burn which now flows round the site in an artificial channel. It is a sheltered spot, hidden from the natural harbour only three miles away at the Isle of Whithorn. To that extent it was protected in the early Christian period from seaborne attack.

By 1991 digging reached a depth dating from the fifth to the seventh centuries, that is immediately after the withdrawal of the Roman legions from the Province south of Hadrian's Wall. The layman's first reaction to what was revealed at the earliest level must have been disappointment. For there was nothing there! No gleaming white church, no convenient inscription, no obvious shrine. Nothing but a multitude of empty holes where wooden stakes had rotted away, curved gulleys where water had drained away, and a highly miscellaneous assortment of rubbish. To the archaeologist the prospect was less unpromising, but it took a year before the preliminary analysis was complete, and longer before the full significance became clear.

It was not until 1993, after digging in the Glebe field had been completed and a season's work had been done on higher ground, that it became possible to discern a double circular enclosure embracing both the Glebe field and the crown of the hill where the ruins of the medieval priory now stand. There was no embankment often associated with early Celtic monastic sites, but the double enclosure was there, and its circles continued to affect the planning of the site for over 1,000 years. Other features and finds had already convinced the archaeologists that they had found an early monastery, and that a monastic community had continued on the site until the Reformation, but here was the final corroborative evidence. It could only be identified once the digging was done, and it was possible to stand back and review the shape and limits of the settlement as a whole.[16]

The earliest feature found in the Glebe field was a metalled road over bedrock, which had been quarried to create a relatively level surface. It runs across the site to the top of the hill, pointing like a finger to some important feature at the summit. The edges of the road had been encroached on by ploughing. A mouldboard plough had been used, protected from erosion by quartz and granite pebbles inserted into the wooden sole. The stakeholes and curvilinear drainage gullies marked a series of small rectilinear stake-walled structures, some of which had bowed sides. All these will have been roofed with thatch.

There was of course, a burial ground, although after so long all human remains have disintegrated, apart from traces of tooth enamel. Graves were found, set among stone flagging with gulleys and post-holes recording a formal lay-out, and possibly the entrances to an enclosure. Three of the earliest graves contained large coffins constructed from split tree-trunks. They will have taken considerable effort to make, and suggest the burial of people of importance. A few such burials have been discovered in northern England and Ireland, but always in a Christian graveyard.

On the northern ridge of bedrock a bank of rubble had been revetted with a wattle fence. The rubble included builders' rubbish, apparently from a nearby building-site. There were lumps of grey lime, sometimes with an incomplete crust

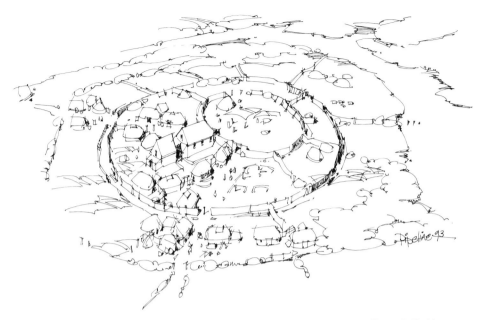

Reconstruction drawing of the Christian settlement at Whithorn around AD 600 (Dave Pollock)

of white calcium carbonate. The lime probably derived from carboniferous lime-stone, burnt and then pulverised and slaked. The calcium carbonate crust would have formed if piles of the unmixed lime had been exposed to the carbon dioxide in the atmosphere. A stone building rendered with this material would acquire a surface that was brilliant white after rain, and dull white in dry weather.

The debris on site also contained many fragments of fine glass, the shattered remains of cone beakers.[17] They evoke the words of the bard Aneirin, recalling the dead northern warriors who 'drank sparkling wine out of glass vessels'.[18] These were post-Roman memories. Commercial contacts with Mediterranean markets in the fifth and following centuries are however indicated by shards of amphorae, used for carrying oil and wine, suggesting a relatively wealthy, sophisticated society.

The insubstantial stake-buildings do not seem to belong to the same world, until their purpose is better understood. They appear to have no parallels in the district, though it must be said that excavations have been few. A Dig at Rispain Camp, some 1.5 km away revealed substantially built roundhouses of perhaps AD 200, with large floor areas exceeding 140 m.[19] The Whithorn buildings are no more than a tenth of this size, and are more comparable with later structures on Irish ecclesiastical and secular sites. An apt word for such houses might well be 'cab-ins'. Not only are the building methods at Whithorn distinctive, but materials have been used on the site, such as the limestone, which are only available north of Solway, 20 miles to the east in the parish of Rerrick, and will have had to be transported by sea.

The quartz and granite pebbles used with the plough were local, but no other site is known in Galloway where they were used for that purpose at this time, although similar plough pebbles have been found in various parts of Europe including Denmark, the Auvergne, the Loire valley, and eastern Ireland. Another innovation appeared in the broken sections of a sandstone mill-stone from a water-mill, probably originally driven by the Ket burn. Once more the material was imported, and the technology, though accessible in the Roman world, was apparently new to the locality.

A pile of haematite was found on the site beside one of the buildings. This is another material that had to be brought in — possibly from the same place as the limestone. Haematite can be used as a pigment, but here it was obviously smelted for iron. There was slag in quantity scattered over the site, the debris of large smelting furnaces, close in construction to Roman models.

By now it is becoming clear that a new monastic settlement had been established in the fifth century consisting of poor, flimsy dwellings, yet employing technologies hitherto unknown in the district. These included, of course, the craft of the masons who inscribed the Christian memorial stones. The imported skills, and the likeness of the memorial stones to models in south-western Gaul, combine with the stories of contact between the bishopric of Candida Casa and the bishopric of Tours to convey a remarkably consistent message.

A MONASTIC COLONY

The apparently simultaneous importation of new technologies and a manifestly Christian milieu with affinities in south-western Gaul, call to mind the commemoration of St Martin at Candida Casa on which the literary sources are unanimous. The character of the buildings on the site — a series of very small, flimsy cabins — is reminiscent of St Martin's community at Marmoutier beside the river Loire, as described by Sulpicius:

> . . . he [Martin] made himself a hermitage about two miles from the city. The place was so secluded and remote that it had all the solitude of the desert. On one side it was walled in by the rock-face of a high mountain, and the level ground that remained was enclosed by a gentle bend of the river Loire . . . His own cell was built of wood, as were those of many of his brethren; but many of them hollowed out shelters for themselves in the rock of the over-hanging mountain.[20]

How Martin's cell was constructed is not clear but the stake-houses at Whithorn were also timber-built. A group of Martin's monks forming the nucleus of a new community at Whithorn, could be visualised as taking with them skilled artisans, either among their number or as lay-brothers or employees. The literary sources support the importation of new technologies, to the extent that Ailred spoke of Ninian's taking home from Marmoutier a team of masons to build his church, and Bede referred to its construction as one with which the Britons were unfamiliar. Touraine is limestone country and industrial processes using lime-stone, both in the surfacing of buildings and as a flux for smelting might be ex-pected to develop there. Mouldboard ploughs and plough pebbles are known to have been used in the Loire valley possibly at the same time as the Whithorn ones.

The huts by the Loire by no means represented the summit of native building skills in Roman Gaul. On the contrary the poorest of peasant hovels were simu-lated in-pursuit of austerity. Northern winters would have rendered their habita-tion even more ascetic. Neither at Marmoutier nor Whithorn did these cabins represent places of retreat from more solidly built monasteries elsewhere. Sulpicius intended his readers to understand that Martin and his brethren at Marmoutier lived in their tiny huts and caves the year round, leading the life of solitaries, sharing meals and resources, but meeting only at church services. They undertook no buying and selling like the hermits of the Egyptian desert who made baskets to sell and support themselves. At Marmoutier the monks bound them-selves not to practise any craft except that of copyist, and that was left to the younger ones, so as to free their seniors for prayer. Martin lived among them, but he was by no means a recluse. Sulpicius makes it clear that Martin's understanding of a bishop's duties might not have been conventional, but he performed the litur-gical functions, and added the work of the healer and missionary. His whole com-munity must have reflected these concerns, so that from the first his brand of monasticism was less introverted than that of the East.

The mid-twentieth-century controversy whether Ninian conformed to the norm of a post-Roman bishop, or whether he founded a monastic community, was based therefore on a false antithesis.[21] For it contrasted the urban diocesan Roman bishop with the head of a monastery in the sense in which the word applied to the great communities of sixth-century Ireland or Iona. The significance of the early commemoration of St Martin at Whithorn was deliberately left out of account, on the assumption that this 'dedication' must have been of later date. But Martin of Tours was both a Roman bishop and a practising monastic, and the archaeolog-ical evidence now forcefully suggests that Ninian's Candida Casa was not merely a monastery, inspired by the example of Martin of Tours, but could have been a cell, or daughter-colony of Marmoutier or Ligugé.

The site in the Glebe field at Whithorn focuses attention on the living quarters, the sources of food production, and the workshops of Candida Casa's eremitic community. There was no sign of the stone church Bede speaks of; but if it was built at the top of the hill, under the present ruins of the medieval cathedral, the 'shining white' building rubbish buried in the revetted bank may be evidence of its construction.

This busy industrial site uncovered by excavation contrasts sharply with condi-tions described at Marmoutier. At first it seems to make nonsense of the idea that the one could be a daughter village of the other. But after a little reflection it begins to make sense. The monks of Marmoutier lived on the outskirts of the Roman city of Tours. Their place of worship was the cathedral in the city, the sources of their frugal diet were in its market and the open hands of well-wishers — they could abstain from work and make prayer their life's occupation. But on the virgin site at Whithorn, chosen probably for its relative isolation, a church had to be built, land had to be ploughed, cereals had to be grown, and a mill provided to grind flour for their daily bread. Graves had to be dug, and a burial ground laid out. The iron smelting may have begun for the manufacture of the new plough, and possibly for finer ironwork within the church.

Self-sufficiency was forced on the new community. In consequence it had apparently employed a work-force under the supervision and training of Gaulish artisans. The variety and sophistication of the industries developed on the site, which may have included glass-working, indicates that the community developed in reaction to the different conditions, along lines contrary to the principles of Marmoutier. Alternatively the settlement may have attracted skilled men from south-western Gaul as a refuge from the disturbed conditions on the Continent at the time.

What induced the Gaulish colony to settle in Galloway? Given that they may have been in some measure political refugees, did the undeveloped country north of Solway, a heavily forested area opened only by one dilapidated Roman road, attract them as offering a 'desert' as veritable as the sands of the Sahara? Perhaps. But while satisfying the criteria of a desert in their eyes, the place was less remote than the immediate environs suggested. It had the advantages of being central to the western sea-lanes, and accessible both to Ireland and North Britain.

Their chosen site may have been uninhabited ground, but the surrounding district will not have been unpopulated. The inscription on the Latinus stone implies a Christian congregation already in existence, and according to the literary sources, Ninian's purpose included building a church with the skill of Gaulish stone-masons. The colony must have come with a missionary purpose among others. It would be difficult to visualise a responsible bishop with a wide rural diocese to care for, inviting in a community of monks who were intent only upon saving their own souls. Some involvement on their part in the needs and purposes of local Christians, or in a wider perspective in the service of the universal church would surely have motivated the settlement. Had the incomers' sole objective been to find a 'desert' they had a host of desert places to choose from. A wider and more specific purpose must have brought them to Whithorn.

ORTHODOXY

That purpose can only be suggested as a speculation. Events in the Western church of the time highlight the anxiety of the Christian communities of Gaul to combat heresy among their fellow-Christians in Britain and Ireland. The Western church suffered a severe crisis throughout the fifth century in the rapid spread of the heretical teaching of a Briton by the name of Pelagius. His critics attributed to him belief in salvation by good works alone, without the intervention of divine grace. Pelagius left Britain and lived for years in Rome; and won many adherents on the Continent. But he had already won over many of the faithful in Britain,

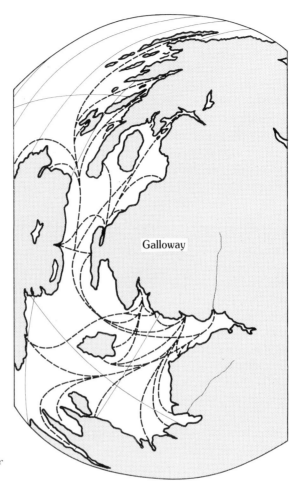

The Irish Sea provinces, showing ancient trade routes and the centrality of Galloway (Scottish Society of Northern Studies)

and probably the Christian minority in Ireland. By AD 429 Bishop Germanus was sent to Britain from Auxerre to combat the heresy, and in the course of his visit became involved in military operations against the Picts. He made a second visit in 434–35, indicating that the first had not eradicated Pelagianism. Meanwhile Pope Celestine had sent Bishop Palladius to Ireland, where he seems to have concentrated his work in the south. Churches founded under the influence of St Patrick were evidently confined to the north.[22]

To judge by the dating of the Latinus stone (*c.* AD 450) the planning and settlement of the colony at Candida Casa must have come within the period of active opposition to Pelagianism. Supposing — and it can be no more than a supposition — that the heresy had reached the Romano-British churches around Carlisle and possibly the young Christian congregations of northern Ireland, the colony at Candida Casa would have been admirably placed for the dissemination of orthodox doctrine. For all his eccentricities, St Martin's orthodoxy had never been doubted, and his teacher St Hilary of Arles had been a prominent champion of orthodoxy against an earlier heresy, Arianism. That tradition will have been preserved at St Martin's communities after his death, and concern for orthodoxy in Britain appears to have been widespread among the churches of Gaul.

Irish sources, often unsatisfactory as single references, are sufficiently numerous to be relied on for their testimony to a monastery at Whithorn by the sixth and seventh centuries, when it had become a training centre for both laiety and priests.[23] Had that originally been its *raison d'être* — to train young ordinands in orthodox theology as an antidote to the spreading Pelagianism? The copying of manuscripts by the younger monks at Marmoutier is evidence of a developing seat of learning there, and something they would have been likely to take with them to Candida Casa. Bede represented Ninian as trained at the very seat of orthodoxy. It has often been assumed that this was Bede's own interpolation dictated by the needs of his own time. It could however have reflected a genuine memory of the founding of Candida Casa to be a northern centre of orthodox Christian learning.

The 'Miracula' and the 'Life' tell of a miracle by which Ninian cleared the good name of one of his priests who had been accused of fathering a child. Within a few hours of birth, the baby was able to speak and identify its true father. Another miracle came out of Ninian's persecution by a certain King Tudwal. The bishop left Tudwal's country, and disaster followed. The crops failed, and the king went blind. Ninian was begged to return. He did so and restored the king's sight. These tales record hazy memories in parable form. Friction between Ninian's clergy and local people might well be explained by Ninian's introduction of a foreign monastic colony. It has been suggested that the original difference between the king and the bishop was doctrinal. Had Ninian denounced Pelagian theology to a spiritually blind heretic?

Tudwal was a Brittonic name and more than one King Tudwal can be traced in ancient Welsh tradition. One, whose date might be placed in the fifth century was associated with the lands of Manau. That could have meant either the Isle of Man or the district of Manau Gododdin, stretching along the southern shore of the Forth between Edinburgh and Linlithgow.

A strongly urged case has been made to identify Tudwal with the Isle of Man;[24] but the alternative is worth consideration. At some time towards the mid-fifth century Manau Gododdin was occupied by the Picts; and as will appear later, became part of Ninian's mission field. The most vivid feature of the Tudwal story in the Miracula is the anguished appeal for help sent by the blinded king to St Ninian. It does not do to build too much on such flimsy evidence, but it is true that the Britons of Manau Gododdin and adjacent territories suffered the double disaster of Pictish invasion and famine in the mid-fifth century, which calls to mind how in the miracle story, the crops failed. Could it have been an appeal from Tudwal that decided Ninian to seek out and preach the Gospel to the southern Picts, so as to restrain their atrocities and enslavement of young Britons? It would not have been wholly altruistic. The Pictish attack on the Britons of Lothian and northern England threatened almost equally the Britons of Galloway.

These speculations highlight the need to define the approximate date of Ninian's episcopate. The excavation evidence is imprecise and will need further analysis before archaeology can help the struggling historian. For the present, every writer about St Ninian and Candida Casa must have the courage to define his or her own chronology and risk being wrong.[25] The sources offer several dates. Ailred put the building of Ninian's church around AD 397. Bede said Ninian's mission to the Picts was long before Columba's (soon after AD 565). Something like a consensus of archaeologists date the Latinus stone at approximately AD 450. The coincidence of the rough dating of the Latinus stone and the approximate date now entertained for the British victory over the Picts seem, in the absence of new evidence, to put Ninian's career as bishop most logically in the latter half of the fifth century.

The Latinus stone can be taken as marking the early maturity of the colony at Candida Casa; and a bishop who has made such an impact on posterity may be assumed to have had a fairly long working life. Nevertheless it is out of the question that Ninian could have been an adult in St Martin's time, and Ailred's date of 397 must (reluctantly) be abandoned. The meeting between the two bishops must be seen as a literary convention, but by no means invalidates an intimate and prolonged contact between Whithorn and Martin's monastic communities after Martin's death. Finally, it leaves room for the full development of Candida Casa as a scholastic and industrial centre at a somewhat later date, around 500, and presupposes the continuation of strong leadership there.

THE CONVERSION OF THE SOUTHERN PICTS

Bede is the main authority for Ninian's mission to the southern Picts. The 'Miracula' and the 'Life' use more words without being more informative. Several generations of historians have doubted its authenticity, or have said the mission failed because it left no trace. It is now possible to see beyond this negativity. Some scattered and enigmatic fragments of evidence survive in Welsh tradition and folklore, where much north British material has been preserved. They are too cryptic to make instant sense; and so long as it was assumed that the Picts of Ninian's time were to be found north of the Forth-Clyde line, any attempt to trace St Ninian's footsteps was astray. The sixth-century writer Gildas said the Picts were south of that line but he was disregarded as an ignoramus. It has taken the work of a number of distinguished scholars, all pursuing their own wider objectives over the past twenty years, to change the signposts and redirect the enquirer.

The first change was brought about in the 1970s by an eminent English place-name scholar, who was not looking for the Picts at all, but set out to explain the meaning of the English place-name 'Eccles' and its compounds.[26] He gave the derivation of Eccles as the Latin word *ecclesia* (church), and pointed out that it would have been current only before a word for church had evolved in the native languages: *llan* (Welsh), *circe* (Old English), and *cille* (Gaelic). He concluded that the Eccles place-names indicated very early Christian sites. Similar place-names in Scotland were reviewed in 1983, and a significant grouping of 'Eccles-' compounds where the first element was followed by a saint's name were identified in the Forth basin, centering particularly on the simplex Eccles, the medieval name for Kirkton of Stirling. The compounds, slightly later foundations, spread out from the original mother-church.

The proximity of Eccles to the stronghold of Stirling was immediately seen as having special significance. For the church of Kirkton has been known since the Middle Ages to commemorate St Ninian. Kirkton lies one and a half miles (two kilometres) from Stirling Castle, a late building on a very ancient site. It has been pointed out that if a Pictish king had given the site for a church, or permission to consecrate a burial ground at Eccles, its distance from the stronghold on Stirling Rock suggested a cautious acceptance of the new religion.[27] Given the possibility of a genuinely ancient commemoration to St Ninian here, authentic evidence of Ninian's mission to the Picts is at last in sight.

The great popularity of St Ninian's cult in the later medieval church caused numerous parish churches, chapels and altars to be dedicated to him, so that without good signs of a genuinely early association with St Ninian on any given site it is unsafe to assume any dedication to St Ninian is earlier than the twelfth century. At Kirkton however, the medieval documentation shows that the chapel in Stirling Castle was dedicated at the command of King Alexander I (1107–24). There was little likelihood of contact between Stirling and Whithorn at that time, for they lay in separate and potentially hostile kingdoms. Alexander's choice of patron saint suggests therefore that St Ninian was already honoured locally — presumably at Kirkton — and that the commemoration there was very old indeed.[28]

The search for St Ninian among the Picts was advanced further in the 1980s when a group of Cambridge scholars re-evaluated the sixth-century writings of Gildas, especially as they related to events in the north. According to Gildas the Picts had overrun territories to the south of the Forth-Clyde line, and after years of intrusion on these lands, were (by the first half of the fifth century) retreating slowly northward. Whether or not in response to an appeal from King Tudwal, it was around the headwaters of the Forth that Ninian found them. They were in retreat and on the defensive, but still managing to hold the Forth basin. Their chief still had his headquarters at the strategic strongpoint of Stirling, and they apparently held other defensible points along the erstwhile Antonine Wall.

If Ninian's mission was to succeed, the conversion of that chief had to come first, and mass conversion of the people could then be expected to follow. The psychological moment had come, when the Picts were confronting the realities of defeat, and could be brought to face the inadequacy of their own gods. Then the Christian Gospel could be offered as holding out new hope and new preoccupations. An enemy both defeated and Christianised would be doubly disarmed.

A JIGSAW

It is at this point that anything like an ordered narrative breaks down. We are confronted with a ragbag of clues and tall stories which nevertheless promise that if they can be somehow put into the right order, truth may be found. An eighteenth-century estate plan, three or four place-names, an allusion to an ancient joke, a tale of two bulls pulling a hearse, and a taradiddle about a gigantic bone and a resurrected robber chief — these are the materials. As a collection they have a surrealist, dream-like quality. Yet once they can be related to one another, each clicks into place as neatly as a jigsaw-piece, and suddenly there is a picture.

CATHURES

The most coherent fragment is a story about a burial ground consecrated by St Ninian at a place called 'Cathures'. It occurs in a twelfth-century 'Life of St Kentigern', the patron saint of Glasgow, written by Jocelin of Furness around 1180.[29] Jocelin says 'Cathures' meant Glasgow, but that seems to have been a gloss interpolated into an older story that Jocelin claimed was his source. The place-name may have been corrupted but it corresponds closely to the Brittonic word for fort — 'cader'. Cadder is now a district of Glasgow on the Antonine Wall. There was already an ancient mother church there when Jocelin was writing; and he implies that a rudimentary religious community existed in St Kentigern's time. Kentigern died in 612.

Jocelin tells of Kentigern's chance encounter with an elderly holy man, Fregus, whom Kentigern finds on the point of death. He dies, and it is Kentigern's clear duty to bury him. So he places the body on a wain and harnesses to it two bulls. The Latin word used to describe the bulls is 'indomitos', meaning unmastered, or unbroken. (Bulls would scarcely be docile draught animals, and in attempting to use them as such Kentigern is demonstrating his powers as a wonder-worker). He orders them:

> to carry the burden . . . to the place the Lord had provided for it. And in truth the bulls, in no way restive or in anything disobeying the voice of Kentigern, without tripping or fall, came by a straight route where there was no track, as far as Cathures which is now called Glasgu, along with Kentigern and very many others accompanying [him], and then with all gentleness they halted near a certain cemetery which had long before been consecrated by St Ninian. [A long biblical allusion follows, then Kentigern buries Fregus] 'in the cemetery in which no man had lain. This was the first body to be buried in that place where afterwards very many were buried in peace'.[30]

Jocelin is claiming that after being consecrated by St Ninian the burial ground had lain unused for more than a century, until Kentigern came along and discovered it — a singularly unlikely tale. So as to present St Kentigern as founder of the church of Glasgow, Jocelin filched two bulls and a cart from Muirchu's *Life of St*

Patrick, and pressed into service an account which had nothing to do with St Kentigern or Glasgow. It was about the burial ground at Cadder consecrated by St Ninian. Jocelin, preoccupied with glorifying St Kentigern would not have mentioned St Ninian if his name had not appeared in the source he was adapting.

If Ninian and not Kentigern is visualised as officiating in the funeral cortège at Cadder in the presence of a crowd of people, the event acquires the appearance of a public demonstration. The Antonine Wall had been demilitarised by Ninian's time, but it retained many memorials to pagan gods. At Kirkintilloch for example, which had been the next fort going eastward from Cadder, a fragment of a relief was discovered only in the last century depicting a bull, a reminder that both the Romans and the Picts worshipped the bull, an enduring participant in fertility rites.[31] The symbolism of the two bulls yoked to the wain is rooted in the pagan perception of the bull in its strength and potency as an aspect of deity.

Now the story of the two bulls pulling a hearse begins to mean something. It was a demonstration that the bull, the god, could be brought down to the level of a draught beast, and put to the service of the true God in taking a body for Christian burial. The yoke had been a symbol of shame and defeat to the Romans; to Christians it is the faith itself: 'Take my yoke upon you,' says Jesus in St Matthew's Gospel, 'and learn of me, for my yoke is easy, my burden is light'.

The people accompanying the funeral procession were witnessing a public act by which the old gods were humiliated and the power of Christ made manifest. The transforming symbol of the yoke, changing defeat into a new life of faith, signified in Christian perception what Ninian was offering the Picts. The figurative presentation of this material suggests it was originally transmitted by oral tradition as poetry or song. The demonstration had meaning only so long as the church was preoccupied with defeating organised paganism. Its significance was lost on Jocelin, in whose time the church did not need to concern itself with conversion.

There are now two hypotheses: a church founded by Ninian at Eccles near Stirling, and a burial ground consecrated by him at Cadder. The identification of the second place explains the jibe at Ninian and his kinsman Peibio (Plebia in Latin) in a very old Welsh folk-story, 'Cwlhuch and Olwen'. In order to win Olwen in marriage from her ogre-like giant of a father, Cwlhuch has to perform a series of seemingly impossible tasks. Among them his prospective father-in-law demands: 'There are two horned oxen . . . One on the far side of Mynyd Bannawg, and one on the near side. I want them yoked together under one harness. Nynnyaw and Peibyaw are they and God turned them into oxen for their sins.'[32]

The oxen represent two celibate churchmen, their pastoral cures lying either side of a range of hills, Mynydd Bannawg.[33] One was clearly Nynia or Ninian; and in Peibyaw the character Plebia may be recognised, whose reproof, according to Ailred's Life, made Ninian blush for shame. Their inability to get on with each other, that the joke implies, echoes in Plebia's criticism of Ninian in the moralising account of the shower of rain.

Where was Mynydd Bannawg? Its identification is critical to the understanding of this evidence, and fortunately presents no problems. It is documented in

The Antonine Wall at Watling Lodge (Historic Scotland)

medieval charters relating to the Stirling area.[34] Mynydd Bannawg was the Brittonic name for the hills now known as the Campsie Fells. Cadder lies at the very foot on the south-western side. On the north-east, in a diagonal line across the hills, lies Eccles or Kirkton of Stirling, now known as St Ninian's. Ninian's mission headquarters there had an outpost at Cadder.

ST CADOG AND CADW

Another story involves Mount Bannog, a translation of Mynydd Bannawg. The 'Life of St Cadog of Llancarfan in Wales' was written by Llifris around the year 1100.[35] It contains two accounts of a visit by Cadog to St Andrews 'in Scotland', and to a place 'this side of Mount Bannog' where on his return journey he built a monastery of stone. This 'visit' to St Andrews may signify no more than the transfer of information to Llifris from the Culdee community at Kylrimont (St Andrews) about a holy man whose name resembled Cadog's. By weaving this into his 'Life of St Cadog' Llifris could enhance the reputation of St Cadog and his monastery. By the year 1100 nobody much cared about an obscure Pictish saint. There could be no objection to attributing his story to the Welsh St Cadog. From the perspective of St Andrew's whence the story came, 'this side of Mount

*Pictish representation of a
bull (Historic Scotland)*

Bannog' would mean the side nearer St Andrews — that is, the north-eastern side
— so back to St Ninian's, Stirling.

There Cadog is portrayed as digging the foundations of a monastery, when he
comes upon an enormous bone 'large enough for a horse and rider to pass
through'. Then a terrifying figure of a giant appears. In front of a crowd of
frightened people, he throws himself down at Cadog's feet. The apparition
confesses to have been in life the Pictish chief Caw (or Cadw), who reigned
beyond Mount Bannog, and had been killed with all his men when raiding the
territory of the Britons. For this crime, he explains, 'we have been tormented until
now by the devouring flames of hell!' St Cadog has compassion, raises the ghost
from the dead, pardons him, and he becomes Cadog's 'fossor' all his days.

There are some very old memories here, of a time when pagan Picts had raided
British territory. The word 'fossor', no longer current in the Middle Ages, was an
order of priesthood in the early Christian church, the functionary in charge of
burials. The term 'fossor' belonged to the same period as the place-name 'eccles'
and indicates that the story told in the 'Life of St Cadog' had a source reaching
back to the beginnings of the Christian church among the Picts.

So a dead Pictish chief is raised to life (an allegory for Christian conversion)

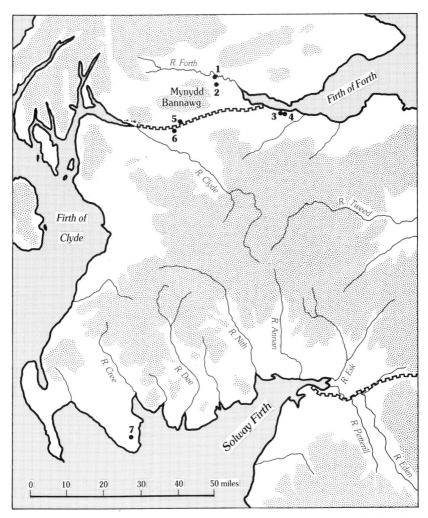

1. Stirling; 2. Eccles; 3. Abercorn; 4. Hopetoun; 5. Kirkintilloch; 6. Cadder; 7. Candida Casa.
North Britain between Hadrian's Wall and the Antonine Wall

and becomes a dignitary of the church. The story has all the drama of a spine-chiller told round the fire on a winter's night. Yet here is news of the Pictish chief whose baptism was the precondition for the mass conversion of his people. The event takes place near Stirling, as might be expected. The source of this material is folklore, mercifully preserved in medieval hagiography; but its authenticity is vouched for in the language of the primitive church. Even the gigantic bone was authentic and helps to identify the site of Cadog's monastery. Many bones, now known to be the remains of Mesolithic whales, have been unearthed in the Carse of Stirling in more recent times.[36]

29

THE PICTISH CHURCH

To sum up, a burial ground at Cadder was consecrated by Ninian where a mother-church developed. Then a burial ground was consecrated at Kirkton of Stirling, and a fossor appointed. No specific date can be set on these events. It is not known when Ninian left his diocese and travelled north to seek out the Pictish king, although there can be little doubt about the route he followed.

The directness of the way to Cadder overland points to his having taken the Roman way through Nithsdale from Dalswinton northward, or from the river crossing at Friars' Carse. This road runs due north through Crawford, Castle-dykes, and Bothwellhaugh to the junction between Cadder and Kirkintilloch on the Antonine Wall.[37] Leaving Plebia in charge at Cadder, Ninian would have continued east along the Wall to the Ardoch road, and thence to Stirling. There, having converted chief and people, Ninian apparently consecrated a burial ground at Eccles and left it under the management of Cadw, whether he was the converted Pictish chief or another. The church that developed at Eccles commemorated Ninian as founder.[38] He is also commemorated at Kirkintilloch.[39]

At Hopetoun, a few miles along the coast towards Edinburgh, Ninian is remembered under the pre-medieval form of his name, 'Nynia', as patron of a holy well. All that remains is the record of a field-name, Nyniwells Field, on an eighteenth-century estate map of the great aristocratic estate of Hopetoun House at Abercorn.[40] In a similar form — 'Ninia'- St Ninian's name was honoured in the Pictish church. For it appears spelt thus in a compilation purporting to be the litany used by the Culdees of Dunkeld.[41]

This outline of the founding of the church of the southern Picts, while necessarily tentative, has the virtue of making sense of material previously obscure and fragmented, and of bringing pattern out of muddle. Its most impressive feature is that it draws ultimately on British and Pictish folklore and on enduring material such as place-names. Once more it is older than the Northumbrian sources, yet the story it tells is consistent with Bede's.

HOME BASE AND MISSION FIELD

According to the literary sources, after Ninian had founded the Pictish church he returned home to Candida Casa, where his name was remembered in a crescendo of devotion. Yet before the Northumbrian church took control in the seventh century, some of the substance of Ninian's biography, and all memory of contacts between Candida Casa and the Pictish church had been lost.[42] It is striking to reflect how very nearly the Northumbrian church re-established that contact. For Northumbria annexed the district around Abercorn from the Picts and set up a bishopric there. It was short-lived; for in 685 the Picts gained a decisive military victory and regained much of the territory they had lost. Bishop Trumwine, the Anglian bishop of Abercorn, fled south and ended his days at Whitby. The effacing of Ninian's memory at Abercorn, (presumably by the Northumbrian church) coincided within a few years with Northumbria's embracing of his cult at Whithorn. Yet the connection between Abercorn and Candida Casa was not recognised.

In the absence of these memories, the faithful were dazzled by the eager hyperbole of hagiographers, and Ninian the real man was obscured in legend. The author of the 'Miracula' set the tone for subsequent writers by representing him as radiating light: 'He attained the high rank of bishop that he might shine out as the lamp of the holy sanctuary . . . and be seen burning brightly from the top of the candlestick.'

Ailred of Rievaulx drew apparently on Irish tradition to epitomise the miraculous powers attributed to Ninian. A young ordinand in training at Candida Casa committed some misdemeanour and provoked Ninian's anger. In panic he ran away, but had the forethought to pick up Ninian's pastoral staff as protection for his journey, 'and flying therefore from the face of the man, he sought diligently for a ship that might transport him to 'Scotia' (the old name for Ireland). The story continues:

> It is the custom in that region to construct a bowl-shaped vessel out of rods big enough to hold three men sitting side by side. By stretching an ox-hide over it they made it not only buoyant, but also impervious to water . . . So the youth found one such ship drawn up on the shore but without its covering of hide.

The power of the staff took this porous vessel safely across the sea to Ireland. The young man landed and stuck the staff into the ground:

> Soon the dry wood shot out roots, and clothing itself in new bark, produced leaves and branches, and afterwards growing into a lofty tree it demonstrates even now the power of Ninian . . . At the foot of the tree a very clear spring burst out and sent a crystal rivulet winding along with gentle murmur . . . both delightful to look at and sweet to drink, while useful and health-giving to the sick by the power of the saint.[43]

The unmistakably Celtic blend of the fabulous and absurd nevertheless stirs the imagination. The bishop's staff or crosier represents St Ninian's power, which extended beyond his physical presence and beyond the grave. It is revealed as the Tree of Life, whence springs the water of healing and salvation. Ninian the miracle man, was presented as a great healer, yet apart from the parable about King Tudwal whose blindness symbolised his spiritual state, there is no authority for that claim older than the eighth century.

Ninian's human achievements were the building of his church, his creation of a community devoted to the principles of St Martin, and his reckless adventure among the merciless Picts. The strength and scope of the community and church of Candida Casa was clearly the achievement of more than one man, but all that the Dig has revealed argues an original guiding spirit of rare imagination. The enlightened courage that went into founding that Christian colony was of the kind that prompted Ninian to offer the Gospel to the southern Picts, his people's

St Ninian's Cave near the Isle of Whithorn, where St Ninian was said to have retreated for solitary prayer. In the words of the 'Miracula', Ninian 'studied heavenly wisdom with a devoted mind in a cave of horrible blackness'. The artist was the great Gallovidian, Sir Herbert Maxwell. (EL)

enemies. Both enterprises implied leadership able to mobilise a major cooperative undertaking. If this was the work of Bishop Ninian, his rewards were to watch his community prosper, and to see the end of the slave-trade, and of his countrymen's harassment by constant war. These were successes for his own time. They were not understood by later generations who took for granted the technologies that were innovations in Ninian's day, and had no experience of organised paganism or the threat of the sudden raid and the slave-gang.

Relatively soon the chances and changes of history cut contact between the episcopal see at Whithorn and the mission field in the Forth basin. Eccles passed out of Pictish control into the hands of the British kingdom of the Gododdin, and subsequently Anglian Northumbria. Cadder, if it ever belonged to the Picts, was claimed by Strathclyde. Galloway, once the land of the Novantae, passed, some scholars think, into the hands of Rheged, the most celebrated of the kingdoms of the North.

Rheged was the realm of the 'hero-king' Urien, whose bard Taliesin proclaimed his conquests. Surviving documentation is minimal. Most historians assume that Rheged centered on the old Roman city of Carlisle. Taliesin hailed Urien as the lord of Catraeth (Catterick in Yorkshire), and linguists have traced the name Rheged in place-names as far apart as Rochdale in Lancashire and Dunragit near Glenluce in Wigtownshire. Whether the kingdom's boundaries extended thus far remains a question over which present-day scholars are sharply divided. Urien was killed in 585, supposedly by treachery, and his name passed into legend. His identity melts and merges after the fashion of dreams with that of the battle-leader Arthur; and it was Arthur who was said to have ruled at Penrhyn Rionyt. When in the seventh century the British kingdoms were destroyed by the power of Northumbria, little remained but a vibrant oral tradition, and a popular devotion to St Ninian.

In recent centuries Candida Casa and its bishop have lain buried under the Glebe field and the ruins of Whithorn's cathedral; and historians, wary of its incantation, have doubted the authenticity of their story. Rightly so perhaps, for before such achievements could be given credence, they had — in the words of Sulpicius Severus — to be 'duly ascertained and tested'. But now it is neither possible to assume that the Northumbrian Angles reconstituted a broken tradition when they took control at Whithorn, nor that Ninian's mission to the Picts failed. Old scepticisms have been discredited beyond expectation. The findings of the Dig and the literary sources together assert with surprising unanimity the scope and distinction of the church and community of Candida Casa, the genius of its founder, and its long continuity as a holy place.

2

SECOND BISHOPRIC:

Pecthelm, his Friends and Successors
(730–836)

For lo, the winter is past, the rain is over and done. The flowers appear on the earth; the time of the singing of birds is come. The figtree puts forth her green figs, and the vines with the tender grape give a good smell.

Song of Solomon[1]

Bishop Pecthelm settled in Whithorn around the year 729–30. His arrival, as the first bishop of a newly created Anglian see, was the start of an episcopate which built up the prestige of Whithorn and shaped Galloway's spiritual life and parish organisation for centuries to come. The Anglian kingdom of Northumbria had established political supremacy in Galloway some time between 650 and 670, and maintained it until the end of the ninth century. This comparatively short period, which coincided with an era distinguished for its Christian learning, vigour and artistic achievement, is astonishingly well documented. Northumbria was peopled by men and women whose curiosity and exuberant creativity compel our sympathy.

The *Anglo-Saxon Chronicle* is a primary source, recording major political events in the English kingdoms, and listing the appointment and death of bishops, including the bishops of Whithorn. Two letters survive written by Anglian churchmen abroad, bearing directly on this narrative. Of the literary sources, Bede's *History* is the most comprehensive and reliable, and although it contains only two or three direct references to Galloway, provides an informative general background. Contemporary Latin 'Lives' of saints, including the 'Miracula' poem, and a corpus of Old English poetry, all contribute to a more fully documented account than was possible in the period described in Chapter One.

ANNEXATION

In the course of the seventh century the Angles had destroyed and supplanted the kingdoms of the North. In their hands the twinned territories of Bernicia and Deira became the kingdom of Northumbria, the Bretwalda for some generations — a term which meant first among all the kingdoms of Britain.

This supremacy had been won by a bitter process of aggression, as the Angles, a land-hungry, pagan people, wrested territory from the native possessors. Their record was disfigured in 603 by the massacre of British monks before the battle of Chester; and the final disaster for all the kingdoms of the North soon followed. It was symbolised in Welsh poetry by the image of a dark roofless hall deserted after the slaughter of its lord, his warriors all dead, and the songs of his bard silenced.

At the last, the British kingdoms had joined together against the common enemy, but too late. The Scots of Dalriada, who supported them, were defeated and reduced to a long-lasting neutrality. The Picts were the last Celtic people to sustain opposition to the Angles. They gave ground, but eventually enticed the acquisitive King Egfrith northward, and inflicted a disastrous defeat on his armies in 685 at Nechtansmere (now Dunnichen near Forfar). Northumbria had to give up territory and annexation ceased, but by that time Galloway was in Anglian hands.[2]

CHRISTIAN NORTHUMBRIA

Northumbria had been christianised in the mid-seventh century, first abortively under King Edwin (627–42) and then by King Oswald who succeeded him. Oswald had been baptised in Iona, and on his accession invited a mission from there to Lindisfarne. As pagans the Angles had likened the life of man to the 'swift flight of a single sparrow through the banqueting hall . . . on a winter's day'. He 'flies swiftly through one door of the hall and out through another. While he is inside he is safe from the winter storms; but after a few moments of comfort he vanishes from sight into the wintry world from which he came'.[3]

After their conversion the Angles gave their church unhesitating commitment. The faith was their only light in that cosmic darkness, and a sure source of perpetual joy. That fervour sounds in all their writing, but most of all in the anonymous poem, the 'Dream of the Rood', which gives a vision of the cross on which Christ suffered:

> It seemed I saw the Tree itself
> borne on the air, light wound about it,
> a beam of brightest wood, a beacon clad
> in overlapping gold, glancing gems
> fair at its foot, and five stones
> set in a crux, flashed at the crosstree . . .

[Then the rood itself speaks]:

> I dared not break or bend aside
> against God's will, though the ground itself
> shook at my feet. Fast I stood,
> who falling could have felled them all . . .

> I shook when His arms embraced me
> but I durst not bow to ground

stoop to earth's surface
Stand fast I must.

I was reared up a rood.
I raised the great King,
liege-lord of the heavens,
dared not lean from true . . .
They drove me through with dark nails:
on me the deep wounds manifest,
wide-mouthed hate-dents.
I durst not harm any of them.
How they mocked at us both!
I was all moist with blood
Sprung from the Man's side
after he sent forth his soul.[4]

That mystical union of God, man and tree touches the heart as the Tree of Life, conjured out of St Ninian's crosier, moves the imagination. The 'Dream of the Rood', inscribed in runes along the sides of the Ruthwell Cross, is a poem for all time.

It came to be said in Christian Northumbria that a woman carrying a new-born babe, could walk from sea to sea without fear of harm. Such a boast conveys the change of values from the bragging of the conqueror and the war hero. This change was accompanied, as in Ireland and among the Picts, with a release of creative energy.

THE ARTISTIC MIRACLE

The Northumbrian church, devout and learned, had rapidly become a patron of the arts. Churchmen visiting Rome and the Continent, returned to enrich their churches with pictures, jewelled chalices and candlesticks, and above all with books. Some like Benedict Biscop brought back craftsmen, glaziers and stone masons with skills still unknown among the Angles. Native skills soon developed under this stimulus. With the inspiration of the Irish traditions of Iona, Anglian sculpture acquired artistic excellence, not only in technique, but in design.

The stone-carving reached its climax in the free-standing crosses. They represent an astonishing synthesis, a coming together, like a confluence of powerful rivers: the classic discipline of Mediterranean culture, with its vine-scroll motif, foliage forms and three dimensional figure representation combine with the Celtic mastery of the curvilinear — scroll, spiral, and interlace; and with these, an affectionate observation of the wildlife of forest and wilderness — of birds, and small mammals. They are drawn according to the demands of filling space, with an elongated fantasy. That last element seems to have been a specifically Anglian contribution. The sympathy with nature voiced in the poetry materialises in tangible form. In the Ruthwell Cross and the fragment from Jedburgh in Roxburgh

Ruthwell Cross, Dumfriesshire. A section of the shaft — birds and animals among vines (Historic Scotland)

the stone itself seems almost animate and sinuous. The same marriage of technique and design appears in Anglian metalwork and bone carving. The illuminated books have all this with the added dimension of colour, and always with the same disciplined subordination of detail to design.

This marvel was all the greater in that it was not confined to one people. It proceeded from the interaction of three — Angle, Irish and Pict — under the stimulus of the Christian vision. The record of the Christian church has not been unblemished, but in north Britain in the seventh and eighth centuries it inspired an outburst of creative energy, and a happy cooperation between Celtic, Mediterranean and Germanic cultures.

The interchange of Christian clerks and scholars between Northumbria, Ireland and Pictland was paralleled by the coming and going of itinerant craftsmen and artists. That is demonstrated in the artefacts themselves, to the point where a common style and a competing standard of excellence often make it difficult today for the expert to identify the provenance of a particular piece. The long twentieth-century debate over the relationship between the *Lindisfarne Gospels* and the *Book of Kells* exemplifies this.

Galloway shared in this creativity, though little is now to be seen. In eastern Kirkcudbrightshire delicate stone-carving and metalwork of high quality were

Part of the cross-shaft from Jedburgh (Historic Scotland)

produced, but can be traced now only from fragments. Parts of two finely carved stone crosses have been discovered in recent years in Auchencairn and Kirkcudbright, and a small metal plate, possibly part of a reliquary, exquisitely decorated with interlace, was picked up in Rerrick old kirkyard (see cover).[5]

A few miles away the Angles took over the Mote of Mark on the mouth of the

A fragment of ninth-century carving built into a house near Kirkcudbright and painted (photo: Alistair Penman)

river Urr, previously a British stronghold, and used it as a workshop for metal working. Apart from such utilitarian processes as iron smelting, luxury crafts were practised. Jewellery decorated with interlace was cast there. Moulds and crucibles, unearthed on the site, project no more than a shadow of elegant brooches in silver and gold. Imported materials such as trailed and coloured glass beads and millefiori rods, set the mind's eye to work, but none of the finished products was to be found.[6] It is hardly surprising. They were presumably marketed — shipped along the coast to places like Whithorn. From its site above the natural haven at Kippford, the workshop was convenient both for the importation of exotic materials and the distribution of the manufactured goods.

THE NEW BISHOPRIC

In Northumbria the zenith of creativity came in a period of political stability and peace. The church was then organised in three episcopal sees at York, Lindisfarne and Hexham. A fourth at Abercorn had proved shortlived and ceased to exist with the defeat of Northumbria by the Picts before the end of the seventh century. An archbishopric of York was in prospect, but did not materialise until 735. In the

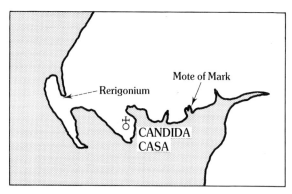

Candida Casa and the Mote of Mark

meantime around the year 730, a fourth diocese was created to embrace Galloway with its centre at Whithorn. Bede's voice informs us once more, this time with the confidence of personal knowledge:

> ... in the province of the Northumbrians, ruled by Ceolwulf, four bishops hold office: Wilfred in the church of York, Ethelwald at Lindisfarne, Acca at Hexham, and Pecthelm in the see known as the White House, where the number of believers has so increased that it has recently become an episcopal see with Pecthelm as its first bishop.[7]

This dates the bishopric as 'recent' in 731.

BEDE AND PECTHELM

Elsewhere in the *History* Bede's references to Pecthelm imply they did not merely correspond, but actually met and became friends. This must have happened after Pecthelm's consecration as Bishop of Whithorn. Hitherto Pecthelm had lived as a monk at the great Mercian monastery of Malmesbury, and Bede seldom left Jarrow, and then to go no further than York. The two men had much in common. Both were scholars, both had undergone long training in a distinguished centre of learning, and they shared a number of interests. Their very conversations seem to be relayed in Bede's *History*:

> I have thought this story [about a man afflicted with demonic possession] should be told in a straightforward way, as I heard it from the venerable Bishop Pecthelm ... Bishop Haeddi of the West Saxons departed to the life of Heaven. He was a good, just man who carried out his duties as a bishop guided by an inborn love of goodness rather than anything learned in books. The most reverent Bishop Pecthelm — of whom more will be said in due course — was a fellow-monk and deacon for a long time with Haeddi's successor Aldhelm. He relates how many miracles of healing occurred through Haeddi's holiness at the place where he died. He says that the people of that province used to carry away earth from it to

40

The Episcopal Sees of Northumbria

mix in water for the sick, and with it many men and beasts who drank or were sprinkled with it were restored to health.

'In consequence', adds Bede, permitting himself a smile, 'there was a considerable pit created by continual removal of the hallowed soil!' [8]
They had memories to exchange. The controversy had only recently been settled which had divided the churches of Britain and Ireland over the computation of Easter. It had affected both their monasteries, and each probably remembered some personal participation. Bede could recall how when he was a young monk, the King of the Picts had consulted his abbot, Ceolfrid, as to how the date of Easter should be calculated, and the Pictish church had been won over to regular Roman practice, and away from the 'errors' defended by Iona. At Malmesbury, Pecthelm's friend and abbot, Aldhelm, had been instrumental in accomplishing a similar change of mind among the churches of the Welsh. Pecthelm had been trained in a strictly orthodox — even missionising — milieu. [9]
A picture of the two men suggests itself, soon after Pecthelm's consecration, ensconced in the most comfortable corner of Jarrow's chilly scriptorium, exchanging reminiscences and stories, and delightedly discovering mutual understanding. At such a time it was not merely likely, but natural that Bede's keen curiosity and Pecthelm's preoccupation with his new diocese, should result in Bede's hearing the half-forgotten story of St Ninian, as Pecthelm had recently heard it at Whithorn. Bede's *History* was all but finished, but there proved to be time and space to insert the short, condensed paragraph quoted on page 12.

THE EASTER CONTROVERSY

Northumbrian Christianity had derived from Iona, and in its early years had depended on close contacts between Lindisfarne, Northumbria's first monastery, and the mother-house. Iona had been midwife and nurse, held in affection and reverence. But as early as the mid-seventh century the Northumbrian church had come of age. The Continental journeys of such men as Benedict Biscop and Bishop Wilfred had strengthened their orthodoxy in the method of calculating the date of Easter which made the reactionary Celticism of Iona appear deviant. Northumbria had stood for the Roman method of computation since the Synod of Whitby in 664, and the conduct of the controversy was at once uncompromising and civilised. For where many churches might have become embattled and intolerant, no personal attacks were made, and the Roman party, as represented by Monkwearmouth-Jarrow and Malmesbury, relied on patience, diplomacy and persuasion to overcome the opposition.

It had taken until 719 to bring Iona to conformity, and meanwhile the Northumbrian church had dispensed with tutelage, and assumed a leading role. It was for this reason that Pecthelm's appointment to Whithorn was made with such care.

The controversy might be over, but sustained effort would be needed if Northumbria were to maintain its spiritual leadership among the Celtic churches and intellectual parity with Iona. A strongly orthodox monastic community was needed, which could build up a reputation for learning, and attract Irish scholars and ordinands seeking training, who would otherwise depend overmuch on the Columban tradition. Whithorn was ideally placed geographically, with Strathclyde and Dalriada to the north, Wales and Cornwall on the southern sea-lane, and Ireland across no more than a narrow strait. The monastery of Candida Casa with its memories of a church and bishop in post-Roman times, would appeal to Celtic sympathies while being able to claim prestigious and orthodox origins. The place was well suited to occupy a dominant position in the west.

This was enough to explain the choice of Whithorn as the centre of the fourth Northumbrian bishopric. 'The increase in the number of believers' might have been urged in favour of Melrose, or Hoddam in Annandale where a monastery in Anglian hands was producing excellent stone-carving; or the new episcopal see might have been centred at the old Roman city of Carlisle, had other considerations been equal.[10]

THE CHOICE OF PECTHELM

Pecthelm as bishop was also carefully chosen, though Tatwine's elevation as Archbishop of Canterbury in 731 may have weighted the choice in his favour. The initiative in setting up the new diocese of Whithorn must have come from the Bishop of York, Wilfred II, but Tatwine as archbishop would have had a say in the appointment. He had been Abbot of Bredon in Mercia, and may have known Pecthelm, a monk of Malmesbury.

Pecthelm was highly qualified for the office, even though his election meant looking beyond the boundaries of Northumbria for the new bishop. Malmesbury, always a house with a learned tradition since its foundation by the Irish monk

Maeldub, had gained added prestige during the abbacy of Aldhe
of Sherbourne (who died in 709). Aldhelm, celebrated both fo
and as a Latin stylist, had also been a church-builder, and had ne
Welsh churches in the matter of Easter. Pecthelm was a fellow ......
with Aldhelm, and had the advantage of having been his pupil, and heir, so ιυ
speak, to this experience.

He was a considerable scholar in his own right. The breadth of Pecthelm's
scholarship is testified by his younger contemporary, Bishop Boniface. He was a
West Saxon who refused high office and a promising career in the province of
Canterbury to become a missionary to the pagan peoples of Frisia and Germany.
Divorced from books and libraries, he wrote to Pecthelm for advice on a point of
canon law. Boniface had close connections with Malmesbury and may have
known Pecthelm personally. Although his tone is ceremonial, his letter suggests
personal acquaintance, and his reliance on Pecthelm's wide reading and judgment
is sufficiently clear:

> To his venerable and beloved fellow-bishop, Pecthelm, Boniface, humble servant
> of the servants of God, kind greeting of love in Christ . . . We have sent you some
> small gifts in token of our love, a sacrament cloth ornamented with white spots,
> and a towel to wipe the feet of the servants of God. These we beg you to accept
> as a remembrance of us.
>
> About one thing too we wish to hear your counsel and judgment: the clergy
> of the whole of France and Gaul, as well as those who speak for them, declare
> that a man is guilty of the greatest crime in marrying a widow for whose son he
> had stood sponsor in baptism. This kind of sin, if it really is one, I did not know
> before, and I have not learned that in the canon or decrees of the pontiffs, in
> writings of the Fathers or the Apostles, it is put in the list of sins. Therefore if
> you have found it discussed anywhere in the writings of the Church, be sure to
> tell me, and give me your opinion on the matter.[11]

It is evident that Boniface was not concerned merely with an academic point.
A hard-pressed missionary, he must have actually had a convert who wanted to
marry his godson's mother. The letter was dated 735, the year of Pecthelm's death,
and it is to be hoped it arrived in time to receive a reply.

Two very late martyrologies claim that Pecthelm's contemporary Acca, Bishop
of Hexham, left Hexham for a period, and 'became Bishop of Whithorn'.[12] Acca
died in 740 and was buried with great honour at Hexham, his tomb within the
church marked by two vine-wreathed crosses, popularly associated with him. The
local legend that Acca left Hexham in 732 and became Bishop of Candida Casa
is almost certainly untrue; but there may have been some truth in the statement
of the twelfth-century chronicler, Richard of Hexham that Acca prepared the see
of Candida Casa for Pecthelm.[13]

Bishop Acca had been the inseparable friend and chaplain of Wilfred of Ripon,
the most brilliant (and difficult) churchman of the age. Acca had worked with him
in furnishing his churches with precious things from abroad, and succeeded him

ιe bishopric of Hexham at Wilfred's request. As bishop, Acca had succeeded
n enticing away from Canterbury Maban, a celebrated singer, to be his master of
music. Music was one of the arts to which the Northumbrian church paid special
attention, and it will have been their common love of music that cemented the
friendship between Acca and Bede. Also a scholar, Acca had provided material for
Bede's *History*. He would have been a welcome helper to Pecthelm in the arduous
business of establishing a new diocese, and had valuable experience to offer in the
planning and furnishing of Whithorn's churches.

It is plain that from the start Pecthelm and his episcopal see were in touch with
some of the ablest and most respected personalities of his generation. Aldhelm
and Bede, both men of European reputation, were his friends. Their monasteries
of Malmesbury and Jarrow were centres of intellectual and spiritual influence. St
Boniface achieved a reputation as a great missionary bishop before suffering
martyrdom. (He was attacked and murdered by a band of pagans in Frisia.) Acca
was both eminent in his own right, and shared much of Wilfred's distinction. The
most reverend Bishop Pecthelm, as Bede called him, was in contact with an elite,
to which it must be assumed that he belonged.

WHITHORN

When the first Northumbrian settlers reached Whithorn in the second half of the
seventh century, the British church of Candida Casa had suffered a period of
decay. Two generations later two chapels had been built on the old site along the
same building line with strong stone foundations and a super-structure of timber
and white plaster. By this time whitened walls had become a local building tradition.[14] This new phase of building had been constructed on ground levelled and
surfaced with 'chips' derived from an iron smelting spoil tip as a basis for paths
and building foundations. It conveniently indicated to archaeologists the limit of
the Northumbrian stratum.

Pecthelm's episcopate marked the maturity of the Anglian settlement at
Whithorn and some achievement in timber building construction. While the
stone church, or a replacement, was presumably still at the top of the hill, an
exceptionally coherent succession of buildings has been discovered on the
excavated site. A church or chapel of some distinction dominated a range of
ecclesiastical buildings including a burial chapel, a children's graveyard, organised
on a rectangular grid, with associated paths and terraces. Probably by the time
Pecthelm had taken up his appointment, the two aligned chapels had been joined
together to form a building 14 m by 4.5 m. Massive vertical posts running the
length of the exterior were then added to form a colonnade with a veranda roof.
A somewhat narrower structure was added probably incorporating an older
shrine. The building and the structures and courtyards surrounding it have been
dated from coins on the site as mid-eighth century. The lay-out was planned by a
master architect, but Bishop Pecthelm and his immediate successor Bishop
Frithwald, whose episcopate lasted until 763, must be credited with responsibility

for much of the development. Whithorn had become a market town and the centre of a large estate. At the same time the intimate relationship between monastery and laiety is made clear by the presence on the excavated site of a children's graveyard. It can be assumed that burial grounds for men and women also lie immediately beyond the limits of the Dig. The pastoral care of the laiety by the religious community could not be more clearly indicated.

The interior of the whole of the timber church was divided by screens. The linen and costly fabrics, and precious chalices and candlesticks that furnished the interior have not survived, but they can be visualised from an account of the church at Hexham, built by Bishop Wilfred between 672 and 678, and furnished by his chaplain and successor Bishop Acca 'with splendid gold and silver ornaments, precious stones, and silks and purples for the altars.'[15]

A stone church, a successor to Ninian's original structure, probably crowned the hill. The Northumbrians were already familiar with such buildings. At Hexham the original crypt of finely dressed stone is still to be seen under the medieval abbey church, and the seventh-century stone church of Jarrow still stands. There can be no comparison with its austere Romanesque dignity: and no means of knowing at present whether the hypothetical stone church on the hill in any way matched it. But the timber church on the excavated site at Whithorn can be pictured by comparison with some of the finer 'black and white' buildings still to be seen in East Anglia and the West of England. Those manor houses and cloth halls were built centuries later, but their structures and appearance would be similar. The combination of oak beams and white plaster has its own comeliness in harmony with a predominantly rural landscape.

Whithorn's Northumbrian church is the finest timber church yet known to British archaeology. As yet, the eighth-century monastic living and working quarters have to be identified. The refectory and the monastery garden provided the background to parts of the 'Miracula', the poem written at Whithorn perhaps a generation later. The poem's very existence indicates the presence of a scriptorium, where the monks wrote, studied and copied manuscripts. Church and monastery comprised a significant centre of a planned urban settlement. It provided a diocesan centre of Christian worship and pastoral care, serving the whole of Anglian Galloway, while offering services to visitors and pilgrims from a much wider catchment area.

Whether or not Candida Casa had been a seat of learning from its beginning, there is some evidence for a primitive university there under Northumbrian rule. Later Irish writers saw Whithorn as a prestigious school, a seminary for ordinands, and a centre of education for young aristocrats from Galloway and surrounding countries. The number of Irish saints credited with a Whithorn training, while not always historically sustainable, was indication enough of the prestige Whithorn enjoyed in Ireland in the eighth century.

Ruthwell Cross. Mary Magdalen washing the feet of Christ. The figure-carving of Christ follows the classical style, but the flatter, broader modelling of the Magdalen, which compares with some modern sculpture, enhances the symbolism and poignancy of the statement (Historic Scotland)

THE CULT OF ST NINIAN

Some memories of Ninian survived the decline of the native church at Candida Casa and its annexation by Northumbria. But it seems to have been the Northumbrian church that made St Ninian a focus of devotional feeling, and brought pilgrims in increasing numbers to his shrine. The foundations of the immensely successful medieval cult may be set down to the credit of Bishop Pecthelm and the bishops who succeeded him. It was promoted both by written propaganda and probably by more practical means in setting up a centre of healing.

The two poems, the 'Miracula' and the 'Hymn', were discovered in a library at Bamberg in Germany in the early twentieth century and were first called to the attention of the English reading public in 1940.[16] Neither is great literature. They were clearly intended to popularise the saint as a miracle worker and healer, and despite a florid, wordy style, the 'Miracula' can be evocative and sometimes touching.

THE 'MIRACULA'

Chapter 7 of the 'Miracula' gives a glimpse of the monastery's refectory and garden when the bishop and his monks were gathering for dinner. The description presumably applied more to the community of the poet's own day than to St Ninian's. The bishop discovers there are no green vegetables on the menu, so he says to a man:

> Run off on twin feet and go to the well watered garden plots, and bring us back the vegetables that are springing from the earth. The brother who was in charge of the garden answered him, 'Look, today I have planted seeds firmly in furrows and they are not yet sending up from the green turf dewy shoots which every kind of vegetation produce from their innermost parts'. But the holy man spoke to his servant from his pure heart, 'Run then and in the faith of the Lord look for vegetables' . . . Then he visited the heart of the garden and saw . . . in spite of his unbelief all kinds of plants sprouting from the seed in the earth, springing up and growing to the full verdure they would reach there in the whole period of the summer.[17]

The recent excavation actually found the monastery garden — or at least a considerable depth of garden soil at sixth or seventh-century level.[18] In contrast to the miracle of the vegetables and similar wonder-works which may have belonged to an older, Celtic tradition, the 'Miracula' relates miracles of healing which are presented as taking place after Ninian's death, at his shrine in the church:

> This is the house of the Lord, which many are eager to visit . . . for many who have been afflicted with a disease of long standing hurry there. They eagerly accept the ready gifts of health-giving healing, and they grow strong in all their limbs by the power of the saint.[19]

Some of these posthumous cures were presented as having taken place in the living memory of the writer:

> A certain man of the people and his wife had a son who was disfigured over all his flesh and shattered over his worn-out frame by a great collection of diseases. The wretched boy moved only with the accompaniment of torturing pain . . . Day by day he began to lose all feeling in his limbs and . . . he lay numb in the shadow of death. His parents brought him to the temple hand in hand with faith and made it their aim to visit the body and ashes of the holy man [St Ninian]. . .
>
> As the day died they left the dying boy . . . Then a light shone forth just at the turning point of midnight at the place where the young boy lay at the tomb . . . suddenly he caught sight of the bishop entering, clad now in snow-white raiment and placing his holy hand on the boy's head. From this hand powerful healing flowed into the wasted limbs . . . when he tried out his feet, he rose safely dancing over the marble floor. After this he received the tonsure and lived a long time within our walls, and was called Pectgils by name.[20]

The story suggests a therapeutic centre, and Pecthelm's interest in Malmesbury's cures associated with Abbot Haeddi would be consistent with his starting faith-healing at Whithorn. It is clear that some arthritic and paralytic cases were treated, and a late medieval poem refers to fasting as part of the therapy.[21] In the absence of scientific medicine, healing by faith and prayer was developed in the monasteries, combined with herbal remedies, exercise, a dietary regimen and the laying on of hands. Some of these are used at Lourdes today.

The commitment and experience required by the healer who uses the laying on of hands, has been movingly described a generation ago by a Church of Scotland minister.[22] A few years ago an article in the *British Medical Journal* compared the miracles of healing reported in saints' 'Lives' of the eighth century (such as the 'Lives' of St Cuthbert and St Wilfred) with recorded, hospital cases where the patient recovered against all expectation and without adequate scientific explanation. In each case the patient was being prayed for and had faith in intercession.[23] Dramatic cures do happen from time to time, and credit must be given to some of the claims the 'Miracula' advanced. The story of Pectgils is particularly convincing.

The success of the 'Miracula' in publicising the legends of St Ninian can be measured by a letter addressed in the very early ninth century by the celebrated librarian and advisor to Charlemagne, Alcuin. At Charles's invitation he spent some years at his court, while retaining close touch with his own community and school of York. He wrote 'to the brethren of St Ninian of Candida Casa', asking for their prayers 'in the church of our most holy father, Ninian, famous for many virtues', and goes on to say that he had been reading of his miracles in the 'songs' (*carmina*) sent to him by his own faithful students and disciples of the church of York. He enclosed a silk veil for Ninian's shrine.[24]

By this time the diocese of Whithorn was subject to the Archbishops of York. It was natural that a copy of the 'Miracula' should be sent to York, and the copies sent to Alcuin from there have been identified with those discovered at Bamberg 1100 years later. Once the 'Miracula' reached Alcuin, its circulation on the Continent followed. For a reference is to be found in the writings of the ninth-century Benedictine monk, Paschasius Radbertus of Corbie (near Amiens), to the miracle which constituted the climax of the 'Miracula'. A priest celebrating Mass in the church at Whithorn prayed that he might be made more keenly aware of the presence of Christ in the elements, and found the living Christ-child on the paten in place of the consecrated bread. The priest is named as Plechgils, and the similarity suggests that this may have been Pectgils, the healed paralytic of the previous story.[25]

Although the tradition of healing at Candida Casa may have derived from St Martin himself, for he was credited with many cures, the 'Miracula' is the primary authority for Ninian as a healer. From the eighth century onward, Ninian's role as the successful missionary and saviour of his people from the slaving raids of the pagan Picts was played down, and his power as a healer emphasised.

THE FETTERS

There may have been one way in which the more authentic tradition was expressed. No eighth-century picture of St Ninian survives; but three medieval portraits or miniatures exist, two of which show Ninian in the vestments of a bishop, either wearing or carrying a severed chain (see cover). This motif appears in the two burgh crests that depict St Ninian — those of Whithorn and Nairn. This symbolism is not explained. A fifteenth-century vernacular poem refers to St Ninian's concern for prisoners, paraphrasing the words of Jesus 'I was in prison and you visited me . . .' but in relation to Ninian, that was quite unhistorical. A Missal of the same period has a Latin verse addressed to St Ninian: 'by land and sea thou dost not cease to liberate Christ's worshippers in chains'.[26]

In the eighth century however, more than one folk story about fetters was circulating in Northumbria, and other Anglo-Saxon kingdoms. Bede tells of a young Northumbrian nobleman called Imma, who was captured as a prisoner of war and subsequently 'sold to a Frisian in London' as a slave. Imma's brother, a priest and abbot, meanwhile believing him dead, was celebrating Masses for his soul. The slave master took Imma away:

> but found that he was unable to fetter him. When one kind of fetter after another had been put on him and none could hold him, his buyer gave him permission to ransom himself . . . It was at the hour of Terce, the customary time for saying Mass, that his chains were most frequently loosed.[27]

It is also related of Bishop Wilfred when he was at odds with the king, that 'despite his holiness and exalted rank' he was handed over to the Sheriff of Dunbar to be kept prisoner. The sheriff was no friend of Wilfred's either, and had him bound hand and foot —

and ordered the smiths to forge iron fetters . . . the irons always turned out either too small and narrow, or else so big and loose that they slipped off the wrists and ankles of God's baptist and evangelist. This terrified the guards so much that they left him unbound.[28]

In Worcester cathedral the figure of a bishop dangling a chain from his wrist can still be seen in the chantry for Henry VII's eldest son Arthur. This figure was identified last century, on account of the chain, as St Ninian; but this has since been corrected. The bishop was apparently Bishop Egwin of Worcester, an older contemporary of Pecthelm, and like him, a friend of Aldhelm of Malmesbury. He performed Aldhelm's funeral rites in 709.[29] The 'Life of St Egwin' tells he resolved to go to Rome to appeal against a decision taken by the King of Wessex and the Archbishop of Canterbury. Before starting out he locked his ankles in fetters and threw the key into the river Avon. In Rome the key turned up inside a fish that Egwin bought (despite his fetters) in the market. A similar story was told by Aldhelm of Malmesbury. The motif of something lost being found inside a fish appears in Irish folk-tales.

The circulation of these stories suggests contact between Jarrow, Malmesbury and Whithorn, and points to Pecthelm as the most probable link. Did he tell the author of the 'Miracula' the story of the newborn baby who spoke? It appears in the 'Life of Aldhelm'; but as the 'Life' was written much later than the 'Miracula', it may be that it was conveyed from Whithorn to Malmesbury rather than vice versa. Similarly it remains a question whether Pecthelm found symbolic fetters already associated with St Ninian when he arrived at Whithorn, or introduced them as an emblem to enhance St Ninian's appeal. St Ninian's broken fetter symbolised his defeat of Pictish slave-trading when he christianised the southern Picts. Not unnaturally it was imperfectly understood centuries later by fifteenth-century devotees; but it would not have been lost on Pecthelm's generation. They knew the story of Imma, sold into slavery to a pagan Frisian in London; and Pecthelm himself was in touch with Bishop Boniface, striving to bring Christianity to the slave-masters of Frisia.

DIOCESAN DUTIES

The duties of an eighth-century bishop extended beyond these concerns. The diocese at large, its organisation and pastoral care was his responsibility and unlike a bishop of the later medieval church, he was without the support of a fully developed parish system, or a hierarchy of deans and archdeacons. The number of priests in full orders at this period was restricted, and the spiritual welfare and orthodoxy of the laity was very much the concern of the bishop.

Similarly church buildings were few, and most congregations relied on a 'field church', that is a consecrated burial ground and a cross (of stone or wood) 'raised high for the daily office of prayer'. A shrine containing relics of the local saint often extended spiritual protection to graveyard and congregation. These places

A fragment of an eighth-century Northumbrian stone-carving from Hoddam in Dumfriesshire. Unfortunately some very fine crosses of this period were destroyed there in the twentieth century. (Crown copyright, RCAHMS)

might be visited by priest or bishop only irregularly, to perform baptisms and burials. But the need was enough to keep bishops constantly travelling about their diocese, in order to watch over the laity in isolated homesteads and nucleated villages miles apart. Some idea of the extent of Pecthelm's diocese, assuming that his ministry was confined to Anglian territories, can be gathered from a study of the Old English place-names, supplemented by church dedications and archaeological data. A comprehensive survey would be tedious, but a sample concentrating around Buittle and Kelton in Kirkcudbrightshire, and defining the boundaries of the Anglian colonies, gives with the help of a map (see page 53) an idea of the diocese of the Northumbrian bishops.

ANGLIAN SETTLEMENTS

Analysis of the place-names of Galloway and Carrick in south Ayrshire, shows three groups of Anglian settlements, each radiating from strategic and administrative centres. From the stronghold of Buittle (near Dalbeattie) a cluster of parishes controlled the Solway coast, its estuaries and natural harbours from the mouth of the Urr westward to the valley of the Fleet. The course of the Roman road threads through this district from east to west, and was crossed at Kelton by the age-old track running due north from the coast up the Glenken and over the watershed into Ayrshire at Carsphairn. The boundaries of this Anglian colony, which seems to have been called 'the Shire', can be identified today.[30]

Two Anglian settlements lie either side of the mouth of the Urr: at Edingham, a few miles from the Mote of Mark, and Buittle. Both were parish names in the twelfth century, and both represent distinctively early Old English place-names. Buittle derives from the OE 'botl', meaning 'hall' or mother-village. This was the site of one of the chief residences of native lords of Galloway until the fourteenth century.

Inland of Buittle lies the parish of Kelton (calf village). The name could be any age, but the place has a long history as a strategic cross-roads where the Roman road intersects with the route up the Glenken. Kelton's pre-Northumbrian name seems to have been Threave (Brittonic tref — homestead), or possibly as suggested in the Prologue, Loctrebe (homestead by the lake) a place-name recorded in Roman times.[31]

The settlement was evidently an important native centre before the advent of the Romans, and the second-century Roman fort at Glenlochar was built, not only to control the strategic cross-roads, but to keep the native *oppidum* under surveillance. Archaeology has demonstrated the wealth and antiquity of this tribal centre. The La Tène Celtic pony-mask (BC 400–200) was unearthed at Torrs Farm, where there is also a stone circle.[32] Carlingwark Loch at Castle Douglas is known to contain a crannog, and a hoard of metal was cast into the loch as a votive offering in pre-Christian times. It can be dated by the Roman military equipment it contained.[33] A strong local cult of a water deity is marked by the Latin name of the river Dee ('Dea' — goddess) less than a mile away. A standing stone near the site of a traditional horse fair at Kelton Hill represented a tribal assembly point. The strategic position of Kelton, and its antiquity as a settlement is unusually clear.

The Angles' presence in and around Kelton fairly early in the period of their supremacy is indicated by more than one undatable place-name. It is established by the church dedication to St Oswald the Martyr, recorded in 1210. This king of Bernicia, who was seen as the founder of the Northumbrian church was killed fighting the heathen Penda in 642. St Cuthbert, especially beloved from the personality that emerges from two almost contemporaneous 'Lives', had died in AD 687. In 698 his tomb was opened, and his body was found to be uncorrupted. This was seen as a mark of special holiness and his cult flourished from that time.

A second commemoration of St Oswald is to be found in the adjoining parish of Rerrick (now better known as Auchencairn). The estate name Kirkcarswell (Kyrassalda 1365) incorporates the saint's name, and the parish church of Auchencairn, built on a new site in 1855, still bears the dedication. It was in this parish that a fragment of stone cross was found a few years ago built into a bridge. More recently part of a metal object — possibly a reliquary — was picked up in

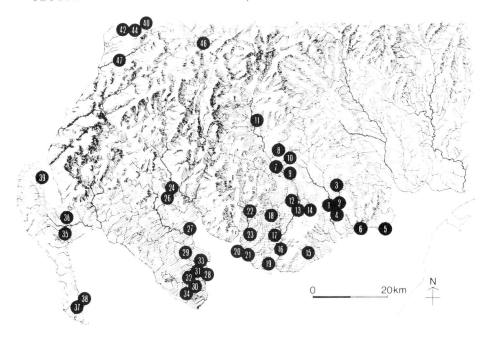

The Northumbrian Settlements in Galloway and Carrick (Dave Pollock)

Key: (d) = lord of Galloway's demesne
　　 [ ] = settlement identified, OE place-name lost
　　 ( ) = obsolete place-name

Map Ref (NX)	Settlement Name	Map Ref (NX)	Settlement Name	Map Ref (NX)	Settlement Name
1	8161	Buittle (d)	18	6559	Miefield	35	0953	Stoneykirk
2	8362	Edingham	19	6546	Senwick	36	1058	Soulseat
3	8367	Blaiket	20	5749	[Ardwall Island]	37	1335	Alton
4	8359	Richorn (d)	21	5948	Porton	38	1435	Cailliness
5	9655	Preston	22	6050	Plunton	39	0368	(Rintsnoc)
6	9056	Southwick (d)	23	6053	Girthon	40	3009	Maybole
7	6672	Burned Island (d)	24	4060	Penninghame	41	?	Scipsate
8	6875	Shirmers	25	?	(Frethrid)	42	2407	Turnberry
9	7169	Parton	26	3864	Mertonhall	43	?	(Coffe)
10	7074	[Glen]swinton	27	4355	Wigtown	44	2607	(Suthblane)
11	6183	Earlston	28	4843	Cruggleton (d)	45	?	(Snade)
12	7163	[Kirkandrews]	29	4248	Claunch	46	3804	Straiton
13	7361	Netherall	30	4440	Whithorn	47	2701	Dailly
14	7660	Kelton (d)	31	4544	Broughton	48	1183	[Ballantrae]
15	7549	[Kirk]carswell	32	4442	Outon	49	?	(Red Hohc)
16	6850	[Kirk]cudbright	33	4645	Pouton	50	?	(Alesburc)
17	6654	Twynholm	34	4339	Rispain			

the old kirkyard. Westward along the coast the port of Kirkcudbright honours St Cuthbert in the OE spelling of his name — Cudbriht. A well-carved stone cross-arm was found in the ancient kirkyard here, and a 'little ancient church of rock and stone' is recorded in a twelfth-century 'Life of St Cuthbert'.[34]

This concentration of Anglian coastal settlements ends abruptly at the Skyreburn ((Glen)skirburne 1494) just west of Gatehouse of Fleet. There Ardwall Island, the site of a seventh-century Irish religious community lies off-shore. Although the stream name Skyreburn is not documented until the fifteenth century it appears to preserve the OE 'scir-burna' (shire stream, boundary stream). The limit of Anglian territory in this area apparently ran from the Skyreburn up-country and eastward to Shirmers on Loch Ken. This was the OE 'scir-(ge)maere' (shire boundary). A British estate-name lay north of this divide, and to the south is a cluster of settlements with OE names, including Parton (Parton c. 1275) deriving from 'pearr-tun' (village within the district). In Loch Ken the stronghold of Arsbotil (1456) (now Burned Island) containing once more the element 'botl', guarded the track up the glen and over the border into Ayrshire.[35]

This well-defined Anglian district is matched by another stretching from the Cree crossing in Penninghame down the east coast of the Machars to Whithorn and Glasserton in the south. This includes lands and villages that can be shown in medieval records to have belonged to the monastic estate of Whithorn. The dominant stronghold in this area at Cruggleton has almost entirely disappeared as the thirteenth-century stone castle subsided down the steep cliff into the sea. Excavation has however revealed a long period of continued occupation on the site consisting first of a roundhouse, then a timber hall which probably dated from the Anglian period, and finally the stone castle built by Roger de Quinci, one of the heirs of the last native prince of Galloway.

A third 'shire' lay in Carrick: five medieval parishes running southward from a 'mother village' at Maybole (another 'botl' name). Church dedications to St Oswald and St Cuthbert extend southward to Ballantrae. The boundary with Galloway is once more identified here. The name of the highest mountain ridge in south-west Scotland, the Merrick (850 m) appears to derive from the OE 'gemaere-rig' (boundary ridge). Coastal outliers from these three 'shires' controlled strategic landing places.

The conclusions of the comprehensive study of which that is a sample, are unexpected. The Angles settled in Galloway in the seventh and eighth centuries more extensively than used to be thought, and mainly in places of continuing importance. Out of a list of 69 medieval parishes in Galloway and Carrick, 30 had Old English names originating at this period. More than this, fairly precise territorial boundaries can be traced between the Anglian colonies and enclaves of British population, presumably rendering tribute to the Angles.

The existence of field churches in the Anglian sectors is shown by the commemorations of Northumbrian saints, and by the fragments of eighth- and ninth-century stone crosses. Fragments of three eighth-century stone crosses can be traced — at Auchencairn, Kirkcudbright, and Tongland. Dedications to

3

STORM BULLETIN:

Raiders, Refugees and Colonists
(836–1128)

> The waves rose high, and the sea that was tranquil before, became dark and
> stormy. Three immense waves coming one after the other half-filled the vessel
> . . . and were immediately changed into blood.[1]

This imaginative evocation of a storm at sea was written in the comparative calm
of the early twelfth century by Symeon of Durham. He was describing with an
intuitive understanding of their terror and despair, the sufferings of his brother
monks fleeing from the Vikings more than 200 years before. Between the mid-
ninth century and the end of the eleventh a prolonged struggle between peoples
for territory and power altered the political geography of Britain. It was an era
when the lives of warriors were short, and the suffering of non-combatants long.
The impact on Galloway is poorly documented, but a dearth of historical records
was general. Early medieval society depended on its monasteries to preserve lit-
eracy, to keep the annals, and chronicle events; and they — undefended and full
of treasures — were the first casualties of Viking assault. As one by one the
monasteries were attacked and their communities terrorised and dispersed, regularly maintained records of important events ceased. Among even greater losses,
recorded history was almost suspended.

VIKINGS

This was less true in the south where the *Anglo-Saxon Chronicle* preserved
accounts of the clash between the Anglo-Saxon kingdoms and incoming Danes
and Norsemen. After much suffering, during which Pagan armies quartered
themselves upon the countryside, and raiding gave way to settlement, the kings
of Wessex emerged as leaders. It was they who eventually checked the
Scandinavian invasion, and welded the territories occupied by Anglo-Saxons and
Scandinavians into a single state. Events in the north are known only in general
outline. Norse and Danish Vikings first raided and then occupied large tracts of
Yorkshire and Northumbria, Caithness, Sutherland and the Western Isles.
Around 840, when disaster appears to have fallen upon Whithorn, Danes established themselves in Dublin, and some years later conquered the Northumbrian
capital of York.

There were sudden savage raids, when leading Norsemen sailed among the islands all summer alternately trading and inflicting atrocities on isolated communities. A highly organised slave-market developed in Dublin trading with the moors of Spain, and there was a regular traffic in young western slaves to eastern Islam.[2] The Norsemen's relations with the native peoples in northern England and Scotland ranged from murder and the annexation of their land, to slaving, rape and outright war. Equally their transactions included commerce, the negotiation of political accommodations, and intermarriage. Under these pressures many natives with families and property to protect, resorted to expedients to buy off armies, or even to join forces with adventurers in profitable maritime warfare. As time went on an unpredictable degree of local assimilation often took place.

As the old kingdom of Northumbria collapsed, other native peoples gained power. The small kingdom of Scottish Dalriada, finding its western coasts and islands penetrated by Norsemen, moved its centre westward to Dunkeld. This ancient stronghold of the Picts came into Scottish hands with the rest of the Pictish kingdom after long warfare, and a final battle of great slaughter. This can be dated around 845. In the next century the British kingdom around the Rock of Dumbarton gained a great swathe of territory to the south including Annandale in Dumfriesshire and the Eden valley in what is now called English Cumbria. The Norse occupied parts of Ireland and the Hebrides, and the western seas between Dublin and Oslo were a battleground.

Until the excavation at Whithorn provided a factual continuum, any account focused on Galloway depended on a few equivocal sources. A raid is chronicled; forlorn refugees wander along the Solway coast carrying a coffin; new settlers are disclosed by 40 or 50 place-names; a succession of stone crosses testifies to continuity through many vicissitudes of some sort of settled Christian life. As the storm rises to its climax, faceless arrivals reach Galloway, their status and power uncertain. A more coherent sequence of events can be achieved as a result of the excavation but interpretation is far from simple, and the scene remains shadowy. Names and personalities are almost lacking from the story.

WHITHORN

The major disruption at Whithorn in the middle of the ninth century which has been revealed by archaeology wrought a dramatic change in the life of the community. The internal furnishings of the church were dismantled and the former chancel was used as a winnowing floor, while level ground a few yards outside the church, was ploughed up. Northumbrian coins date the change of use fairly narrowly around the year 844.[3] The Anglian community of Galloway was responding to a local disaster, a reduced standard of living, and the unsettled state of Northumbria itself, by retrenchment and reorganisation. Within a few years the deconsecrated church and burial chapel took fire. The thatched roofs and the draught of the winnowing floor had perhaps combined to cause an all too common accident. Or perhaps it was no accident?

58

ALPIN

The local disaster which precipitated these changes is opportunely explained by a written source. A Scottish chronicle — one of very few that refers directly to Galloway at this time — records a raid on Galloway in the year 841. The attacker was Alpin, the father of the Scottish king, Kenneth MacAlpin, who in 845 was to unite the kingdom of the Picts with the kingdom of Scots. Medieval chroniclers proudly tracing the lineage of the kings of Scots from Kenneth MacAlpin may have invested Kenneth's father Alpin with a royalty not properly his.[4] Alpin remains a shadowy figure — a chief perhaps, certainly an adventurer, based in western Argyll. An ancient chronicle of the Scottish kings records that he died in 841 'in Galloway after he had entirely destroyed and devastated it'.[5] A variant version dating from a thirteenth-century document gives more detail: 'He was killed in Galloway after he had destroyed it, by a single man who watched him in a thick wood above the entrance to the ford of a river while he rode with his men.'[6]

The stark account of a raid in which Galloway was laid waste and Alpin was killed has acquired the accretions of legend. Apart from the vivid story of a single assassin watching the raiders from a wood, Alpin's death has been localised in Glenapp just over the Ayrshire border and his burial marked (it is said) by a monolith subsequently known as the Taxing Stone a few miles away, near the eastern shore of Loch Ryan. The stone stands just south of the Carrick border on the farm now called Little Laight on the eastern shore of Loch Ryan, adjoining Meikle Laight on one side and Laight Moor on the other. Alpin's connection with Glenapp can be questioned. The medieval name of Glenapp was 'Gleann-ob' which in Gaelic means, not Alpin's glen, but valley with a shallow river, topographically an apt description.[7] This story of the death of an early Scottish hero has been so romanticised, probably after Galloway was absorbed into Scotland, that the raid itself might be dismissed as a fabrication, but for the sober witness of an obsolete place-name.

Lands closely associated with Little Laight were recorded with minor variants at least eight times between 1203–7 and 1492, as Lachtalpin.[8] The Gaelic place-name 'leac-' or 'Lacht-Alpin' means Alpin's grave-stone. Somewhere near Loch Ryan, where raiding ships could make landfall, a chief called Alpin met his death and was buried. The raid upon Galloway becomes more credible.

The raiding party apparently met opposition, or were ambushed as they returned to their ships in Loch Ryan. They had, perhaps, been as far east as Whithorn, but where else they had struck at villages and farm lands is not certain. The chronicle's implication that Galloway had been devastated from end to end may be exaggerated. The devastation may have been confined to the western districts. The damage such a raid could inflict on the local subsistence economy was nevertheless almost beyond calculation. For it would not be a matter of firing one year's crops. Growing and stored grain would have been burned, including the precious reserve of seed corn for planting the following season. Cattle that

'Lacht Alpin' (or the Taxing Stone) 1.7 m high, said to mark the grave of the Scottish raider, Alpin. It may have been an ancient standing stone (Wigtown District Museum Service)

could not be driven away would be slaughtered. Villages and communities will have been attacked, the inhabitants killed or driven into hiding, the roof-timbers of their houses burned. The word 'destroyed' employed by the chronicle was not so inexact — food and shelter and some of the people alike were gone. Recovery from such devastation might take, not a season, but a generation. The drastic adjustment at Whithorn was the price of survival. The ploughing up of the church precinct illuminates the urgent need for grain. The record of Alpin's raid is wholly consistent with the archaeological evidence, and symptomatic of the disturbed times.

THE GALLGAIDHIL

That was further illustrated by entries in the *Annals of Ulster* for the years 856, 857 and 859. Warbands called in the Irish annals 'Gallgaidhil' (pronounced Gall-gael) were operating both on land and sea in the local wars between Irish chiefs and the Norsemen. On one occasion the Gallgaidhil were supporting an Irish prince

The bridge at Glenapp. By Hugh Thomson from the Rev C A Dick: Highways and Byways in Galloway and Carrick, *2nd edn, 1927 (EL)*

against the Norsemen, and on another they were fighting with the Vikings against the Irish. The Gallgaidhil were apparently mercenaries — freelance fighters at the disposal of any warlord whose activities promised sufficient plunder. Judging by the Irish term applied to them they may have come from Galloway, for though it can be interpreted to mean 'foreign Gael', the name could have been a gaelicisation deriving from the Brittonic name for Galloway.[9] It was almost to be expected that Gallovidian mercenaries would be operating in the conditions of social breakdown of the mid-ninth century.

WHITHORN: THE CHURCH RESTORED

The disruption at Whithorn at any rate was temporary. A new church was built. It was shorter than the old timber church, but stoutly constructed on low stone walls with a timber superstructure. That it was intended for a ritual use, replacing the former church, is plain from Northumbrian compass-drawn designs of a cross and a 'marigold' of seven intersecting circles scratched on paving stones on the floor and just outside the building. The old burial chapel was also refurbished.[10] A succession of small buildings to the north show renewed settlement. A new village had grown up on the south side, which was to prove long-lasting. The surviving Anglian community seems to have re-established itself, restoring and redeveloping the monastic village and the lay settlement on a more modest scale.

After so much effort at reconstruction it comes as a surprise to find that within a couple of generations the new church was systematically and carefully dismantled. The main timbers were removed and reserved for further use, and the structure was allowed to collapse inward upon itself. No other consecrated building was erected there, perhaps because the demolition signified the building or re-building of a church on the top of the hill. The life of the Gallovidian Angles remained precarious. They were on the defensive both against fresh raids, and perhaps from fear that their vulnerability would tempt the British native population up-country, to attack them. This state of insecurity could have lasted as much as 50 or 60 years.[11]

REFUGEES

About the year 882, refugees from Lindisfarne reached Whithorn in search of food, shelter and safety, after a seemingly interminable journey. They had set out seven years before after the second raid on Lindisfarne in 875. The Danish leader Halfdan, already established in Dublin, had harried Northumbria, destroyed Carlisle, and occupied the city of York and the surrounding countryside. In 876 he was sharing out the whole province of Northumbria between himself and his men and 'together with the army, cultivated the land'.[12] It is left to the imagination what happened to the dispossessed landholders.

In 875, the army had sacked Lindisfarne. Since the raid of 793, the monastery had been unmolested, the monks carrying on their old life of prayer, and making few concessions to changed times. They were still illuminating books with lettering of silver and gold in the tradition of their gospel book, produced before the Vikings had become a threat.[13] Nevertheless when the Danish attack came, Bishop Eardulf and Abbot Aenred showed decisiveness and some forethought. They hustled their monks down to the boats, and left the island, taking time to collect the heavy coffin of St Cuthbert from its shrine, and the gospel book in its jewelled case. They took to the road, travelling south and west, carrying the coffin. At first, because they were held in such respect by the people, they were given food and hospitality in the villages. People brought gifts, rich or simple according to their means as long as there were things to give. The route they followed was probably the Roman way from Berwick-on-Tweed to the river Aln, and thence via High Rochester or Chesters and Corbridge. Some of the time they will have traversed forest and hill-country. It was not easy on foot, carrying the coffin. When they reached settled land again their difficulties increased, for the region had been stricken with epidemic and famine, and was terrorised by the Vikings. There was very little food to be had.

The account written 200 years later recalls a stricken countryside where 'No man dare put a hoe in the ground for fear of the Norsemen.'[14] Its topographical vagueness indicates that the refugees themselves were often uncertain of their whereabouts. The essentials were remembered — their hunger, and how at one point in the seventh year of their wandering, the only provisions they could get were a cheese and a salted horse's head. The whole tone of the account suggests the wanderers either travelled alone through a deserted and famine-stricken countryside, or that they went by hidden ways through the forests, not daring to approach the homesteads and villages lest the Vikings were in possession. Memories of this nightmare were handed down from generation to generation of monks, and recalled once the community had at last found a place to settle at Chester-le-Street. The accounts now extant were written in the early twelfth century probably from older narratives, when the community had made a permanent home in Durham. But for seven years, the chroniclers claim, Bishop Eardulf and his companions journeyed from place to place, homeless outcasts, constantly having to move on.

Initially they struck westward into Cumbria, through desolated country. They felt that a duty had been laid upon them to preserve and find shelter for St Cuthbert's relics in his own land of Northumbria. But when they reached the mouth of the Derwent (Workington) despair overtook them, and they decided to give up the struggle and embark for Ireland. They set out in good weather, but a storm 'forced the ship on its beam ends'; and in the ensuing panic the precious gospel book was swept across the heeling deck into the sea.

The bishop and his monks saw the storm as the wrath of God. In penitence, mourning the loss of their treasured book, they put back into port. Then a diminished party set out overland once more, through unfamiliar country, in search of food and a safe abiding place. In this extremity one of the monks called Hunred, dreamed that St Cuthbert spoke to him, and told him how to find a horse to pull the coffin, and so ease their journey. He urged him to search for the lost gospel book on the shore. 'Now at this time,' the account goes on, 'they had reached the place called the White House, or more commonly Huuitern'. Here, at an abnormally low tide after walking for three miles and more they eventually found 'the holy volume of the gospels with its gold, gems, and all its outward splendour, as well as its letters and leaves, and all its inward beauty, so sound and perfect, that it looked as if it had not been touched by water'. Inspired by this proof of St Cuthbert's care for them, Hunred recalled the rest of the saint's instructions in his dream. They were to look for a bridle hanging on a tree, and a red horse, that would run up and offer itself to be harnessed. This happened according to plan, and the party set out once more with the horse drawing the coffin behind them to the relief of the monks who had been carrying it on their shoulders.

Provided the reference to Whithorn is taken to mean they were in the diocese of Whithorn rather than the town, the gist of the story is not improbable. The description of the Solway at low tide is recognisable if exaggerated, but it fits the upper Solway better than the more open sea near Whithorn. Wide expanses of mud and sand, firm enough to walk on in places, are exposed when the tide goes out. These flats adjoin the fords of Solway, a route for horsemen in the Middle Ages, exposed for a perilously brief interval at low tide.

The story does not include any description of Whithorn town or of the refugees' reception there. Had such memories remained, a medieval writer might have painted a highly coloured picture of the monks' tears of joy. No welcome was

A storm at sea: from an illuminated MS. The central figure is St Cuthbert himself (by permission of the British Library: Yates Thompson MS. 26. f 26)

remembered and there is no assurance that the refugees penetrated as far west as Whithorn. The loss and recovery of the *Lindisfarne Gospels* suggests perhaps, that some help was received towards its preservation until better times; but the strongest impression that the story conveys is desolation. The wanderers seem to have been alone in a strange and oddly unpeopled land. They managed to get cheese and salted horsemeat, but in a horse-breeding country, it had taken a miracle to procure a horse. Evidently they met no Norsemen in the diocese of Whithorn; but they seemed to meet few other people. It was nearly 50 years since Alpin's raid had devastated Galloway, and although the scars of that devastation might still have rendered the countryside comparatively inhospitable, there is a possibility that the epidemic and famine that struck Cumbria had visited Galloway also, and left it partially depopulated.

NORSE SETTLERS

British pressure on the Anglian population of Galloway was almost certainly increasing by the year 900, as the kingdom of Strathclyde, the kinsmen and natural allies of the Gallovidian Britons derived increasing power from the collapse of Northumbria. If the Angles were at the same time depleted in numbers by epidemic or famine, their need for reinforcement would explain the arrival about the same time of Norse-speaking settlers on Anglian territory.[15] A thin belt of place-names deriving from Old Norse extends along the coast of Galloway and southern Carrick. Most of these settlements occupy good cereal-growing land. They are too closely confined to the coast, and too few in number to suggest wholesale conquest by Norsemen. The evidence points to a negotiated deal between the incomers and Galloway's Anglian rulers.

The Scandinavian settlements in northern England had such an effect upon the Middle English spoken in the north that many topographical terms deriving from Old Norse were adopted into the vocabulary of English-speakers. Words such as dale, fell, holm (island or water meadow), gill (narrow valley), ness (headland), and kirk (church) and the suffix -bie, or -by (homestead) cannot be regarded without supportive evidence as signs of Norse settlement. In Galloway however, a number of place-names, especially in the parishes of Glasserton and Borgue, can be unhesitatingly identified as Norse. Ravenstone in Glasserton was originally 'hrafn's skogr' (Hrafn's wood) and the personal name Hrafn may represent one of the leaders of the warband who originally settled in the district. Kidsdale and Physgill (fish valley) nearby and several other estates within a short distance trace the outlines of the settlement around Whithorn, while to the east Kirkdale (church valley) and Borgue (from 'borg', a fort) with Boreness (fort headland) close by, lie between Gatehouse and Kirkcudbright. The fort was an old Iron Age fortification, Castle Haven on the shore at Kirkandrews, reoccupied at some time by Vikings. Rerrick ('hreyrr-eyk' — cairn-oak, or boundary oak), Hestan Island (Estholm — east island), and Southerness (originally Salternes — headland of

A page from the Lindisfarne Gospels. *The manuscript was written 'in honour of God and St Cuthbert' by the scribe Eadfrith; bound by Aethilwald; an Old English translation inserted by Aldred; and the jewelled case, now lost, was wrought by Billfrith. All four were monks of Lindisfarne. Two later became bishops of Lindisfarne (by permission of the British Library: Colton MS Nero. D.IV.1.139)*

66

the saltpans) are examples from a list of nearly 40 Norse-named settlements stretching along the coast.[16]

These estates gave the incomers easy access to the best harbours in Galloway — the Isle of Whithorn, Kirkandrews, Kirkcudbright and Kippford — as bases for fishing, trading and piracy. A sculptured stone at Kilmorie on the western shore of Loch Ryan clearly establishes by its style and Christian symbolism, the presence there of Norsemen newly converted to the faith. An incised crucifixion scene portrays the crude strength of Thor the Mighty rather than a Christ manifesting the still alien qualities of sacrifice and compassion.

Late medieval records preserve evidence that some of the most important of the estates with Norse names had at some time been communities of free men — a ship's crew or a warband dating perhaps from the start of the tenth century. At Kidsdale in Wigtownshire and Borgue in Kirkcudbrightshire, both large grain producing estates, the land had been portioned out between free peasants holding their land directly from the rulers of Galloway.[17]

When the ninth Earl of Douglas, lord of Galloway, was dispossessed by the crown in 1455 the lands were managed on the king's behalf by a local Chamberlain reporting to the Exchequer. The *Exchequer Rolls* give details of their management for the next 50 years. For the most part they were run as they had been for centuries by the lords of Galloway, respecting the rights of the customary possessors. Most were managed on a manorial pattern with a lord of the manor between the peasantry and the superior, Galloway's hereditary rulers. At Kidsdale however there was no lord of the manor. The lands were let direct by the superior to the peasants themselves, on a steel-bow arrangement by which they cultivated the land and paid the crown an annual rent in kind, retaining seed corn each harvest for the next sowing. The Latin term applied by the Exchequer for these producers was unique in Galloway estate records — it was 'coloni'.[18] The word has no servile implications, and can be translated husbandmen or even colonists. A document of 1282 refers to the freemen of Borgue.[19]

Land-holding patterns, like estate boundaries, are proverbially long-lived; and provided this late evidence is not strained unduly, it is an attractive speculation to trace a connection between the tenure of the 'coloni' of 1455 and Norsemen settling the lands by arrangement with the Anglian rulers around the year 900. Good land was handed over as the price of coastal defences, which possibly preserved in much later records vestiges of a Norse social pattern. At Ravenstone the leader of the Viking colonists may have taken over an estate for himself. Elsewhere if our daring speculations may be entertained, Norse settlers held land directly from the Anglian rulers, and farmed communally on an open-field system. Part of the bargain struck may have included the Vikings' acceptance of Christian baptism. That is clear, not only from the Kilmory stone, but from undeniable evidence that well organised Christian observance continued throughout Galloway during the undocumented period. While the political events can be inferred only in shadowy outline, evidence of the continued vitality of the church is more explicit.

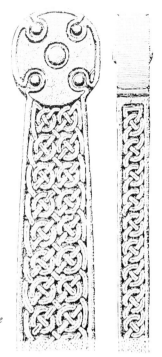

The Monreith Cross, one of the most handsome crosses of the tenth and eleventh centuries by the Whithorn school (DGNHAS, EL)

THE TENTH-CENTURY CHURCH

The conversion of the incoming Norsemen, the possibility of a new church built on the crown of the hill at Whithorn, and a vigorous parish system can be traced in the tenth century. The administration of this apparently diocesan organisation is suggestive of the bishopric's continuity.

Numerous stone crosses dating from the tenth and eleventh centuries have been identified widely distributed over the countryside, some associated with the Angles, and some with the British population. Round-headed crosses decorated with interlace have been classified as the 'Whithorn school'. There are something like 150 of them. They are not all now in their original positions, but were apparently sited either singly or in groups mainly in eastern Wigtownshire, spaced so as to suggest a pattern of parishes around field churches. Simpler, incised crosses have been found in other districts, particularly the British territories.[20]

Neither the carving nor design of the Whithorn school reach the quality of the eighth-century Anglian crosses at their best, but the sculpture is not to be despised. The crosses are carved with assurance and some are undoubtedly handsome. While they show affinities to contemporaneous work elsewhere, as a group they have a unique style. It implies a school of local craftsmen training up their own apprentices from generation to generation, and a local aristocracy with the wealth, Christian commitment, and taste to be their patrons. These monuments stand for a measure of social stability during the undocumented period, and for the continued vitality of the church. They must surely have marked old Northumbrian field churches, where what was perhaps originally a wooden cross had been replaced and improved on, and possibly a pattern of parishes extended to include new field churches. A burial ground, and perhaps a shrine, given added identification and dignity by the cross, was the local gathering point of the faithful. Some were, doubtless, erected by noble patrons for their own households.

Later documents make it clear that some church buildings existed at this period. In Kirkcudbright a church of 'minster' type, with a resident community of canons training up novices, was reported as late as 1164. They were still apparently serving the pastoral needs of the laity for baptism and burial, and celebrating High Mass on holy days. The twelfth-century writer who described it, related disapprovingly that the 'Scolofthes' (novices) baited a bull on consecrated ground on St Cuthbert's day, to the discredit of this old-fashioned establishment. But his reference to the 'little ancient church of rock and stone' leaves no doubt of its antiquity.[21] This type of 'mother-church' extended its pastoral care to scattered villages by a circle of small chapels. Some are still traceable. Similar centres may be discovered elsewhere, for instance at Barhobble in the parish of Mochrum, Wigtownshire, excavation has revealed a church and burial ground of some size and importance. Several fragments of crosses (including one hammer-headed cross similar to the one at Kilmory) have been found. The church has been identified as Celto-Norse, and dates from the early eleventh century. A stone church was built around the middle of the twelfth. The whole sequence suggests a regional centre connected with the diocesan centre at Whithorn.[22] At Edingham near Dalbeattie another mother-church has been traced from later documentation; and there may have been others.[23]

Two distinct models of parish organisation existed — the mother-church with its extended 'plebania', and the field church centering on a cross, possibly within a noble estate. They reflected on the one hand the survival of church buildings from the Northumbrian supremacy, and on the other, later initiatives by lay patrons in raising crosses or renewing older ones, where there were no church buildings.

The survival of the bishopric into the tenth century is further evidenced by an almost obsolete Norse place-name at the Isle of Whithorn. Bysbie Cottage preserves the name of an old estate recorded in 1305 as Biskoby or Biskeby, and in 1454 as Biscoby.[24] This derives from the Old Norse 'biscop-byr', meaning Bishop's farm, and suggests lands owned by the bishop who commanded the natural harbour at the Isle. Such a name would hardly have been coined in the late ninth or early tenth century on the strength of a bishop's having lived there before 840. Equally it cannot represent a late use of the Norse suffix 'byr' (which did remain current into the twelfth century in some places) because by the time the bishopric was permanently restored in 1128 the connection between the bishop and Bysbie was probably already forgotten. By 1305 the lands were claimed by Dundrennan Abbey (founded 1142) as part of their long-standing estate. Their value to the monks was obvious, for by then they were exporting wool, and needed a harbour for their ships. Their right was disputed in the fifteenth century by Whithorn Priory, a competing exporter of wool, while the bishop of the day complained to the Pope in 1408 that he had no residence nearer to Whithorn than ten miles away.

Once reinforced by Norse colonists to defend their coast, the Gallovidian Angles seemed by the tenth century, to have achieved something like prosperity and continuing good order. Two of the carved crosses of this period — one at Whithorn and one in Ninian's cave — testify independently to the survival of the Anglian ruling class. Both are inscribed with Anglian runes, and one appears to have been marked with the personal name 'Donferth', an Anglian name in a tenth-century form.[25] Just as the bishopric may have been retained, so for a time yet the Angles managed to maintain a power balance with their British neighbours. The Gallovidian Britons were by tradition cattle and horse breeders to whom the hill pastures were a natural habitat. They were also miners, and occupied the areas where silver could be extracted and gold panned in the streams. (The iron and copper deposits lay in the Anglian lands.) Both peoples hunted and fished; but the wildlife and game of the forests and waters were abundant enough for both. Competition for arable land may not have been a source of friction, and the seclusion of one settlement from another by wide tracts of forest, helped to maintain a rub-along peace.

Both peoples seem to have occupied islands and crannogs, a tradition reaching back to Roman times and beyond. They were easily defensible against wolves and aggressors, but the fortifications were light. Each people maintained their little strongholds at strategic points, and equilibrium seems to have been maintained until events beyond Galloway's borders upset the balance.

BRITISH POWER

The independent kingdom, Strathclyde, with its stronghold on the rock of Dumbarton, had been hemmed in (so long as the Northumbrian power lasted) to a limited territory centering on the Clyde valley. Once Northumbria had collapsed, and the kingdom of Scots was preoccupied in assimilating erstwhile Pictish lands and institutions, Strathclyde was free to expand. The rapid annexation of the strategic southern corridor of Nithsdale, Annandale and the vale of Eden brought its southernmost boundary to the Rere Cross on Stainmore.[26] The speed with which these territories were acquired was almost certainly assisted by continued ease of movement along the old Roman ways.

This development in the early tenth century argues that the kings of Strathclyde were able to rely on the acquiescence of the Scots and the Hiberno-Norse, who had replaced the Danes in York and Northumbria.[27] The effect was briefly to renew Strathclyde's strength. The Gallovidian Britons inevitably benefitted. The old balance between Briton and Angle tipped in the Britons' favour, and the Angles were caught in a nut-cracker grip. Strathclyde and Galloway had a common border along the southern limits of Ayrshire, and Strathclyde's hold on

Nithsdale and Annandale divided the Gallovidian Angles from their traditional homeland of Northumbria. They were apparently compelled to draw back to the river Urr.[28]

Important place-names containing the Brittonic 'tref-' (homestead) lying between the Nith and Urr, were probably survivals of Strathclyde's occupation: Troqueer on the west bank of the Nith, and Terrauchtie in the parish of Lochrutton (Traachty 1487). These, several more in Nithsdale, and eight or nine in Carrick, probably mark centres of power and wealth in these enclaves of tenth-century Strathclyde. Terregles, also on the west bank of the Nith, may be a much older survival, containing the primitive Christian element 'ecles', meaning a church, although medieval forms suggest the later 'eglwys'.

West of the Urr, older settlements of the Gallovidian Britons can be traced. The old name for the parish of Balmaclellan, Trevercarcou (1275), and Troquhain suggest British settlements north of the Anglian shire in the Northumbrian period, and Threave at Castle Douglas, a pre-Northumbrian tribal centre. An equally ancient stratum of Brittonic place-names survives in the parishes and great estates of Wigtownshire west of Whithorn. Most of them incorporate the word corresponding to the Welsh 'maen', signifying a stone, usually a standing stone: Monreith co-terminous with the obsolete parish of Kirkmaiden; Mindork; and the large multiple estate now called Craighlaw, and in 1296 Manhincon.[29] It included the medieval parish of Longcastle (Lengast). This name contained the Brittonic 'lann' (church). Several crannogs were found there when Dowalton Loch was drained in 1862, and it was here among the artefacts unearthed, that a Roman *patella* (skillet) stamped with the mark of the first-century foundry of P Cipius Polibius was found — a tangible suggestion that the crannog was inhabited in Roman times. Another important British enclave dominated the Rhins, with its centre in what became the medieval barony of Leswalt.

The antiquity of these multiple estates can be clearly established. Their survival to the very threshold of the twelfth century emphasised the strength of the Brittonic element in Galloway's medieval culture. British kindreds under a recognised chief were still an important part of the social organisation of Galloway and Carrick in the fourteenth century.[30] The Brittonic administrative division, the cantred, can be traced in both districts.

PEASANTS

Great estates required a large work-force. British peoples may have attached less importance to arable production than the Angles, but they ate bread and other cereal foods, and produced the grain to make them.[31] Mineral extraction and timber felling called for intensive labour. Very little is known about the organisation of the work force, and the social structure of the British enclaves at the lower levels, or how the structure came about. By the tenth and eleventh centuries the kindreds were probably served by a servile class of Gaelic-speakers. Dialect words 'gossok' and 'kreenie', still current in the nineteenth century, suggest as much.

'Gossok' has been shown to be a survival corresponding to the Welsh 'gwasog' which originally implied a person of servile status. 'Kreenie' deriving from the Cruithnich of northern Ireland, seems to have been a synonym; and became a contemptuous word, almost a term of abuse. Evidently the 'kreenie' had been subject to a Welsh-speaking aristocracy who called them 'gwasog'.[32]

OVERLORDS

Strathclyde's rise to power in the tenth century coincided with intervention by the kings of Wessex in northern affairs. In 927 Athelstan challenged the pagan Hiberno-Norse lord of York for the control of Northumbria. The kings of Scots, allying with Strathclyde and the Hiberno-Norse, opposed the house of Wessex. On occasion, when compelled by military necessity, they submitted; but the struggle for Northumbria continued. It had the effect of bringing the horizon of the Scottish kings southward. By negotiation with the Saxons of Wessex they annexed English Cumbria. Meanwhile they gradually reduced Strathclyde to the status of a client-kingdom under their overlordship.

THE KINGDOM OF SCOTS AND THE 'GALLGAIDHIL'

In the first 20 years of the eleventh century the distribution of power between peoples in North Britain and Ireland changed decisively. In 1014 the Battle of Clontarf smashed the power of the Hiberno-Norse of Dublin. In the east four years later, Malcolm II King of Scots heavily defeated the Northumbrians at Carham in Northumberland. He had been supported by Owen, King of Strathclyde, who may have been killed in the battle. At any rate he died the same year, and Malcolm was able to enforce a claim to his throne. So ended the ancient British kingdom. The Scots had gained Lothian and Strathclyde (then called Cumbria) that stretched from the Rock of Dumbarton to the Rere Cross on Stainmore in Westmorland. It comprised Clydesdale, Peeblesshire and Ayrshire, and penetrating southward, Annandale and Nithsdale in Dumfriesshire, the Eden valley in Cumbria, and the coast south of Solway. The kingdom of Scots had Galloway surrounded on three sides.

This general outline of events is documented, but the impact within Galloway is not. At this crucial point, and for the century that followed, Galloway's history is virtually blank. That blankness may be eloquent of the turmoil it concealed.

An obscure prince of the Scottish royal house was known as the 'king of the Cumbrians' signifying his dominion over the erstwhile Strathclyde. Heirs apparent of the Scottish kingdom assumed the title of the Prince of Cumbria. To what extent they were able to exact tribute from the old Cumbrian nobility is not recorded. Equally it is not known how extensively Scottish nobles penetrated the newly acquired territories, but the spread of Gaelic place-names, for instance into Lothian, is some indication. By 1106 Alexander I was levying tribute in Ayrshire, and his heir (David I) left documentary evidence of his power over the erstwhile

Cumbrian church.[33] The status of Galloway meanwhile is obscure, but it seems to have remained distinct, with its borders more narrowly defined.

Over the same period Hiberno-Norse Vikings were leaving Ireland and settling in whatever districts they could in western Britain. These people were of Scandinavian stock whose families had spent a generation or more in Ireland. Their mothers and grandmothers were often Irish. They were Christians, and apparently Gaelic-speakers. As merchants, fighting men and seafarers they were seen as Vikings, but their numbers must have included churchmen and craftsmen.

Wherever they went, their arrival was mainly undocumented, and their numbers may have been exaggerated. In the Western Isles and Kintyre, areas already under Scandinavian control, their presence can be inferred from Irish sources and later Scottish records. In these documents they were called 'Gallgaidhil'. It has been assumed they also settled in Galloway.

Evidence has been elusive,[34] but the Dig at Whithorn has at last provided significant information bearing on the second half of the eleventh century and the early years of the twelfth. This reveals the presence of a new culture and unfamiliar personnel. The construction of a new double enclosure round the monastery on approximately the same site as the ancient one, but slightly off-centre, is an indication that the new order was investing both capital and energy into the reform of the church and monastery of Whithorn. A few artefacts and much workshop debris and waste from iron smelting indicate that crafts and technology were once more being given a prominent place there. The crafts were comparable with the work of Hiberno-Norse craftsmen in Dublin. New housing, arranged radially within the outer enclosure, was of Irish type, suggesting the life-style of late Celtic or 'Culdee' monks.

Here at last is evidence of the Hiberno-Norse in Galloway! The antiquarian view of the 'Gallgaidhil' derived from late and unreliable Irish sources. It portrayed them as conquerors who populated Galloway, gave it its name, its Gaelic speech, and incurred its medieval reputation for savagery. They were represented as godless pagans and despoilers of churches. Their arrival and the circumstances of their arrival are unrecorded. To come upon them first, engaged as enthusiastic monastery-builders and reformers is unexpected. Nevertheless once the presence of Hiberno-Norse churchmen has been identified at Whithorn, their presence elsewhere in Galloway can be traced.

AFTER THE STORM

Glancing back to the early tenth century, Galloway had then been divided between the British enclaves in the north and west and the Anglian shires in the south where Anglian power had been reinforced by invited Norse settlers. Then came the information-gap of 100 years, and when records begin again, that Anglo-Brittonic culture had been replaced by something quite different. The unrecorded process of change leaves unanswerable questions: how far had the Anglian aristocracy survived the rocket-like rise and fall of Strathclyde and the new potency of the kingdom of Scots? Were the Gallovidian Britons able to withstand Scottish pressure? And what were the circumstances of Hiberno-Norse infiltration? The course of events can only be reconstructed from what had changed in the meantime.

THE LANGUAGE CHANGE

A host of Gaelic place-names had come into existence. The multitude of topographical names and the relatively few habitation names suggest that many were the work of the peasantry. At the same time the personal names of the upper classes had become gaelicised. The churchmen and nobles surrounding the rulers of Galloway in the twelfth century are named as witnesses to the first few available charters. Among them are names like Gilcrist mac Gilwinnen, Gillecatfar, Gilmore Albannach, Gilchohel; later we hear of Gillecolum and Gillepatrick. The prefix 'Gille-' is Gaelic, signifying 'disciple' and the second part of these names honour a multitude of saints, Catholic, Northumbrian, Irish and British. Among the many 'Gille-' names the occasional form appears such as Cospatric, where the saint's name is preceded by the Brittonic 'gwas' (servant or disciple). Here the actual process of a swing from the northern equivalent of Welsh to Scots Gaelic is clearly visible, marking the language change as recent, or actually still in progress.

The 'Gille-' names were of course current in the traditionally Gaelic- speaking communities of Ireland and Scotland north of the Forth-Clyde line. By the twelfth century they and their transitional forms are traceable in Peeblesshire and Dumfriesshire as well as further west. This spread supports the well established linguistic view that as the Britons of Strathclyde fell under Scottish overlordship, Gaelic became predominant.[35] The vitality of Scots Gaelic at this period was so great that it affected even the Norse-speaking Western Isles despite their political allegiance to the Norwegian kings.[36] In all these districts it was the language rather than the population that had changed; and the Gaelic-speaking kindreds of Galloway and Carrick preserved traces of their British descent into the high Middle Ages.

The view that the Hiberno-Norse invaded in strength and populated Galloway is not sustainable against this evidence. Nor, in my view, did they give Galloway its much more ancient name; but it is clear that they infiltrated the country as churchmen and church patrons, and it must be presumed they exercised political power. Their presence probably accelerated the language change and the fashion for 'Gille-' personal names, initiated under Scottish influence. Their patronage would explain the unprecedented influence of Iona in the diocese of Whithorn.

IONA

The monastic community of Iona had suffered several vicissitudes during the Viking age, including sojourns in Ireland during the worst times. By the mid-eleventh century the monks were once more in Iona and the Columban church was recovering its influence and prestige under the patronage of both the Norse lords of the Western Isles and King Malcolm III of Scotland and his consort Margaret.

In Galloway saints honoured in the Columban church are commemorated in the Rhins, along the Kirkcudbrightshire coast, and in southern Carrick. These Columban dedications include seven parish churches, three dedicated to St Colman of Elo, and the rest to St Aed Macbricc, St Bride, St Cormac and St Cummene. New churches were apparently established and dedicated to St Colman of Elo at Buittle, Urr and Colmanell in southern Carrick. The new church at Buittle super-seded the chapel or field church at Kirkennan, and the new church at Urr replaced the moribund mother-church of Edingham. Four neighbouring churches were taken directly into the care and control of Iona, and were apparently served by its monks: the mother-church of St Oswald the Martyr of Kelton and its pendicles of Barncrosh (now in Tongland), St Andrews of Balmaghie, and Kirkcormack near Gelston.[37] The last may have been founded while the rest were under Iona's control. Iona's intervention here, and especially at Buittle, shows how deeply the new cultural influence penetrated the erstwhile Anglian power base in eastern Galloway.

The parish name Kirkcolm in Wigtownshire has often been taken as com-memorating St Columba, and the well beside the church has been mapped by the Ordnance Survey with that dedication; but the pronunciation of the parish name has apparently always been 'Kirk-Cum'. A papal letter of 1397 explains this, for it gives the patron saint as St Cummin or Cummene, and not Columba at all.[38]

The dedication to St Cummene helps to date the whole group, for he was the seventh Abbot of Iona, who died in 669. The early prestige of Iona had declined by then, especially in the eyes of the Northumbrian church, as a result of the Easter controversy, finally settled in favour of Roman practice by the Synod of Whitby in 664. St Cummene wrote the earliest 'Life and Miracles of St Columba' in an attempt to reinstate the reputation of both saint and monastery. The Northumbrian annexation of Galloway had followed, and Whithorn was soon being held up as a model of orthodoxy to Iona's disadvantage. It would have been unlikely that Galloway's dedications to Columban saints were made then, or in the period of Northumbrian supremacy; and by the ninth century Iona was under attack from Vikings. The eleventh century was the most likely time for the hon-ouring of Iona's saints in Galloway.

It is unlikely that the King of Scots' writ ran in Galloway at this time. Gallovidians may have fought under Malcolm III's banner in answer to his tribal muster, or as allies or mercenaries; but there was no sign that the kings of Scots were able to levy cain (food-rent), their traditional taxation, south of the Carrick border or west of the river Urr.[39] The church dedications themselves point to the Hiberno-Norse.

Commemorations to St Colman of Elo, St Cormac, St Cummin and St Aed MacBricc are not apparently to be found in the territories then under Scottish control. St Colman of Elo was honoured in Kintyre; St Cormac (Charmaig) in Knapdale in southern Argyll and in the Isles — all districts associated with the Gallgaidhil. The only known churches of St Cummin, apart from Kirkcolm, were at Glenelg on the north-west coast of Invernesshire, and Fort Augustus as the foot of Loch Ness. St Aed MacBricc, an Irish saint, honoured in the parish of Kirkmabreck (Kyrkemaberc 1351: Kirk Makbrik 1466) in Kirkcudbrightshire, and apparently on a less important site in Wigtownshire 'Kirkmabrick', does not seem to have been commemorated elsewhere in Britain.

In total however the patrons of the new Gallovidian parish churches seem to have been in contact with the Scandinavian culture of the Isles and the west coast. The generous investment in renewing what may have been a decaying church, suggests wealthy and possibly *parvenu* patrons anxious to purchase respectability and local acceptance.[40]

By the end of the unrecorded centuries, the Anglian nobility and the descendants of their Norse allies can no longer be identified. The survival of British law, social and administrative organisation, and the great British estates, on the other hand, emphasise the wealth and power of the British Gallovidians at a very late date. Their posterity is still identifiable in the kindreds of the fourteenth century. It must have been as the allies of the Gallovidian Britons rather than as their conquerors that the Hiberno-Norse acquired a say in political affairs. Some transfer of power may have taken place, for example by the marriage of a Hiberno-Norse chieftain to a Gallovidian heiress. Inevitably this account of the undocumented years has to conclude with a speculation.

It was not until the third decade of the twelfth century that records begin to reveal Galloway with any clarity. Then the emerging society shows all the contradictions of a mixed culture. The fighting men display the verve and savagery to be expected of a people with strong Celtic roots and acquired Viking standards. The names of the clergy and aristocracy proclaim the recent influence of Iona. Yet bishops and princes prove staunchly loyal to the Archbishops of York. An Anglo-Saxon parish system and Gaelic speech co-exist with a British social structure. As rulers of that complex community, a dynasty of able and determined princes appears in the spotlight of the first handful of documents, representing those diverse influences in their personalities and policies.

4

THE HOUSE OF FERGUS:

King of the Gallovidians
(c. 1120–60)

Thy kindome and thy grit empyre
Thy ryaltie and thy riche array,
Sall nocht endeur at thy desyre,
Bot as the wind will wend away.

Robert Henryson: 'The Abbey Walk'[1]

Fergus of Galloway stepped out of darkness into recorded history already a mature man and a political force. His parentage, youth and marriage all lay behind him in the obscurity of the preceding age. To that extent Fergus himself remains an enigma, a prince without a pedigree, whose influential dynastic marriage can be traced, although his wife's name is unknown. His subsequent career is documented only fitfully, and it says something for his personality that in a northern context, he is one of the most vividly perceived historical figures of the twelfth century. Here at last is a secular ruler of Galloway who can be identified. His descendants were to rule Galloway for two centuries.

THE BISHOPRIC

Correspondence survives from the year 1125 about the election of a bishop of Whithorn. Pope Honorius wrote to Gilla-Aldan, whom he addressed as 'his dear son the elect of Candida Casa' commanding him to seek consecration from Thurstan, Archbishop of York, his rightful metropolitan.[2] This, Gilla-Aldan obeyed and his profession of 1126 ran:

> To his lord and father the reverend Thurstan, by the grace of God Archbishop of the Province of York, Gilla-Aldan, the humble elect of Candida Casa, greeting and obedience. I have understood, as much from the authentic writings of the fathers as from the trustworthy testimony of elderly men, that from ancient times the bishop of Candida Casa has owed respect — and in those things that are God's obedience — to his mother the archepiscopal church of York. Wherefore I, Gilla-Aldan elect of Candida Casa of the holy Church of York, promise both to you Thurstan, and to your successors canonically appointed, due submission and canonical obedience, as established by the holy fathers.[3]

Until the formidable character of the church and community of Whithorn in the undocumented centuries had been made clear by excavation it was thought that there had been a prolonged vacancy, and that Galloway had been without a bishop for 300 years. It is now evident that this cannot have been so. The significance of the correspondence just quoted is that it marked the 'turning back' of the see of Whithorn to its traditional metropolitan — York — and away from the church establishment of the Western Isles and Man (and ultimately Norway). So long as Whithorn looked to Iona for spiritual leadership the diocese might have been served from the Isle of Man. A list of Manx bishops and a garbled metrical chronicle of York suggest that a Bishop Gamaliel or Gamelinus held both sees — Whithorn and Man — in the late eleventh century; but the sources are not wholly reliable.[4]

How soon Gilla-Aldan was consecrated after his profession is not altogether clear. Nor is it recorded that Fergus was in control in Galloway in 1126, but the probability is that he had been ruling for some years, and that the decision to seek the approval and protection of the archepiscopal see of York was in line with his policies. It served his interests well that the bishopric should demonstrate its traditional obedience to the archbishops of York. Iona and the Western Isles were under the sway of the Norse Lords of the Isles, whom Fergus and his house regarded as opponents. The Province of York on the other hand, represented for Galloway a defence against domination by the Scottish crown.

When in 1120 David I (then Prince of Cumbria) had founded the bishopric of Glasgow, he and Bishop John had gone to the length of defying expressed papal instructions to accept York as the rightful metropolitan. John had delayed taking up his charge to travel to Rome and argue the case that a Scottish bishop should not be subject to the Archbishops of York. In requiring this stance David was following the lead of his elder brother King Alexander I, and it became the established policy of the Scottish royal house, supported by the Scottish clergy. Consequently nothing could declare more plainly that the church (and political realm) of Galloway were independent of Scotland, than Gilla-Aldan's carefully worded profession. As early as 1128 the ruling principle of Fergus of Galloway's life and and policies was made known.

Gilla-Aldan remained Bishop of Whithorn until his death in 1152. Unfortunately surviving records leave us guessing at the trend of his policies. His loyalty to the Province of York seems to have remained all that he professed in 1126, and as far as it is possible to tell, occasioned no conflict with his adherence to Fergus. Much of Fergus's generous giving to the church must have been done with his cooperation, and under his influence.

It was soon apparent that Fergus intended to pursue his opposition to Scottish control by diplomatic means rather than open hostility. He is first documented in 1136 as an honoured guest at the Scottish court, his young son at his side. After the music and ceremonial of a sung Mass, during which the newly completed cathedral of Glasgow was dedicated to God and St Kentigern, an endowment of land for the new church was recorded in a royal charter. The document was engrossed and witnessed by a small elite at David's court. The scribe sat patiently, his pen charged with ink, ready to list the witnesses in order of precedence.[5] By witnessing the charter, those present were endorsing its authenticity, and at the same time giving personal guarantees that they would honour the grant. So at the foot of the vellum, after the names of an abbot and three Scottish earls (David's premier noblemen) next in honour is written the name 'Fergus of Galloway' (Fergus de Galweia), followed by a string of Celtic notables.

The Knights of St John of Jerusalem (the Hospitallers) preserved a record of a grant of land Fergus himself gave them, describing Fergus as King of the Gallovidians (*Rex Galwitensium*). The record was apparently quoting from Fergus's own charter, and this was the style he applied to himself.[6] Scottish and English documents give him lesser titles, such as lord (*dominus*), ruler (*regulus*) or prince (*princeps*), or the simple Fergus of Galloway. By his own declaration, however, Fergus was a king. And while he was consistently styled in other men's charters as ruler of Galloway, it was as the King of the Gallovidians that he saw himself. A territorial title might class him with David's new Anglo-Norman vassals, like Robert de Brus 'lord of Annandale' who derived his power and dignity from David's grant of land 'for the service of ten knights'. The King of the Gallovidians' on the other hand, declared Fergus's unconditional and hereditary right to rule Galloway, not on the say-so of the King of Scots, but with the consent of Galloway's traditional nobility and people. Fergus's conservatism and his pride in an ancient heritage was expressed in one phrase.

Significantly, the Latin word Fergus's scribes used for Gallovidians (*Galwitenses*) is the Brittonic form. Commoner in the Scottish and English documents of the twelfth century was an alternative form deriving from the Old English — 'Galweienses' (as recorded in 1130). The two stems had developed over the long period when Galloway had been partitioned between Britons and Angles. Even today that linguistic duality is perpetuated by the currency of the alternatives: Galwegian and Gallovidian. If Fergus had been an upstart adventurer installed in Galloway by the King of Scots, as used to be thought, he might have arrogated to himself the title King of the Gallovidians, but he would scarcely have used a form of the name that was already becoming archaic.

Fergus's kingdom of Galloway was smaller than the wide expanse of territory, originally the southern part of the Caledonian forest, to which in the twelfth century the topographical term 'Galloway' could still be applied. That extended to the northern boundaries of Ayrshire and in the east to Annandale. The country within Fergus's political control was confined to what were later known as the counties of Wigtownshire and Kirkcudbrightshire, with the eastern march cut off at the river Urr. Here lay the boundary with David I's territory — the old principality of Cumbria within the kingdom of Scotland. The local rulers under David between the rivers Nith and Urr were the native princes of Nithsdale. Westward, and stretching as far as the Irish Sea, lay Fergus's Galloway. His northern border may have extended as far as the river Doon, thus enclosing the hills and pastures of Carrick (southern Ayrshire). Documentation implies that Fergus's son Gilbert later controlled Carrick, but whether Fergus's jurisdiction went as far is not recorded.

FERGUS'S MARRIAGE

Relations between Fergus and David I demonstrated the realism and diplomatic skill of both men. Neither wanted a confrontation with the other. They played a patient power game — neither pushing the other too far, nor yet releasing him from constraint. One of Fergus's main supports in this well-mannered duel was his alliance through marriage with Henry I of England. Henry had only two legitimate children, a son and a daughter, but his natural children are believed to have numbered 19. Many of them were brought up in a family group at his court, and Henry married off the girls to ruling princes whose territories bordered his own, both in France and Britain.[7] The lady Sybilla, for example, among the eldest of these ladies, was the wife of David I's elder brother, King Alexander I.

Documentation in the succeeding generation points to Fergus's wife as one of Henry's natural daughters, though her name is not known.[8] Each of Fergus's three children: Affrica, who married King Olaf of Man, Uchtred and Gilbert are recorded as having been related to Henry II. Two different chronicles refer to Uchtred and to Godred of Man (Affrica's son) as Henry's cousins, and in a letter of 1213 King John of England called Duncan of Carrick (Gilbert's son) his kinsman.[9] This relationship stood Fergus in good stead throughout his life, and as long as Henry lived, was a support in his dealings with David I. Yet for David also it had a stabilising effect. His own close relationship with Henry — they were brothers-in-law — kept the balance between Fergus and himself. For David, Fergus's alliance to the English royal house may have made him inconveniently independent, but it was preferable to an alliance between Fergus and the disaffected dynasty of Moray, which challenged his own right to the Scottish throne, or with the unruly Lords of the Isles who professed allegiance only to the kings of Norway. It would not have been surprising therefore if David, when Prince of Cumbria (1113–24), had negotiated Fergus's marriage to one of Henry I's daughters.

ANGLO-SCOTTISH RELATIONS

Henry I died in 1135, still grieving for the death of his one legitimate son, who with several natural siblings, perished in the White Ship disaster. In his last years Henry worked single-mindedly to gain support for the unopposed succession of his legitimate daughter, Matilda. Unfortunately few royal ladies have been more ill-equipped than Matilda was, by a disagreeable temper, to keep support and win popularity, but that emerged later. Henry had done all he could to persuade the English nobility to swear support for her against the pretensions of her cousin Stephen. (The first to take that oath had been her uncle, David I.) Stephen nevertheless seized the crown within days of Henry's death, and Matilda's only resource was to raise an army and prepare for civil war.

David I had every intention of keeping his oath, but he deferred action in Matilda's cause while he negotiated with Stephen to return Cumbria to Scotland. The gathering at Glasgow in 1136 served to celebrate the successful conclusion, and David may have taken the opportunity when all his Cumbrian magnates were gathered together to raise support for an invasion of Northumbria, ostensibly in Matilda's cause. A more pressing motive was to secure Northumbria for his son Henry, in the right of his mother, Maud de Senlis, whose inheritance it was.[10]

GALLOWAY AND SCOTLAND

To Fergus, who judged it expedient to be present at the dedication of Glasgow cathedral in 1136, there was not much to celebrate. For Scotland's occupation of the city of Carlisle and Cumbria, south of Solway, completed the encirclement of Galloway by Scottish territory. Fergus's powerful father-in-law (Henry I) was dead, and the English connection, hitherto advantageous, now represented weakness rather than strength. David was in a strong position to ask for, or possibly demand, Fergus's military assistance in his projected attack on Northumbria. But Fergus could yield with dignity. He too was related to Matilda (his wife's half-sister), and an element among his own people were more than ready to go to war for whatever spoils it would afford them. The issue whether David could command Fergus's military aid as his overlord, or had to negotiate for it, could therefore be comfortably obscured.

The relationship between the two rulers remained equivocal. David might address the occasional charter to his 'good men, French, English, Scottish and Gallovidian . . .' so long as they were in arms together, but throughout his reign David was never in a position to impose his sheriffs and royal officers upon Galloway, or to seek land for his new Anglo-Norman vassals within its borders. Fergus kept the peace, or went to war in alliance with David. For the next 15 years the two men played diplomatic chess with self-discipline and skill, and apparently with good humour. Meanwhile a social revolution overtook the enlarged realm of Scotland at David's bidding, compelling Fergus and his sons to make a choice between the old order and the new.

As heir to the Anglo-Brittonic culture of Galloway, with its Hiberno-Norse veneer, Fergus had to witness the coming of the Anglo-Norman aristocracy into Scotland and Cumbria. David's background had not been so different from his own, for he was the youngest child of a Gaelic-speaking Scot (Malcolm III) and a Saxon princess. The death of his parents within one week when he was still a boy, had caused him to make his home at the court of his sister and brother-in-law Henry I. There he was educated in the Norman fashion, so that when he became King of Scots in 1124, and found himself with a divided kingdom, it was natural to him to resort to Norman solutions. Caithness, Sutherland, Orkney and the Western Isles owed allegiance to the kings of Norway. Moray was disaffected, and Galloway jealous of its independence. David had little choice but to people his court with the younger sons of Anglo-Norman magnates, many of them from his wife's estates of the Honour of Huntingdon, on whose loyalty and superior military technology he could rely. These were the knights and barons to whom he granted lands in Scotland as his feudal vassals.

This Anglo-Norman elite reached the north some 60 or 70 years after their fathers and grandfathers had conquered Saxon England. They came north as individuals and groups at David's invitation. In no sense were they an invading army; but they changed the character and structure of Scottish society within two generations. These men were the products of Norman culture, and like the twentieth-century devotees of all things American, judged the new ways to be better than the old. This conviction ran through Anglo-Norman society, in matters ecclesiastical as well as secular. The new ruling class — foreign by extraction, and committed to a rigid, militarist social and legal hierarchy — had cosmopolitan loyalties and family connections. The laity were matched with an austere and highly organised church dedicated to correcting old laxities, while acquiring wealth and influence. The reformed monastic Orders, particularly the Cistercians, rapidly became dominant, and at times resembled the multi-national commercial enterprises of today in their far-reaching power and freedom from accountability.

So long as Fergus ruled, the Anglo-Norman landowners settling in Scotland under David I's patronage, found no corresponding welcome in Galloway. The power and numbers of Galloway's aristocracy and fighting men left no place for the new knights. Like David, Fergus's choice was limited. He had to retain the support of his people. He had to protect Galloway from Anglo-Norman acquisitiveness, and Gallovidian autonomy from David's inherited claim to be its overlord. The opposition between the two men became more than political. It was a trial of strength between a traditional native culture and Anglo-Norman innovation.

This opposition of cultures was only partially obscured when the armies massed on the Northumbrian border under the command of David and his son Henry in the latter part of 1137. In more than one sense it was a multiple army. The traditional Scottish war-host, on foot, bearded, kilted and lightly armed, were not always distinguishable from the Galloway forces. The Gallovidians were famed as fighters, especially for their skill at middle distance with the thrown spear. They and probably their allies, the men of Nithsdale, apparently numbered berserkers and war dogs in their armament. Their tactics included making the maximun noise with war-cries to terrify their opponents. In striking contrast to these traditional Celtic forces, David's Anglo-Norman and Flemish knights, clean-shaven under conical helmets, their bodies protected by chain-mail, resembled the defending Northumbrian army more than their own allies. These knights rode to battle but dismounted for combat, where they depended on the long sword, their own body-armour, and the archery of their men-at-arms.

Fergus's participation in the ensuing hostilities is not recorded. The chroniclers who recorded the campaign and the decisive battle were intent on glorifying the Northumbrian army, or exculpating David I personally from the commission of atrocities.[11] Two 'Gallovidian' leaders, Ulgric and Dovenald, were mentioned.

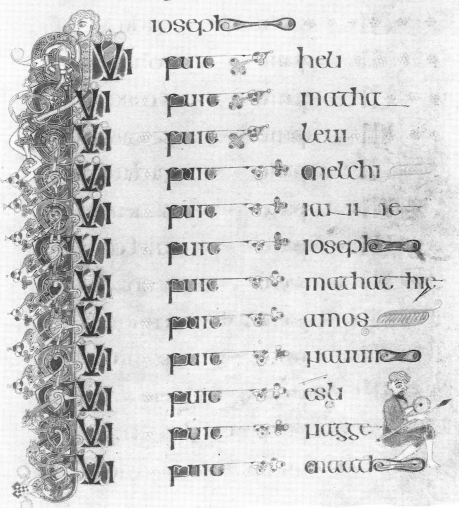

filiatest tues filius meus dilectus mihi
bene conplacuit mihi

Ipse ihserat mapiens quasi an
horum trighita utputabatur filius

ioseph
uit heli
uit matha
uit leui
uit melchi
uit iannae
uit ioseph
uit mathat hie
uit amos
uit nauum
uit esli
uit nagge
uit maath

Book of Kells: *The Genealogy of Christ. Note the seventh-century Celtic warrior in right-hand corner.
The twelfth-century Gallovidian fighting men were no better equipped for battle. They wore no armour,
still carried the small round shield, and their principal weapon was still the long-throwing spear*
(Trinity College, Dublin)

They were probably native princes of Nithsdale, leading the men of Nithsdale. It is however, safe to infer that the main Gallovidian host was led by Fergus and that his elder son Uchtred, and possibly his younger son Gilbert, took part. We are not told what attempts Fergus made, if any, to control his troops in their outrages against civilians.

David I had been involved in skirmishes in the summer of 1137, and had concluded a truce at the intervention of Thurstan, Archbishop of York. It was December 1137 before the whole army crossed the border into Northumbria. Northern English chroniclers described it as a heterogenous multitude: 'that wicked army was composed of Normans, Germans [Flemings], English, of Northumbrians, Cumbrians, of the men of Teviotdale and Lothian, of Picts [who are commonly called Galwegians] and of Scots; and none might know their number.'[12]

This conglomerate force lived off the countryside until the following summer, commandeering or burning the gathered harvest, and using up stored food supplies. They attacked villages and isolated homesteads, leaving a trail of desolation wherever they went. A minor battle at Clitheroe in early summer was counted a victory, largely owing to Gallovidian forces, but in general the campaign was not successful. Strongholds were stormed or besieged, but most of them were defended by Norman castles, built in the previous generation, able to withstand the mainly Celtic war-host without heavy loss. In frustration the rank and file turned upon civilians.

> So that execrable army, savager than any race of heathen yielding honour to neither God nor man, harried the whole province and slaughtered everywhere folk of either sex, of every age and condition, destroying, pillaging, and burning the villages, churches, and houses. For they slaughtered by the edge of the sword and transfixed with their spears the sick on their pallets, women pregnant and in labour; the babes in their cradles, and other innocents at the breast.[13]

All through the spring and summer of 1138 the campaign continued. Atrocity stories multiplied, and although they were undoubtedly exaggerated, the suffering of ordinary people was bitter. The twelfth century was a cruel age, but the torturing and killing of women and children alleged in accounts of the campaign, and the capture of women and girls, to be driven off like cattle as slaves, over-stepped the limits of twelfth-century morality. The harrying and slaving were not unprecedented. The Scots, and possibly the Gallovidians, had repeatedly invaded Northumbria in the preceding century, laying waste the countryside and taking slaves.[14] What was new in 1138 was the presence in Northumbria of Norman defences, the military superiority of the defending Normanised knights, and the Norman morality of Northumbrian churchmen, from the Archbishop of York to the monks who chronicled the event. The new dominant culture practised its own brutalities, but was outraged by those of the invading armies. The Christian church had always denounced slavery, but the Norman church all over Europe, for all its faults, with characteristic efficiency, stamped out the Viking heritage of the

A bronze pyx. Norman knights wearing chain-mail, conical helmets, and carrying long swords and large protective shields (The Burrell Collection)

slave-trade. The action of the Scots and Gallovidians in 1138, must have been one of the last manifestations of its survival in north Britain.

When the army's savagery was turned upon monasteries and churches, David I could not suffer it. It was with dismay and superstitious dread that he heard reports that men under his command had broken into chapels and terrorised monks and clergy. His reaction was to issue formal instruments of protection addressed to his entire army (which must have been read aloud) granting his peace to the monasteries of Hexham and Tynemouth. The charter to Tynemouth survives:

> To his lieges, French, English, Scots, and Gallovidian: know that I with the consent of my son Henry, have granted my peace to the church of St Mary and St Oswyn the Martyr at Tynemouth and all who on St Barnabas's Day [11th June] 1138 were under the protection of that church, for the souls of my father and mother, and King Alexander, my brother . . . as long as the monks and men of that church conduct themselves peaceably.[15]

According to Richard of Hexham however, the Priory of Tynemouth 'paid the King of Scots and his followers 27 merks of silver to buy for itself and for those that resided there, peace in the present need'.[16] Hexham Abbey, by his account relied on a higher power for its protection.

> . . . in the madness of this stormy time the noble monastery of Hexham, although placed in the midst of the course, and as it were, in the way of that wicked army . . . yet the marvellous merits of the saints Andrew the Apostle, and Wilfred, bishop and confessor, and the rest of its patrons, to wit saints Acca and Alemund, and Eata, bishops and confessors, and of the other saints who rest in that church, by God's help afforded the stablest peace to its residents and all who fled to its refuge, and it was to them all the safest shelter from all hostile attacks.[17]

Despite such shelter, the suffering of the people stirred the indignation of Archbishop Thurstan. In August he personally raised an army and took the lead against the invaders. He met them on Cowton Moor, near Northallerton. There he set up a pole fixed to a wagon, and 'they called it the Standard'. According to an eye-witness: '. . . upon the summit of this tree they hung a silver pyx with the body of Christ [the consecrated host or communion elements] and the banners of St Peter the Apostle and the Saints John of Beverley and Wilfred of Ripon.'[18]

The battle that followed was called the Battle of the Standard. By many who took part, and the chroniclers who recorded the course of the battle, it was perceived as the climax of a holy war, in which the people of God, with divine help, defended their own against the forces of evil.

Thurstan was supported by the Anglo-Norman magnates of northern England. These knights and their men-at-arms had all the advantages of the new military technology and systematic training that dominated the education of boys of their militarist caste. Their men-at-arms were archers who for centuries to come were to be the most formidable force in England's war-machine. Their accurate shooting was crucial in the engagement on Cowton Moor.

When battle was joined, the Scots army advanced shouting 'Albannaich! Albannaich!' [the Scots! the Scots!]; 'and the column of the Gallovidians, after their custom gave vent thrice to a yell of horrible sound'.[19] Thurstan's force likewise employed intimidating tactics with the loud, weird boomings of horns called 'petronces'. Several reporters, evidently informed by eye-witnesses, remarked on the appalling noise of the fighting. The Gallovidians attacked with such force that the Northumbrian front-line of spearmen had to give ground 'but they [the Gallovidians] were driven off again by the strength of the knights' who were as impenetrable as a wall of iron.[20] While held against that wall, Gallovidians took the brunt of the archers' deadly accuracy. Their berserkers fought on oblivious of wounds, each 'like a hedgehog with its quills . . . bristling all round with arrows, and nonetheless brandishing his sword, and in blind madness rushing forward'. 'Then,' the same account goes on: 'the Gallovidians could sustain no longer the shower of arrows and the swords of the knights'. One report says that Earl Henry rallied them as they broke; another that a trickster held up a head of one of the slain and shouted that the king had been killed, though it is hard to believe he was heard above the din; but a third chronicler relates that the men of Galloway broke and ran once Ulgric and Dovenald had fallen. According to the chroniclers, retreat became a rout. David's knights were unable to reach their horses, and 'the plain was strewn with corpses; very many prisoners were taken, and the King and all the others took to flight'. Several days later King David's son Henry reached Carlisle on foot, accompanied by one knight.

No one has commented on the fact that while the Normans and Scots under David I's command were opposing Thurstan, a churchman whom their own bishops held in defiance, the Gallovidians found themselves in arms against their own archbishop and saints they had honoured for centuries. They had been overwhelmed, not only by a superior and unfamiliar war technology, but by spiritual powers too real and familiar to withstand. The others might face death in battle: they saw themselves braving damnation. The deaths of Ulgric and Dovenald came as the last straw, recalling the Celtic superstition that no battle can be won after the death of a chief. Their flight was a foregone conclusion.

The peace negotiated in April the following year was surprisingly favourable to the Scots. David was not required to do homage to King Stephen, but his son Henry did, and on performing this ceremony was confirmed in the earldom of Northumbria. The Scottish earls and David's closest friend, Hugo de Morville, were required to hand over their sons as hostages. A papal legate, Alberic of Ostia, came to Carlisle to assist in making peace. He personally supervised the return of the women and girls driven away as slaves, and the Gallovidians were the scapegoats for the brutality of the Scots as well as their own. They and their allies, the princes of Nithsdale sustained heavy casualties, and they had gained nothing from the war but an indelibly bad name in northern England, where chroniclers for generations afterwards stacked up atrocity stories against them. It was a bitter experience Fergus did not want to repeat.

David I continued intermittently in arms for some years, in support of his niece Matilda, or to keep Cumbria and Northumbria for Scotland; but there is no record of Fergus's ever having fought under his banner again. Indeed apart from a defensive action to repulse an attack from Man in 1152, he does not appear to have taken up arms again until 1159. He had learned the lesson that his war-host, for all its formidable reputation, was no match for the knights and archers of the new order.

THE PEACE

The war behind him, Fergus turned to preoccupations of a different kind. One of the first will have been the marriage of his elder son, Uchtred to a daughter of a Cumbrian nobleman. Gunnild was a grand-daughter of the great Earl Waltheof of Northumbria, and heiress to some manors in Allerdale, Westmorland. It was a very suitable match for a Gallovidian prince, for it gave Galloway a foothold south of Solway. It brought Uchtred into contact with a more Normanised milieu than he was accustomed to at home. This was to influence the rest of his life.

WHITHORN CATHEDRAL

Perhaps as early as 1125–35 Fergus had founded a new cathedral church on the hill at Whithorn. It was Romanesque in style, cruciform in plan, with a short nave, and has been compared with contemporaneous churches built in Wales.[21] Glasgow was not alone in having a cathedral. Fergus's other endowments consisted of land from his demesne estate, but the patronage of the new church almost certainly involved finance. Fergus may have contributed timber from his woods and stone from his quarries, but the eventual bill had to be paid in money. We can only speculate that some of the numerous small properties which he appears to have granted to the Military Orders, were handed over for cash or even a loan, to finance the cathedral. The Templars and Hospitallers were unique in Christendom in their financial dealings and their loans of money for interest, which was forbidden by canon law as usury.

The new cathedral chapter was manned by the old religious community. It was unusual for a cathedral chapter to consist of monastic canons rather than secular clergy. The monastery of Whithorn was old-fashioned, and would have been regarded as irregular by such sticklers as Archbishop Thurstan. Some attempt at making the community more acceptable may have been made by introducing a small group of Augustinians, but if it was, it is not documented, and in the long term did not satisfy the stricter churchmen of the Province of York. As late as 1170 a Cistercian writer jibed at the 'monks of a sort' to be found in Galloway. The Whithorn community was not finally regularised (by Premonstratensians) until 1177.

In 1139 Fergus was visited by a distinguished churchman and archbishop, Malachy O'Moore, papal legate to Ireland. He was a monk, and a friend of

Bernard of Clairvaux, the leader of the growing Cistercian Order which Malachy much admired. He was later to found a Cistercian monastery in Ireland at Mellifont. It was en route from Clairvaux to Ireland that he came to visit Fergus in his stronghold at Cruggleton. It was apparently no mere courtesy visit but a mission from Bernard himself. The founding of Dundrennan Abbey, which was established as a working community by midsummer 1142, was the outcome. Its endowment by Fergus can reasonably be traced to Malachy's approach in 1139. It later emerged that a second Cistercian house had been planned in the Rhins. These decisions must have had the support of Bishop Gilla-Aldan.

It was clearly with some enthusiasm that Fergus settled a centre of Cistercian influence at Dundrennan in 1142. So long as it was assumed that this was David I's foundation (an exploded theory) the full significance of the foundation was overlooked. The abbey came into existence as soon as was humanly possible after the conclusion of the Northumbrian campaign of 1138. It was a magniloquent gesture by Fergus, partly to demonstrate his parity with David I (who was planning a second Cistercian abbey on Scottish soil at Newbattle, in addition to Melrose). It may also have been in expiation of war crimes, including the destruction of the Northumbrian abbey of Newminster, and for taking up arms against Archbishop Thurstan.[22] Whatever Fergus's motives, he gave Galloway its finest and most dignified monastery, which even now as it stands in ruins, compels admiration.

DUNDRENNAN ABBEY

The date of the foundation has been disputed. The two surviving records are both flawed. A Cistercian source garbles the name 'Brundrem' but gives the date in full as 23rd July 1142; and the *Melrose Chronicle*'s entry is inserted in an otherwise reliably contemporaneous set of annals, in a thirteenth-century hand.[23] The weakness of this evidence for the date 1142 can nevertheless be exaggerated. Unsatisfactory literary evidence has been advanced to prove that the abbey was not completed for at least another decade and perhaps more. A miracle story relates how the Abbot of Rievaulx on his annual visitation to the daughter-house in the 1160s, was lodged in a leaky hovel. It was an unlikely tale.[24] Any Abbot of Dundrennan in his right mind would have given up his own bed and slept on the floor rather than let such a thing happen! The Cistercians made it their practice not to take up residence until living quarters adequate for the community were completed, though some of the less important buildings may have been of timber construction as some of the earliest buildings had been at Rievaulx itself.[25]

The intimate contact between the abbeys of Dundrennan and Melrose in the thirteenth century is more telling, and supports the date 1142. In 1239 the Prior of Melrose, who is believed to have written part of the chronicle, became Abbot of Dundrennan. A note on folio 46v of the chronicle records: 'Be it remembered that the Abbot of Dundrennan borrowed the chronicles of Melrose in which were 14 quires 5 score and 19 pages' and this entry was made in 1262. It was highly improbable that Melrose should have got the date of Dundrennan's foundation wrong or left it uncorrected. The monks of Dundrennan in the thirteenth century would have been accurately informed as to the date of their abbey's foundation.

Fergus endowed the abbey generously with the entire parish of Rerrick (saving the old ecclesiastical estate of Kirkcarswell) and the parish of Kirkpatrick Durham. This appears to have been the foundation endowment, although not documented until 1305.[26] Lands in the northern Glenken, possibly in Minigaff, and in Wigtownshire belonged to Dundrennan later, but it is not clear that they were given by Fergus. An acreage of this size of some of Galloway's more productive land represented capital outlay which Fergus may well have been able to afford, but this and his other grants distinguish Fergus as second only to David I in north Britain in beneficence to the church.

SOULSEAT ABBEY

In 1148 Malachy returned to the Rhins from Ireland and took up another of Fergus's promised endowments at Soulseat. Malachy was once more on his way to Clairvaux, where shortly afterwards he died. Before leaving Soulseat he established there an abbot and a community of monks from his newly founded Cistercian house of Mellifont in Ireland. So much is testified by St Bernard.[27] It has been a puzzle therefore how within a very few years this Cistercian community came to be supplanted by Premonstratensian canons, and the Premonstratensian Order recorded that Fergus was the founder.[28]

ECCLESIASTICAL POLITICS

At the same time as Fergus and his bishop Gilla-Aldan were modernising and developing the church in Galloway, events were taking place in York which they could not ignore. One way or another each of them will have been compelled to declare where he stood in a rancorous dispute.

Archbishop Thurstan died in 1140, and his successor, William Fitzherbert, was elected in the same year. The election took place under political pressure from King Stephen to whom Fitzherbert was related. An uproar arose over the legitimacy or otherwise of the new archbishop's election. The whole ecclesiastical province was split by the controversy, and eventually the entire Cistercian Order, under the leadership of Bernard, Abbot of Clairvaux, opposed Fitzherbert's appointment as archbishop.

The subsequent career of Archbishop William: the enquiry by the papal Curia into his election; his consecration and reign for six years; Bernard's relentless campaign for his deposition; William's deposition by the Cistercian Pope Eugenius IV in 1147; his voluntary exile, restoration, and alleged murder, and his eventual canonisation as a saint, is one of the neglected dramas of northern history.[29] Feeling in William's favour (as well as against) ran so high that after his deposition, his Cistercian successor, Henry Murdac, dared not stay in York for fear of the citizens, and with the archdeacons who had opposed William, took refuge at

Dundrennan Abbey. The mixed round and pointed arches date the building to the first half of the twelfth century (Historic Scotland)

Fountains Abbey. William's supporters then raided Fountains, doing a good deal of damage, and castrated one of the elderly archdeacons whom they saw as having started all the trouble. The polarisation of ecclesiastical feeling and opinion in the Province of York lasted nearly 12 years. This ferment must have affected the suffragan diocese of Whithorn. Where did Bishop Gilla-Aldan and Fergus of Galloway take up their stance?

Fergus and Gilla-Aldan showed no enthusiasm for Cistercian principles after 1142. The delay in replacing the traditional house of canons at Whithorn with a reformed Order was indicative. So was the withdrawal of support from the new Cistercian community at Soulseat, and their replacement by Premonstratensians. The change was certainly made at Soulseat shortly after Archbishop William was deposed. The strongest lead as to Fergus's attitude was the hostility of Ailred of Rievaulx towards him and towards Galloway, which otherwise seems inexplicable considering that Fergus had founded Dundrennan Abbey. Ailred had been prominent in the Cistercian opposition to William Fitzherbert, conducting the case against him before the papal Curia, and he remained a close personal friend of Henry Murdac, Fitzherbert's rival for the archbishopric.[30] If Fergus had indeed withdrawn his patronage from the Cistercians in support of Archbishop William, he had made some dangerous enemies. The effect of their animosity is a story which must be put aside for the moment as Fergus put it aside for the urgencies of the day. By 1154 Bishop Gilla-Aldan, Archbishop William Fitzherbert, and

Bernard, Abbot of Clairvaux were all dead. There was a new Bishop of Whithorn, Bishop Christian, a Cistercian sympathiser, and for Fergus pressing political events swept other considerations aside.

Between the years 1152 and 1154 two sudden deaths had tipped the balance of political power in a way familiar in medieval affairs. In 1152 David I's son and heir apparent, Earl Henry, a man in his prime, died. He left two young boys, the elder just old enough to be escorted round the kingdom at his grandfather's behest, for a succession of ceremonies in which he was shown to the people as king designate. He was to be Malcolm IV, and David's death in 1153 made him King of Scots at the age of 12. David had been one of the ablest kings Scotland ever had, and with his death the realm that had for so long been strong, while England was weakened by civil war, was suddenly vulnerable. When within a year Stephen died, England's erstwhile weakness was replaced by the formidable strength of Henry II. He was hard, able and young, and heir not only to England, but to a considerable Continental empire.

The change was to Galloway's advantage, and especially once Henry (in 1157) had come to Carlisle and persuaded the hapless Malcolm to surrender Cumbria to England. The kingdom of Scots no longer held the southern shore of the Solway, and Henry II was too preoccupied with his Continental possessions to be a threat. The weakness of the Scottish crown had already given rise to trouble in Moray, where the son of Malcolm Macheth, imprisoned for his attempt in 1134 to gain the Scottish throne, was abetted by his uncle, Somerled Lord of the Isles.

The sons of Fergus, now grown men, began to mutter that it was time Galloway looked to her own advantage. Uchtred had his eye on Cro, the territory between the Nith and the Urr, which David I had held as ruler of Cumbria. It was mainly a moribund ecclesiastical estate ripe for annexation, and would bring Uchtred nearer to his Cumbrian lands. A similar tract of country lay behind the eastern watershed in the upper Clyde valley. Provided the men of Nithsdale could be persuaded to cooperate, the way through the Dalveen pass and across the moors lay open for the passage of a Gallovidian foray.

Gilbert was the more clear-sighted of the brothers and his eye was on the future. Fergus was aging. Who was going to rule after him? Uchtred might be the elder, but the principle of primogeniture counted for nothing in Galloway. The fittest of the royal kindred became ruler. Gilbert was in no doubt who that was. A contest for power and the direction of policy arose between the brothers, bringing each into collision with their father. Fergus might be too old to espouse wildcat schemes to annex Scottish territory, but he was not yet ready to be back-numbered. The Gallovidians' reaction to external events illustrated their preoccupation with their own divisions. A revolt in Moray was put down, and there was a record that Donald Macheth, one of the insurgents, fell into the king's hands in Galloway. It was an unlikely thing to happen. and the story may have been confused with an earlier rebellion in Moray.[31] Somerled of the Isles was involved in some sea-fighting off the west coast, and in 1158, ravaged Man, the domain of Fergus's son-in-law, Olaf. No one in Galloway attempted reprisals on his behalf. Galloway was too preoccupied with its own internal dissensions.

It was at that point that Ailred of Rievaulx saw fit to make his annual visitation to Dundrennan, possibly in response to a nudge from Bishop Christian. Walter Daniel describes the situation in Galloway at the time:

> . . . the princes of the province [were] quarrelling with each other. The King of Scotland could not repress nor the bishop soften the hatreds and rancours in their minds and their despotic acts towards one another, whilst day by day the unfortunate little country bore the stain of much bloodshed, as sons rose against their father, the father against his sons, and brother against brother. Aelred the peacemaker brought them all together. With words of peace and goodness he bound the furious brothers in the firmest of pacts and in a single bond of affection.[32]

This was sensationalist rhetoric. The King of Scotland, for example, far from any thought of repressing trouble in Galloway, was wild to be made a knight, and was shortly to go traipsing off with his Anglo-Norman barons to besiege Toulouse under the banner of Henry II, in hope of winning his spurs. It was an ill-judged move to leave Scotland undefended, and it played into the hands of the war-party in Galloway who could urge they would meet no significant opposition in crossing the border into Scottish territory. It was now or never; such an opportunity might not occur again. Fergus, rather than rely on the sincerity of their reconciliation, may have been desperate enough to feel that action against a common enemy might resolve the dissension between his sons and their supporters.

Malcolm IV returned home in the early summer of 1160, full of confidence in his new knighthood, and made his way to hold council in Perth. There his elder noblemen, the earls of Scotland, met him like outraged parents waiting up late for an erring teenager. What passed was hushed up, and consequently has for a long time been misunderstood. The chronicler of Melrose, somewhat in the dark, recorded:

> And when he had come to the city that is called Perth, Earl Fereteth and five other earls (being enraged against the King for going to Toulouse) besieged the city and wished to take the King prisoner; but their presumption did not at all prevail. [The chronicler goes straight on in the next sentence:] King Malcolm went three times with a great army into Galloway and at last subdued them.[33]

If the two entries are read together the final word 'them' appears to refer to the earls. The result has been that these fundamentally unrelated pieces of news have been inflated into a major military operation, beginning in Perth, where the earls of Scotland, who seven years before had stood round the Stone of Destiny at Malcolm's investiture, his godfathers and sponsors, took up arms against their young king for his first mistake. Worse, Fergus of Galloway has been taken to be one of their number. (Neither of the parties would have been flattered.) Finally the scene was shifted and the earls of Scotia, in retreat, took the unlikely course of seeking safety in Galloway, an alien countryside, instead of heading northward to their homelands. Despite the absence of any evidence that any of the six earls were penalised for this grave threat to the crown, the misunderstanding has passed into the standard history of Scotland under the name 'the Revolt of the Earls'.

There can be no doubt that the earls were angry with Malcolm and did not scruple to say that if he could not act more responsibly towards his kingdom he would be taken back into tutelage. There can be little doubt either that (with his barons at his back) young Malcolm stood up to them, revealing himself to be more effective a king than they had feared. Then he undertook to make good the ill consequences of his absence, and set out on a punitive expedition into Galloway. Such a sequence of events makes reasonable sense.

The Holyrood annalist, who had reason to know better than his counterpart at Melrose what happened in Galloway at the time, made no reference to the young king's carpeting by his elder statesmen in Perth. It was not a story that anyone present wished to spread. The *Holyrood Chronicle* simply says: 'King Malcolm went three times with a great army into Galloway and after he had subdued his confederate enemies he returned with peace and without loss'.[34]

The words 'his confederate enemies' refer of course, not to the earls of Scotia, but to Fergus and his sons, and probably the native lords of Nithsdale in whose territory the Dalveen Pass lay. There is not a scrap of writing to explain why Malcolm took a punitive expedition into Galloway. The forays into Clydesdale and Cro are no more than surmise, but surmise supported by subsequent events. Within a year or two documents reveal Uchtred in possession of Cro (between the Nith and Urr). At much the same time Malcolm IV can be traced parcelling out the lands between Crawford and Biggar among a family group of Flemings, the toughest of his knights. Their leader, Baldwin, became lord of Biggar, and the personal names of the rest sound in local place-names: Folcard (Folkerton), Lambin (Lamington), Robert (Roberton), Simund Lockhart (whose name was preserved in Symington), Tancred (Thankerton), and Wice (Wiston). By establishing these feudal vassals here for military service due, Malcolm was effectively closing off access to the Biggar gap from the south-west, as if strengthening a gate that had recently been forced.[35]

In the meantime the Gallovidian forces had been crushed. Fergus's careful diplomacy over nearly 40 years, by which he had preserved Galloway's autonomy, had been brought to nothing for the sake of a few weeks' plundering — for a cattle raid. Property was no doubt burned, cattle driven off, and people terrorised and perhaps killed. Malcolm IV showed his mettle in bringing the marauders to book. It had evidently not been easy, for it had taken three attempts. Whether that meant three engagements with the same army or battle with separate forces under the command of Fergus and his sons, the outcome had been hard won. It was less conclusive and more costly than the chronicles made out. The peace terms show that.

For the Gallovidians victory had been very near. They had put up a hard fight, but at the last they were beaten. Uchtred was bound over as a hostage while peace terms were agreed. Fergus knew that for him the defeat was final. The kingdom of the Gallovidians was at an end. All that he had feared had come to pass. He had seen the mad courage of his Gallovidians pitched once more against the impenetrable mail of Anglo-Norman knights, and decimated by their merciless archers. With the resource of long experience he warded off the memory, and stood and bargained with the young King of Scots for his sons' patrimony. It may have been then that Uchtred was given title to the lands of Desnes Cro. Certainly the brothers were to hold the rest of Galloway between them, doing homage to Malcolm for it.

Fergus would not do homage. Malcolm was courteous, conscious that Henry II claimed kinship with the Galloway royal house. To put Fergus to death was out of the question. Imprisonment then? Malcolm Macheth had spent 23 years in prison for his rebellion. The young king, preferring to be magnanimous, hesitated and took counsel. Then a time-honoured solution was found. Fergus asked that he should be allowed to retire to a monastery of Malcolm's choosing. With relief Malcolm named Holyrood Abbey, the community of Augustinian canons his grandfather had founded in Edinburgh.

Before Fergus left Galloway for the last time, he gave orders that the land and churches of two parishes on the east bank of the Dee below Kirkcudbright, Galtway and Dunrod, should be given to Holyrood in his name. It was a characteristically munificent gesture with which to make his exit from the world. He died a year later.

It is a political principle much older than Machiavelli that it is not enough to defeat your enemy: you must discredit him. In the decade after the defeat of Fergus a group of writers began what looks very much like a concerted attack on the reputation of Gallovidian fighting men, Galloway society at large, and the character of its abler princes. Many of the accusations related back to the military campaign of 1138 as reported by Richard of Hexham nearly a generation before, repeating and enlarging upon his account, and multiplying the accusations of barbarity to the civil population. For the next 30 years these allegations were copied and embroidered by other writers further afield, in southern England and even Normandy. Their language has been called hysterical, and the further away the teller was in time and distance, the wilder the stories became.[36]

Fergus's resistance to the kings of Scots might have explained hostility on the part of Scottish chroniclers, but the annalists of Melrose and Holyrood (where Fergus was known in his last days) preserved an objective and temperate tone in their references to Galloway. After Richard of Hexham, who was of an older generation, the initial attack came from a tight knot of northern English clerics, writing between 1160 and about 1185: John of Hexham, Reginald of Durham, Ailred of Rievaulx, and his younger contemporary and brother monk, Walter Daniel. They were all Augustinian canons or Cistercian monks.

The detraction seemed to start from accounts of the military campaign of 1138. Richard of Hexham, the nearest in time and place to the actual events, called the whole of David I's forces 'that execrable army more savage than any heathen', but

he singled out the Gallovidians, whom he called 'Picts' and described them breaking into the chapel of St John Lee. The narration of this incident illustrates how
the accusations grew with telling. Richard said:

> ... two of the same nation of Picts came to a certain oratory of St Michael situ-
> ated on the northern side of the river Tyne and belonging to the same church of
> Hexham. They broke open its door and took away what they found there.
>
> (Richard of Hexham)

Some 30 years later the Gallovidians were not distinguished from the Scots, but
the crime had worsened:

> ... the Scots also broke into the sanctuaries of the Lord and in the consecrated
> places irreverently committed acts violent, lewd, and execrable.
>
> (John of Hexham)

By the time the story had reached southern England it ran:

> ... ecclesiastics were put to death for possession of their churches.[37]
>
> (John of Worcester)

Richard of Hexham's most serious charge had been that the Gallovidians captured women and girls and drove them off to sell as slaves:

> ... these most bestial men who regard as nothing adultery and incest, after they
> were weary of abusing these hapless creatures after the manner of brute beasts,
> made them their slaves, or sold them to other barbarians for cows.

One of the surprising features of the propaganda was that this very grave charge
was seldom repeated. Twenty-five years or so later Ailred of Rievaulx reduced the
ill-treatment of women to the generality: 'the most cruel nation of the
Gallovidians raged with unheard-of brutality and spared neither age nor sex'. His
historical treatise 'De Standardo' included a number of horror stories about the
torture-killing of old men, pregnant women and young children. Perhaps the
most haunting is this:

> ... in the same house were several little children. A Gallovidian stood, and seiz-
> ing one after the other by both feet struck their heads against the doorpost, and
> when he had piled them in a heap, he laughed.
>
> (Ailred of Rievaulx)

The same writer's most quoted phrase described the Gallovidians as 'not men
but brute beasts devoid of humanity and piety'. It is of some importance however
that 'De Standardo' was not a chronicle, but a highly dramatised narration of the
Battle of the Standard, written more than 20 years afterwards. Many of the much
quoted atrocity stories do not purport to be eyewitness accounts except insofar as
they were told in set speeches attributed to persons then living such as Walter
Espec and Robert de Brus. These were Anglo-Norman barons with David I, who
were portrayed as trying to dissuade him from battle.

The Romanesque doorway to Whithorn cathedral—a survival from the cathedral built c. *1125 (Historic Scotland)*

All through time armies in enemy territory, keyed up by fear and mass hysteria, have done and still do, terrible things. Richard of Hexham gave a touch of honesty to his account when he said that the same things were done in other wars, but to a greater extent in this. The commission of atrocities on foreign soil by its fighting men did not mark Galloway as any different from other societies of the time. More damaging was the condemnation of its people in general:

> It is a wild country where the inhabitants are like beasts, and is altogether barbarous. Truth there has nowhere to lay its head . . . There chastity founders as often as lust wills, and the pure are only so far removed from the harlot that the more chaste will change their husbands every month, and a man will sell his wife for a heifer.
>
> (Walter Daniel)

This is apparently a reference to Celtic customary marriage common to Galloway, Wales and Ireland, which so horrified Cistercian celibates. Charges like these were so often repeated that the people of Galloway became a by-word for all that was stupid, savage and lecherous. 'That miserable race, on whom God's curse, the Gallovidians who covet wealth', wrote Jordan de Fantosme;[38] and another writer added godlessness and neglect of church-going to the list of their sins.[39]

While Christian observance was being denied, the churches and religious communities of Galloway came in for contemptuous criticism. When around 1170 Reginald of Durham wrote his book about St Cuthbert (at Ailred's suggestion) he told the story which has already appeared in Chapter 3 about Ailred's attending Mass at Kirkcudbright on St Cuthbert's Day in 1162. The bull-baiting on consecrated ground which was the main theme cast a slur on the old mother-church. By the time Reginald was writing, Fergus's son Uchtred had been persuaded to disband the unreformed community of canons at Kirkcudbright. He placed the church and its revenues in the hands of the canons of Holyrood. Reginald's anecdote served a double purpose. It introduced a miracle (the bull gored a blasphemous novice at the behest, we are to suppose, of the gentle St Cuthbert). It also served to justify the dissolution of the old community.

All but the monks of Dundrennan Abbey colonised by monks from Rievaulx in Yorkshire, received the full force of Walter Daniel's scorn:

> certain men of that land, if regularly established in a religious house, have been veritably transformed into monks of a sort, though under the guidance of others; they scarcely have the perseverance to reach out after perfection by their own efforts. They are by nature brutish, having animal appetites that incline them always to the pleasures of the flesh. Rievaulx made a plantation in that savage environment, which with the help of God who gives increase to a new planting, is now yielding plentiful fruit.[40]

Dundrennan Abbey was however not entirely spared. The story of the guest house with the leaking roof did nothing for its reputation. Having vilified the country and its people and even disparaged the churches and the newest, finest monastery, it comes as no surprise when Walter Daniel's references to Fergus are derogatory. He not only belittled him by calling him 'the petty king of that land, incensed against his sons', he went as far as to state that he was responsible for the death of thousands. Even the dignity of Fergus's last act had to be diminished. Walter claimed that the ubiquitous Ailred took part in the peace-making and it was he who persuaded Fergus to retire to Holyrood.

The conspicuously central position occupied by Ailred in the vilification of Galloway is by now apparent. He was a link between Rievaulx and Hexham, Dundrennan and Durham. He visited Durham frequently, and was admired by Reginald, his younger contemporary. Ailred was a son of the last highly respected married priest of Hexham and Treasurer of Durham Cathedral. He began his career in the household of David I to whom he remained loyal, writing his eulogy as well as the historical piece 'De Standardo'. Ailred performed the feat of preserving David's good name, and he did this partly by scapegoating the Gallovidians.

While still a relatively young man Ailred joined the Cisterican Order. He was wholly converted to its ethos and rapidly rose to the attention of its most distinguished members. He became Abbot of Rievaulx before he was 40 almost certainly through the influence of Bernard of Clairvaux. As Abbot of Rievaulx, his visitations to Dundrennan Abbey must have been frequent, and he took an active interest in Galloway's affairs. He evidently replaced the late Malachy O'Moore as Bernard of Clairvaux' unofficial informant on such matters, and once Bishop Christian became Bishop of Whithorn in 1153, he found in him an ally.

In his own time Ailred was an eminent scholar and writer, and twentieth-century scholars have heaped praise on his learning and personal integrity. Whether his animosity towards Fergus and his people was kindled by their support for Archbishop William Fitzherbert cannot be reliably established. Fergus's stance in that controversy can only be inferred. Even if it was at the root of Cistercian animosity it must in justice be said that the traditional native society which Fergus championed against Anglo-Norman values shocked Cistercian morality. Wider loyalties motivated Galloway's detractors. Under its ablest princes, Fergus and his son Gilbert, Galloway offered the Anglo-Norman establishment in the north its most formidable challenge. In every major military engagement Anglo-Norman armour, weaponry and tactics defeated the Gallovidian war-host for all their skill with the thrown spear, their reckless courage, their berserkers and blood-curdling battle-cries. But the terror that host inspired envenomed the writers' pens.

A fresh outburst of bitterness followed the events of 1174-75, to be described later in this narrative; but the deepest motivations were clear from the start. In the north, the vilification of Galloway was uniquely parallel with the Englishman's dislike and contempt for the Welsh. They were 'different', and worse, they had been defeated.

5

THE REALM PARTITIONED:

Brothers

(1160-85)

Serious cause of dissension is the habit of Welsh princes of entrusting the education of each of their sons to a different nobleman living in their territory . . . The
most frightful disturbances occur in their territories as a result, people being
murdered, brothers killing each other, and even putting each other's eyes out . . .
It follows that you will find that friendships are much warmer between foster-
brothers than they are between true brothers.

Gerald of Wales[1]

The new order imposed on Galloway by Malcolm IV was soon brought home to
the sons of Fergus. Shortly after the peace Malcolm promulgated a charter
addressed to 'Uchtred son of Fergus and his brother Gilbert' informing them that
he had given his firm peace to the canons of Holyrood travelling towards or lodg-
ing in Galloway on pain of forfeiture.[2] Since the canons' business in Galloway
arose from the gift of the churches and lands of Dunrod and Galtway by Fergus,
the implication that his sons might impede the canons' enjoyment of them or
allow it to be impeded, must have been resented. For the first time the King of
Scots could enforce his will in Galloway through his own appointed officers, and
he did not scruple to make this plain. Scottish power in the south-west had probably never been so strong. Uchtred and Gilbert were at one in yearning for the day
when they might be free from this constraint. They were united in little else.

The partition of Galloway between the brothers seems to have been made at
the river thereafter called the Cree (from the Gaelic 'crioch' meaning boundary).
Uchtred held the territory to the east, adding to it the district of Desnes Cro, with
his external boundary at the river Nith, and his strongholds at Buittle and Burned
Island. Gilbert had the western districts (now called Wigtownshire) with his chief
stronghold at Cruggleton, and appears to have had possession of Carrick in southern Ayrshire, with his boundary at the river Doon.[3]

Malcolm's charter treated Uchtred as the senior, and subsequent royal documentation emphasised Uchtred's superior status. Uchtred had been about 15 or 16
in 1136. He was presumably born around 1120, and married between 1138 and 1140.
His son Lochlan, who came to be known by the Norman-French name Roland,
was probably born within a year or so of Uchtred's marriage, and may himself have

married around 1170.[4] These informed guesses would make Uchtred about 40 when Fergus was deposed, and Gilbert in his thirties. Both men were already established in life, experienced in the conduct of affairs and the leadership of men.

William the Lyon succeeded as King of Scots on Malcolm IV's premature death in 1165. A charter made shortly afterwards referred to Uchtred by the title Lord of Galloway, but this was not repeated. That title was never extended to Gilbert. As a royal charter witness Uchtred was usually given the precedence his father had enjoyed — immediately after the Scottish earls or the royal office-bearers. On the one occasion when Gilbert witnessed a charter of William the Lyon in Uchtred's absence, his name was relegated to a lowlier position. This discrimination will have done nothing to ease Gilbert's neurotic jealousy of his brother.

RELATIONSHIPS

Gilbert's youth is unrecorded, as is his marriage. His elder son Duncan was always treated in Anglo-Norman circles as a legitimate heir. Another son, Malcolm, may have been a good deal younger. Uchtred had a foster-brother, Gillecatfar, which suggests that both brothers had been fostered in childhood, true to the Celtic traditions of their family. The custom was widespread in Ireland and Wales. The Anglo-Norman church frowned on it, and official disapproval sounds through Gerald's reference to Welsh practice with which this chapter began. Gillecatfar's gaelicised Brittonic name, relating to a Welsh saint Catfach, proclaims him a member of the old Gallovidian aristocracy.[5] He witnessed a charter of Uchtred's around 1164, and another in 1170 when his adult son was with him. The friendship between Gillecatfar and Uchtred survived the passage of youth, marriage and family responsibilities.

Separation in childhood coupled with no clear expectation which brother was to succeed their father, may have been the primary causes of jealousy between Uchtred and Gilbert. Their upbringing and tradition conspired to estrange them, though it is doubtful if either foresaw the extremity their increasing alienation was to reach. A humbler, easier temperament than Gilbert's might have softened the mutual hostility, and less divisive circumstances might have mitigated the occasion for it. As it was, opposing loyalties in a conflict going far beyond the personal scale, embittered their relationship with an epic inevitability. Both engage our sympathy, for both were victims of the social revolution and the political necessities that further divided them.

UCHTRED

Uchtred's marriage to Gunnild of Allerdale had been one of his father's diplomatic achievements, for it linked the house of Galloway with the family of the ancient earls of Northumbria.[6] Gunnild was the daughter of Waltheof, Lord of Allerdale, the second son of Gospatric, the Earl of Northumbria, dispossessed in 1072. She

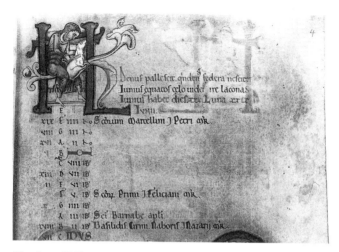

Illuminated MS c. 1140: Man shearing a sheep (Bodleian Library, Oxford)

was dowered with the lands of Torpenhow, and Uchtred's manors south of Solway had a decisive effect on his life. They had given him some independence in his father's lifetime, and brought him into close contact with Cumbrian landowners, both of the hereditary aristocracy and the new feudal baronage. His relationships with these families were well documented. By nature easy-going and adaptable, Uchtred gradually adopted the Anglo-Norman attitudes of his Cumbrian neighbours.

Once Uchtred was in control of eastern Galloway and the newly acquired territories of Desnes Cro, it was to these people that he looked for friends and vassals to be his tenants and the defenders of his half of Galloway. Richard son of Truite and his brother Robert, the sheriff of Westmorland, were members of the ruling caste in Cumbria, and Richard was among the first whom Uchtred infeft in the lands of Desnes Cro. Truite was an Old English woman's name, and these brothers were apparently sons of a Cumbrian heiress. Uchtred granted Richard the lands of Lochkinderloch (later New Abbey) near his eastern border, for the service of one knight. The charter referred to Uchtred's obligation to pay 'chan' (Gaelic: 'cain' — tribute in kind) to the king of Scots:

> . . . and he shall give me yearly for his free service £8 of silver and by this he shall be free and quit of all service and customary dues to the king of Scotland, to me and to my heirs . . . and when I shall be free and quit of the payment of chan, he shall hold freely the aforesaid lands for the service of one knight.[7]

This document has been taken as evidence that Uchtred (and Fergus before him) payed cain (the traditional food rent) to the King of Scots for Galloway as a whole, but it was not necessarily so. The charter implies that Uchtred, having acquired the old Cumbrian lands of Desnes Cro from Malcolm IV, was obliged to pay cain for them. A similar reference to an obligation to render the King of

Illuminated MS c. 1140: Man with a scythe (Bodleian Library, Oxford)

Scots military service in Desnes Cro is mentioned in relation to lands Uchtred leased to the Cumbrian abbey of Holm Cultram.

It is fairly clear that Uchtred and Gilbert owed military service for the rest of Galloway. Whether they had also to pay cain is less certain. Their father evidently did not. The charter to Richard son of Truite implies, moreover, that the obligation to pay tribute for Desnes Cro had some term set upon it, and that Uchtred expected to be released from it in a relatively short time. The main purport of the charter was however to place in the border-parish of Lochkinderloch a baron who could defend it. Richard son of Truite was to hold it for the service of one knight. A similar infeftment for the defence of his lands north of Solway concerned the parish of Borgue between Kirkcudbright and Gatehouse of Fleet. Here the actual charter is missing and the grant has to be deduced from a subsequent document by which Hugo de Morville granted the parish church of Borgue to Dryburgh Abbey.

The de Morvilles were among the wealthiest Anglo-Norman families in Cumbria. Hugo de Morville had been David I's Constable and friend, whom David had infeft in wide acres in Ayrshire, Lauderdale and Westmorland. He and his wife Beatrice de Beauchamp had founded the Premonstratensian abbey of Dryburgh. Their son Hugo II succeeded to the lordship of Westmorland and custody of the castle of Knaresborough, and it was to him that Uchtred granted the lands of Borgue. This Hugo — Hugo de Morville II — was Henry II's favourite, and one of the knights responsible for the murder of à Becket. He was eventually dispossessed of his English lands, not for his part in the murder, but for adherence to the Scottish cause in 1174. Some ten years or more before these events Uchtred negotiated a marriage for his son Roland with the daughter of Hugo II's brother, Richard. It was a distinguished match and proved advantageous beyond expectation.

Hugo II was probably the builder of one of the motte and bailey castles in Borgue. They consisted of a timber (later stone) bailey or tower-house erected on a steep conical mound or motte. These man-made hills are still a conspicuous feature of the Galloway countryside. They represented an innovation in strategic defence-works, which Uchtred welcomed into Galloway as defence against attack from the King of Scots from the east or his brother Gilbert in the west. One of the earliest and best preserved of these Norman strongholds in Galloway — the motte of Urr — was almost certainly built by Walter de Berkeley.

Walter, who was Chamberlain of Scotland under Malcolm IV, held the barony of Urr from before 1165. His estate impinged on land that Uchtred had already leased to the Cumbrian abbey of Holm Cultram. A boundary dispute arose in which the Abbot of Holm appealed, not to Uchtred but to the King of Scots, William the Lyon. Whereupon as well as granting Holm a charter of protection in their lands of Galloway and confirming Uchtred's charter, the king sent a written command to Uchtred to hold an enquiry into the boundary dispute and 'to convene the older men of the district to make a sworn perambulation of the marches of Kirkgunzeon on behalf of Holm Cultram Abbey and Christian, Bishop of Galloway'.[8]

ECCLESIASTICAL POLICY

Uchtred pursued a vigorous and coherent ecclesiastical policy, very clearly influenced by Bishop Christian, for it was essentially Anglo-Norman, and specifically Cistercian in direction. Uchtred's attachment to Bishop Christian was expressed in a charter made before 1164, granting a croft and toft in the township of Troqueer and a ploughgate of land to St Peter's Hospital in York. As part of the deanery of Desnes Cro, Troqueer lay in the diocese of Glasgow, but the charter makes no reference to the Bishop of Glasgow, which would have been normal as a matter of courtesy. The gift to St Peter's declared Uchtred's loyalty to the ecclesiastical province of York, with which the Bishop of Glasgow would have nothing to do. Uchtred nevertheless went out of his way to do honour to Bishop Christian. He addressed the document to 'his lord and father, Christian, Bishop of the Gallovidians'. Christian and the archdeacon of Galloway witnessed it, and the rest of the witnesses were Cumbrians, including the abbot, prior, and cellarer of Holm Cultram Abbey, the powerful Anglo-Norman Hubert de Vaus, lord of Gilsland and Brampton in Cumbria, and the two sons of Truite.[9] The charter speaks plainly of Uchtred's political and social alignments.

Uchtred's lease of an extensive grange at Kirkgunzeon to Holm Cultram Abbey for a sheep walk was one of his most positive acts of benevolence to the church. It suggests the influence of Bishop Christian and of Uchtred's brother-in-law, Alan son of Waltheof. Holm Cultram was a Cistercian monastery, and Alan had endowed it with hunting grounds. Uchtred's lease, soon after 1161, included a salt-pan at a suitable place to be chosen along the coast (the abbey chose a site at Colvend). The grange at Kirkgunzeon brought the abbey into collision with

Illuminated MS: A boar (Bodleian Library, Oxford)

Walter de Berkeley, and with Dundrennan Abbey, whose lands in Kirkpatrick Durham included unenclosed pastures on which Holm's flocks tended to stray. Dundrennan and Holm Cultram both being Cistercian houses, negotiated a settlement:

> It is agreed that Holm shall not acquire more land or build more houses or sheep-cotes on the western side of the river Nith . . . the flocks of Holm are not to go in the adjacent pastures so far that they cannot return at night to their own grange, until Dundrennan has got land for a grange to enclose these pastures and prevent intrusion by the flocks of Holm. The pigs of Kirkgunzeon can go into Uchtred's woods between the grange and the river Nith, but in time of pannage [the acorn crop] the pigs of both abbeys shall get pannage outside.[10]

The charters of Holm Cultram, blessedly surviving, conjure these vivid views of a countryside with square miles of unenclosed pasture and great flocks of sheep, shepherded home each evening. This was Cistercian sheep-farming on a commercial scale. It was changing the landscape, and on the charters' evidence, sweeping away villages and their open fields and their parish churches. Droves of pigs rootling vociferously in the riverside woods, explain place-names like the Gaelic Munnenmuch ('monadh-na-muic' — pig hill) and Lotus (Loschus) that in Old English meant piggery. These places lay on the marches of Kirkgunzeon, which were detailed in two successive 'bounders' or boundary charters. The documents convey almost audibly the elderly men of the district panting up hill and down, to point out the crossed oaks and the stone markers that identified the limits between the monastic grange of Holm and Walter de Berkeley's estate (see p. 107). The saltpans along the coast, owned and operated by several monasteries, were each serviced from a small house, fuelled by timber cut in the woods, and provided with enough land to sustain a horse and a few cows. Those details reveal the diversity and industry of a busy, productive countryside. The pity is there are so few such documents.

Uchtred has been credited with founding the Benedictine nunnery of Lincluden but on doubtful authority. The site in Desnes Cro makes it conceivable that the founder was David I, or one of the princes of Nithsdale. It was so near to the very old religious centre at Darcungal (Holywood) across the Dumfriesshire border, that an older foundation for the nunnery is possible.[11]

THE PARISH STRUCTURE

Rather than found more religious houses Uchtred and Bishop Christian were more preoccupied in reorganising the diocese of Whithorn at parish level by dismembering the old mother-church groupings, and entrusting the churches and estates to the newer reformed monasteries. Thus the complexes of chapels and lands centering upon the 'minsters' of Kirkcudbright and Edingham near Dalbeattie, Uchtred gave to Holyrood Abbey for the canons to administer the estates and serve the churches. Cistercian and Augustinian disapproval of the mother-church of Kirkcudbright had already become apparent; and the breaking up of its 'plebania' (the constituent churches and chapels within its control) may have begun when Fergus gave Holyrood the churches of Dunrod and Galtway.

The canons of Holyrood responded rapidly and conscientiously. They established a cell of their abbey — the priory of St Mary's Isle — on the long tongue of land stretching into the river Dee south of Kirkcudbright. This was part of the lands of Galtway. The canons were able to live in community at the priory while serving the surrounding churches and chapels of the old mother-church — celebrating Mass, performing baptisms and burials, and caring for the spiritual welfare of the laity. It may have been mainly practical considerations that caused Uchtred to annex one of the remaining churches within the plebania to Holyrood — Tongland. David son of Terrus, Lord of Twynholm, gave them Twynholm parish church at the same time.

In Desnes Cro the moribund plebania of Edingham was similarly handed over. Holyrood was granted the church of St Colmanele of Urr, and the chapels of St Brigid of Blaiket and St Constantine of Edingham. The Bishop of Glasgow undoubtedly had rights in the old minster of Edingham. It had been identified as part of his 'mensa' (personal income as bishop) about 1120. This appears to have been forgotten, an instance either of Uchtred's hostility to the Bishop of Glasgow, or his capacity to give unintentional offence.

A similar reorganisation of the ancient mother-church of Kelton was undertaken by King William the Lyon himself. The church of St Oswald the Martyr and its pendicles — Kirkcormack, St Andrews of Balmaghie and the chapel of Barncrosh — were transferred by royal charter from Iona's control to Holyrood around 1173. He preferred to increase the power and wealth of Holyrood Abbey in his own burgh of Edinburgh to leaving Galloway churches within the control of Iona and the Lords of the Isles. By 1174 no less than ten churches and two

The motte of Urr, probably built by Walter de Berkeley (Crown copyright, RCAHMS, aerial photograph)

chapels in Uchtred's half of Galloway depended for their priests and administration upon Holyrood Abbey, and one (Borgue) upon Dryburgh Abbey.

The granting of the cure and revenues of parish churches to monastic houses became very general in the medieval church. It was done piecemeal, usually on the initiative of lay patrons, but no doubt with the encouragement of the monasteries and bishops. It reflected the high esteem in which the reformed monasteries were held in the twelfth and thirteenth centuries. The consequent loss of income and status among the secular clergy however, benefited neither the laity nor the church as a whole. It led to the deterioration of pastoral care. From the outset these annexations enriched the new monasteries at the expense of the old local religious communities or minsters. What happened to their resident canons is not known. Presumably they were disbanded. Some may have been absorbed into the new Order.

It is not easy to be sure how the Gallovidian nobility and people saw this radical change. Too little is known of the vitality, manpower and resources of the traditional minsters. Some may have been so rundown and depleted that any reform was welcome. There is a hint that this was so at Edingham for example.[12] In some parts of the north a local shortage of trained priests may have necessitated the reform. The apparently vigorous intervention in Galloway's affairs by Iona almost a century before gives no certain guide. It is however doubtful whether Uchtred ever asked himself if his policies, so acceptable in Anglo-Norman circles, might be seen by conservative Gallovidians as a wanton assault on respected religious communities for the profit of newer institutions beyond Galloway's borders.

UCHTRED AND GILBERT

The comparatively well-documented period of Uchtred's rule shows him to have been an active and conscientious ruler within his limitations. He espoused the Anglo-Norman interest without reserve; and it is ironical that his patronage of the Cistercian abbey of Holm Cultram and the Augustinian canons of Holyrood coincided with vituperative attacks on Galloway and his father's memory by Augustinian and Cistercian writers. Perhaps he was not aware of it. His charters trace his gradual shift of loyalty from the Gallovidian nobility and clergy in his youth, to increasingly closer bonds with Cumbrian and Anglo-Norman knights and barons as time went on. He seemed to retain the ideal of an independent Galloway without recognising that its achievement would be incompatible with the policies and people he identified with. His brother Gilbert saw this all too clearly.

As a landowner in Westmorland Uchtred was a tenant-in-chief of his cousin, Henry II of England, a circumstance which may have reduced his irritation at his subjection in Galloway to the King of Scots. That was constantly forced on his notice. He could not promulgate a charter in Galloway without seeking its confirmation by the Scottish king. William the Lyon's interference in the dispute between Holm Cultram Abbey and Walter de Berkeley, and his direct action over the churches of Kelton would have been unheard of in Fergus's time. Uchtred's relations with William may have been more distant than his dealings with Malcolm IV had been.

Gilbert's rule of western Galloway is undocumented. As long as the land in his territories was seen as belonging (in theory at least) to the folk or kindred, its ownership rarely changed. In practice a large proportion of it comprised the very large demesne estate in Gilbert's hands. He was not a man to give much away. Apart from an occasional hypothetical gift to a religious community such as Soulseat Abbey or Whithorn Priory by Gilbert or one of his nobles, no transactions needed to be recorded, and the habit of framing charters was not formed. Legal title was inscribed in oral tradition — the memories of 'elderly and respectable men', the traditional arbiters in the event of dispute. It was only when newcomers were given possession of estates on pledge of military service that landowners had any need to prove their ownership.

In one instance only it is probable that Gilbert broke his general rule and granted land to an Anglo-Norman incomer, and that has already been mentioned. Roger de Skelbrooke may have held and defended Gilbert's northern boundary on the river Doon, as he certainly did under Duncan, apparently on feudal contract. Gilbert was always a pragmatist rather than a man of principle, and it would have been consistent with his known character if he was prepared to make use of Anglo-Norman military expertise when it suited him.

Nevertheless he and his Gallovidians watched Uchtred's wholesale parcelling out of estates in the eastern territories with growing alarm. Uchtred's feudalisation of Desnes Cro, his introduction of Anglo-Norman knights into Borgue and Twynholm were as unwelcome to Gilbert as the intrusion of royal officers and favourites like Walter de Berkeley on the initiative of William the Lyon. Innovations on this scale struck at all that Gilbert and his father had stood for. The integrity of Galloway and the security of its traditional aristocracy were being eroded — a process Gilbert resolved to reverse as soon as opportunity offered.

Uchtred seems to have acquired along with his Norman polish, such insensitiveness to the feelings of his own people as to be unaware of the offence he was giving. Perhaps he placed too much faith in the ability of his feudal vassals to defend his territory and himself against the forces of conservatism, whatever the provocation.

WAR

The opportunity Gilbert had been waiting for came in 1174. The rebellion of Henry II's sons, supported by the King of France, challenged Henry's power over his empire, and promised to keep him preoccupied on the Continent. This was William the Lyon's chance to invade Northumbria and create a diversion on behalf of the French king. He called out his war-host, his Anglo-Norman knights, and his vassals, Uchtred and Gilbert with their Gallovidian forces. Uchtred found himself like his Cumbrian neighbours in a conflict of loyalties. Cumbria had passed from Scotland to England as recently as 1157, and many native landowners and Anglo-Normans as well, found themselves having to make a difficult choice between their erstwhile loyalty to the King of Scots and their present fealty to the King of England. Some supported one and some the other, but Uchtred had no option if he was to maintain his hold on Galloway, but to join his brother in supporting William the Lyon. They and their Gallovidians mustered with the Scottish forces and went to invade Northumbria as their father had done in 1138.

The conduct of the campaign was somewhat aimless. The invading army harried the countryside and attacked several castles. Then one misty Northumbrian morning near Alnwick, King William and a party of mounted knights were careless or unlucky enough to be surprised by a company of English cavalry. In the skirmish that followed William's horse fell and rolled on him pinning him to the ground, and he was taken prisoner. The threat to Henry II's northern border thus collapsed, and it was a calamity for which the Scots were unprepared. The chronicler, William de Newburgh, told how some of William's vassals who had not been present at his capture, gave themselves up to the English king 'thinking it honorable to share the peril of their lord'.[13] No such chivalrous impulse moved either of the Gallovidian princes.

To Uchtred and Gilbert the Scottish king's capture seemed heaven-sent. Temporarily they were free of his control, and it seemed within their grasp to make that freedom lasting. Gilbert's reaction was instant and decisive. He turned his horse and rode homeward followed by his army. Uchtred, ready to forget past differences in the elation of the moment, went with him.

Together they sent off a messenger to Henry II. An English chronicler recorded how:

> ... they very urgently besought the king and father of England, and offered him very many gifts, that he would snatch them from the dominion of the king of Scotland, and reduce them to his empire.[14]

At this point the brothers' brief collaboration probably ended. Gilbert turned immediately to the purge of royal officers and Anglo-Norman landowners from Galloway's territory:

> ... and all the English and French they could seize they slew and all the defences and castles which the king of Scotland had established in their land they besieged, captured, and destroyed, and slew all those whom they took within them.[15]

Archaeology has given weight to this account. Excavation of the motte of Urr, suggests that Walter de Berkeley's castle was burnt. Walter was presumably absent, and later regained his estates. Richard de Morville, Richard son of Truite, and David son of Terrus, on the other hand seem to have abandoned their Galloway possessions in Gilbert's reign of terror. The chronicles suggest that Uchtred participated in the violence, but this seems unlikely. He would hardly have turned upon his own friends and vassals; and the consequence of their expulsion was, for him, dangerous isolation.

Primary sources have made it possible in the foregoing paragraphs to trace the years during which the horizons and objectives of the brothers increasingly diverged, and offence was given too grievous to be easily forgotten. The English chroniclers who reported the events that immediately followed, though well-informed at the time, had no means of knowing the growing alienation that had gone before, and were exercised to account for Gilbert's hostility towards Uchtred. William de Newburgh, who assumed Gilbert was the elder brother, attempted to explain it:

But Gilbert, the elder, grieved that he had been defrauded of the entirety of his father's right, and ever hated his brother in his heart, although fear of the king restrained an outburst of the wrath he had conceived. But when the king was taken he was freed from this fear.[16]

The foundations are laid here for the traditional view of Gilbert as psychopathic and unnatural, rather than a ruthless politician of his time and culture. One portrait may be no more amiable than the other, but it may have the advantage of psychological accuracy. The chronicle attributed to Benedict of Peterborough, with rather better information, gives a political explanation:

Uchtred and Gilbert, Fergus's sons, were at strife as to which of them should be lord of the other and have dominion over the Galwegians: and had great hatred between them so that each of them lay in wait for the other to slay him.[17]

The prospect of being freed from Scottish suzerainty revived with a new urgency the old debate who was to be the lord of Galloway. To what extent Uchtred was aware of his own danger is not clear, nor is there any means of knowing whether his thoughts were as violent toward Gilbert as Gilbert's towards him. Deprived of his Anglo-Norman supporters he was vulnerable. He seems to have seen to it that his son Roland was not in Galloway. He might have done well to retire to Allerdale himself. But to quit would have meant surrendering, not only his hopes of ruling, but his half-share of Galloway and the lands of Desnes Cro. Uchtred's solution was to repair to the stronghold where he felt most secure, and wait for a reply from Henry II.

CATASTROPHE

The chronicler who takes up the story here left a blank where the name of Uchtred's stronghold should be. Some historians have assumed that it was Lochfergus, a moated hall outside Kirkcudbright. For several reasons the island castle of Arsbotl or Burned Island in Loch Ken is more probable. It was in a deeply wooded and thinly populated glen, where a sudden attack, especially by night, could be accomplished with very few being the wiser. Since the building of the hydro-electric dam on the Dee the water level of Loch Ken has risen. Burnt Island is still identifiable but it is now smaller than in the twelfth century — too small to accommodate a defended homestead. This was not necessarily a stone castle. A timber hall similar to the one excavated at Cruggleton was more likely, though some masonry, perhaps a stone landing quay, has been seen underwater in recent years.[18] The island lies near the west side of Loch Ken some distance from the shore. It would have been approachable by canoe, the traditional craft used to link populated islands and crannogs with dry land.

On a moonless night a landing party could have reached the island without sound beyond the plash of water against the paddles, and surprised the occupants of the island castle. But in the event the place was not taken by surprise. Gilbert's

son Malcolm, who led the landing party apparently found the doors of the stronghold barred:

> And Malcolm son of Gilbert . . . came and besieged the island of [blank] in
> which abode Utred, brother of his father . . . and captured him, and sent his
> butchers, commanding them to put out his eyes, and to emasculate him and cut
> out his tongue: and so it was done. And they went away leaving him half-dead:
> and shortly after he ended his life.[19]

The stark report expresses the stunned incomprehension with which the news
was received. The envoys from Henry II for whom Uchtred had been waiting
arrived on 23rd November, too late to save him. They reached Galloway to be
greeted with the news of Uchtred's death.

The 'Chronicle of Benedict of Peterborough' is now thought to have been written by one of the envoys, Roger de Howden, and at this point in the narrative car-
ries the authority of an eye-witness. His Anglo-Norman education had not
prepared Roger to understand the significance of the mutilation of Uchtred, and
he represented it as death by torture to gratify hatred. That misses the point: several such atrocities can be quoted in the twelfth century. Logmann son of Godfrey
Crovan of Man was blinded and castrated in 1095; Wimund, Bishop of Man in
1143; Welsh hostages were similarly treated at the command of Henry II in 1165;[20]
the blinding and castration of Magnus Sigurdson is reported in the
Heimskringla;[21] and in the 1190s William the Lyon had this done to Thorfinn
Maddadson, a hostage in his hands.[22]

Regardless of the effects of shock, haemorrhage or infection, this mutilation
was mainly inflicted on rulers and royal claimants. It may have been rooted in a
pre-Christian taboo against killing a king. Or it may have arisen as a way of avoid-
ing payment of a king's blood price. The object was not to kill but to disable,
making it impossible for the victim to rule. The principal functions of a medieval
king were denied to him. A blind man cannot fight or lead his men in battle. A
castrated man cannot beget heirs or command the respect of other men. A speech-
less man cannot deliver verbatim judgment, so cannot dispense justice.

According to Roger de Howden the emissaries from Henry were so shocked
and revolted by what had happened, that they refused to negotiate with Gilbert,
and returned home to report. There is no record that Gilbert ever disclaimed
responsibility for Uchtred's mutililation and subsequent death, and posterity
has no choice but to believe it was done on his instructions. Roger de Howden
certainly thought so. He had been sent by Henry, accompanied by the Cumbrian
magnate Robert de Vaus, to negotiate with the Gallovidian princes on Henry's
behalf in response to their plea for his protection. It is evident that Henry II had
been ready to come to terms with Uchtred and Gilbert, as Roger de Howden says,
'to draw them to his service'.

In the changed circumstances Gilbert offered to pay Henry 2,000 merks in silver, 500 cows and 500 swine annually for his goodwill, but Henry was too angry
at the death of Uchtred initially to discuss terms. His anger was all the greater

because Uchtred was his cousin. A second envoy was sent to Gilbert, commanding him to come before Henry. Gilbert refused.

In August 1175 the kings of England and Scotland met at York and a general peace was negotiated. It was a humiliating peace for Scotland, but Henry II 'gave and conceded to the king of Scotland permission to advance an army into Galloway and subdue Gilbert'.[23] There is no record of a military encounter, but William brought Gilbert to Henry at Feckenham in October 1176, 'and this Gilbert made peace for the death of his brother . . . and became his man [that is Henry's] and swore to him fealty before all men; and to have his love, gave him a thousand merks of silver' (half the sum originally offered). In addition, Gilbert's son Duncan was handed over to Henry as hostage 'for the preservation of peace'.[24]

The strict laws of inheritance practised in Normanised England required that once Uchtred was dead, his property in Galloway as well as Cumbria should pass to his son and heir apparent, Roland, who would have to do homage for them. Since the settlement was imposed by Henry II it must be assumed that Galloway remained partitioned for the next ten years, between Gilbert and Roland.[25] Under feudal law Duncan's rights as Gilbert's heir were protected by Henry. What precise sum of money Gilbert promised Henry is not clear, but it seems to have been more than 1,000 merks. It was not paid, of course, or very little of it. The task of collecting it fell to Robert de Vaus, and his accounts to the English Exchequer record long after Gilbert's death in 1185 an outstanding debt of over £800.

WHITHORN PRIORY

The King of Scots' humiliation at the hands of Henry II led to renewed attempts by the Archbishop of York to exert authority over the Scottish church. An appeal from Scotland to the Pope brought Cardinal Vivian from Rome in 1177 to hold a council with the Scottish bishops, and the Pope pronounced that the Archbishop of York had no right to act as metropolitan in Scotland. The cardinal assembling the council of Scottish bishops called upon Christian, Bishop of Whithorn. Christian refused to attend on the grounds that he was not a Scottish bishop, but a suffragan of the Archbishop of York. The cardinal, misunderstanding the justice of Christian's claim, excommunicated him and suspended him from office. 'But the bishop of Whithorn did not accept this suspension,' records Roger de Howden 'being protected by the support of Roger, Archbishop of York, whose suffragan he was'.[26]

The documentation of Cardinal Vivian's mission concentrates on this incident and is otherwise undetailed. Vivian arrived in England in May 1176 and negotiated a safe conduct to proceed further north into Scotland. It was evident that his purpose included a general tour of the Celtic provinces to bring ecclesiastical regularity where it was lacking. By the end of the year he was on his way to Ireland via the Isle of Man, where he spent Christmas with the King of Man. During the festivities he induced the king to go through a ceremony of canonical marriage with the Irish princess whose son by him was already three years old. The cardinal was a stickler for morality and canonical regularity. His embarkation from the Isle of Whithorn was recorded on Christmas Eve 1176, and argues a preceding stay in Galloway.

The coincidence of this visit with the replacement the following year of the old house of canons serving the cathedral church of Whithorn with a reformed Premonstratensian chapter, suggests that the cardinal was a potent influence in bringing the change about. He must have arrived in Galloway less than three months after Gilbert's submission to Henry II, when he had given such expensive promises to propitiate Henry for Uchtred's death. Gilbert now needed ecclesiastical approval as well as the goodwill of the English king; but it was unlikely that Bishop Christian of Whithorn, Uchtred's friend and spiritual father, would ever be reconciled to him. They might pull together in asserting Galloway's traditional loyalty to the Archbishop of York, but closer cooperation would have been out of character.

Into this situation came the cardinal, perhaps already aware of Bishop Christian's recalcitrance about attending his projected council of Scottish bishops, and quick to criticise the community at Whithorn. After nearly 15 years of Gilbert's rule in western Galloway, the environs of the cathedral and monastery were looking distinctly run-down. Buildings were crowded and the water-table had risen, causing a flood.[27] Its physical surroundings served to emphasise that the community of canons was still effectively unreformed. Gilbert has rarely been credited with an ecclesiastical policy; but he must have been involved in the decision to introduce at Whithorn a colony of Premonstratensian canons from Soulseat; and this may well have been in response to Vivian's prompting. Christian, committed to oppose the cardinal over attendance at the Scottish council, could do little but accept the decision, and his name is recorded by the Premonstratensian Order as one of the founders of Whithorn Priory. The choice of Premonstratensians was consistent with Fergus's policy in planting them at Soulseat Abbey. To that extent it was a natural and unexceptionable choice. Christian might have preferred Augustinians at Whithorn, more closely allied to the Cistercian Order.

Reginald of Durham, an Augustinian, writing a 'Life of St Godric' a few years later alluded to the antagonism between Gilbert and Bishop Christian. St Godric was a hermit living under the protection of the canons of Durham. He was a contemporary of Reginald of Durham, Ailred of Rievaulx, Bishop Christian and Gilbert son of Fergus. Ailred of Rievaulx visited Godric regularly, and it was at his suggestion that Reginald of Durham wrote his Life shortly after Godric's death in 1170. It contains a story about a nun of Galloway (possibly of Lincluden) who made the journey to Durham in order to visit the holy man:

> . . . the man of God began to enquire of her among other things whether she was acquainted with Christian, the bishop of that country. She marvelled how he should know the bishop, whom he had not seen in the body, and began to question in what state of being he came to know this man at such a distance. Then

Carved figure probably a twelfth-century representation of St Ninian (found in a bog near Whithorn). Poles could be thrust through to allow the effigy to be carried in procession (Royal Scottish Museum)

he said 'in the court of the Lord, where I have often seen many things, I have gazed on him. Wherefore until I see him again, advise him for me to bear patiently his injuries from a certain wealthy man, who has persecuted him for so long. Let him endure them with a quiet mind. For [that man's] ship is ready, and within this year he will be departing from this world to regions to him unknown. So it behoves the bishop to suffer his wrongs patiently since they are to last now for so short a time.'

There was a certain man in that land about whom he was prophesying who was very wealthy, but [he was] the bishop's unrelenting persecutor, a dissipator of the Church's goods, most hostile to the bishop.[28]

There can be little doubt that the 'very wealthy man' was Gilbert. Godric was famed for his predictions, and whether by this power or because Reginald wrote after Christian's death in 1186, the prophecy proved true, for Gilbert died in 1185. The charge that Gilbert persecuted Bishop Christian is not directly supported by recorded facts, but about that time Bishop Christian left Galloway and worked as a spare suffragen bishop for the Archbishop of York, filling in for the Bishop of

Carlisle while that diocese was in vacancy. His absence from his own diocese of Whithorn no doubt suited Gilbert, whose political opponent he undoubtedly was. The last word may have been uttered in Christian's decision to be buried at the Cistercian abbey of Holm Cultram in preference to his own cathedral church at Whithorn.[29]

Age did not subdue nor mellow Gilbert. As the vassal of Henry II he had a free hand in Galloway. Henry was preoccupied with his Continental possessions and his unruly sons. Gilbert exploited the advantages of that vassalage. As Henry's man he was immune from any punitive action by William the Lyon, to whom he apparently offered persistent provocation, by hit and run raids along his borders. In 1184, William took advantage of Henry's absence in France, to muster an army against Galloway. The 'Chronicle of Benedict of Peterborough' takes up the story:

> Meanwhile, the arrival of the King of England being made known, William King of Scotland — who had just collected his army to subdue Gilbert son of Fergus and the other Welsh who had wasted his land and slain his vassals and would not make peace with him — allowed his army to go home.[30]

One can almost most hear Gilbert laughing! Within months, however, Benedict recorded with satisfaction that on the first of January Gilbert son of Fergus, 'prince of the Galwegians, the enemy of his lord the King of Scotland' died. By his own lights, and the ethos of his culture, Gilbert had been highly successful in outwitting the Anglo-Norman establishment of both Scotland and England, and had been staunchly loyal to his people and his tradition. It is scarcely surprising after such a career, and especially the events of 1175, that another violent, if more subtle, attack was launched on Galloway's reputation.

A BAD NAME

The prevailing fashion for Arthurian romance, which rose to its peak in the mid-twelfth century, opened up a fantasy world where authentic Brittonic folklore gathered from Wales, Strathclyde and Brittany, and perhaps Galloway, was used as material for tales of chivalry, thus romanticising the militarism of Anglo-Norman society. Writers of Norman-French romances presented Galloway as 'a very evil land with a very perverse [wicked] people'.[31] Chrétien de Troyes, writing mainly before 1182, presented it as a kind of underworld, a realm of sinister enchantment: 'No knight who has ever gone that way by road or field has been able to come back; for that's the boundary of Galloway which a knight can't cross and then return again.'[32]

While in the writings of Chrétien, Galloway is 'off stage' and only occasionally mentioned, a certain Guillaume le Clerc devoted a whole poem to the 'Roman de Fergus', or as the latest translator calls it, 'Fergus of Galloway'.[33] This work of elegant fiction takes the ancestor of the princes of Galloway as its central character while wittily lampooning the uncouthness and barbarity of Galloway's people. The butt of the satire is one 'Soumoillet'. He is presented as Fergus's father, but

A medieval 'doodle' in the margin of a manuscript musical score (National Library of Scotland)

his real identification with a living member of the family would have been no problem to Guillaume's audience. The poem is a light-hearted, celebratory piece, probably composed in compliment to a member of the Gallovidian princely line, to be read aloud for a special occasion — probably a wedding.

'Fergus' himself is a composite character, bearing little resemblance to the father of the Gallovidian dynasty. While bearing his name, and performing the role of the knightly hero, he is clearly meant to be identified with another member of the princely house, in compliment to whom the story was written. He is portrayed as an *ingénu* setting out from an exaggeratedly bucolic background to acquire through a series of adventures, the polish and skills befitting a knight. He achieves both knighthood and the love of the beautiful (and bountifully dowered) Galiena, Lady of Lothian. The lovers marry: 'He loves her as his tender sweetheart, she him as her noble lover. . . . This is the end of the romance. May great joy come to those that hear it!'

Both the historical Fergus and his grandson Roland are merged in the fictitious hero. He is easily identified as Roland, Uchtred's son, and champion of the Anglo-Norman party in Galloway. His eventual marriage to the Lady of Lothian, whose inheritance points unmistakably to Roland's wife Elena de Morville, is the climax of the story. The Lady of Lothian is a stock Arthurian character, just as the buffoon Soumoillet is the stock Arthurian churl or hobbledehoy.

It was suggested at one time that the romance was composed for the wedding of Alan of Galloway, Roland's son and successor, to Margaret of Huntingdon. This does not fit the facts.[34] Alan's wife Margaret was of the Scottish royal house: the granddaughter of Earl Henry, and great-granddaughter of David I. Alan of Galloway, wealthy and distinguished though he was, undeniably gained prestige from this marriage. It is impossible to imagine the composition written for the wedding of Alan and Margaret which failed to make a great deal of the bride's royal blood. Guillaume le Clerc never once suggests the Lady of Lothian was a royal lady, she was heiress of Lothian alone. Yet he compliments the women of Ayrshire on their beauty — 'none more beautiful in the world' — and it was Roland's wife, Elena de Morville whose family estates lay both in Lothian and Ayrshire. More than this, the Lady of Lothian is the daughter of 'the King's Chamberlain'. Elena's father was Constable of Scotland. It is quite clearly Roland who must be regarded as the hero of the romance 'Fergus', and Guillaume's patron.

A character that has attracted much attention is 'Fergus's' so-called father, Soumoillet. He is a peasant to his very soul, described as a rustic who 'on account of his remarkable wealth had married a wife of very noble rank'. Here reality is touched momentarily with a reference to the historical Fergus whose wife was a king's daughter. It was not however, the writer's intention to lampoon the historical Fergus, his patron's noble ancestor, but Roland's detested uncle, Gilbert. Gilbert's resistance to Anglo-Norman culture and manners laid him open to representation as a clownish provincial, and this the audience would have appreciated to the full. He is depicted as living in a place which is a faithful description of Cruggleton in Gilbert's time:

> On the road out of Galloway, in a castle down a valley, lived a peasant . . . very close to the Irish Sea. He had his dwelling splendidly situated on a great rock, encircled by clay and wattle walls. The hill was topped by a tower that was not made of granite or limestone: its wall was built high of earth, with ramparts and battlements. The peasant was very well off to have such a handsome home by the sea. If he looked out he could see for thirty leagues all around. Nobody inside could feel threatened by any maker of siege equipment or from any assault, the rock being high and massive. The peasant governed and held in his possession the whole of the country which had been his for a very long time, and nobody could take it from him.[35]

The emphasis on Gilbert's wealth echoes the nun's story; and if (and it is more than likely) Gilbert amassed wealth at sea by raiding and piracy, the name Soumoillet, the Norman-French form of the Norse 'sumar-ledi' (summer rover) would have identified him instantly to his critics and contemporaries. There would have been little satisfaction in such satire after Gilbert's death, and ridicule would have been out of place once Roland's father Uchtred had been done to death at Gilbert's instigation. Only a very much more bitter tone would then have been appropriate. These considerations reinforce the case for associating the romance with celebration, not of Alan's wedding, but the wedding of his parents, Roland and Elena de Morville, probably around the year 1170.

There are jibes at the barbarity of Galloway — 'it is the custom in Ingegal', the fictional name for Galloway, 'to bear arms [a club] when ploughing or harrowing'; and the young knight Fergus horrifies his lady by carrying human heads on his saddle bow. But the satire goes to the heart of Galloway's weakness — its out-dated and inferior war technology that handicapped the Gallovidians in pitched battle. The young 'Fergus' asks his lumpish father for arms with which to set out on his adventures, and he 'found some old arms, very old-fashioned and rusty, in a chest, and gave them to his son who put them on over his rough clothes'. The Lady of Lothian's father comments that he deserved better. The laughter of the wedding party was assured.[36]

Galloway's bad name, bestowed first by the Augustinian and Cistercian writers in savage earnest about the same time, passed into literary convention. That is not to say that it became no more than an upper-class joke. It remained a crude real-ity. In the mid-thirteenth century the very name Gallovidian had become in the vernacular synonymous with thief. An enquiry was conducted in Dumfries before a jury of burgesses — the skinner, and dyer, and others — into the death of Adam the miller. He had met a certain Richard in St Michael's cemetery 'and Adam there defamed Richard, calling him a thief viz Galuvet [Gallovidian].' The insult was so foul that a few days later Richard killed Adam in the street in front of wit-nesses. Richard was nonetheless acquitted, because 'Adam was a thief and a defamer.'[37]

For all their less sombre tone, the literary attacks were as damaging in their con-tempt as the accusations of the chronicles and hagiography. An English poem, 'The Owl and the Nightingale', written about 1190 carried on the ridicule, though its barbs were directed at the Scots as much as the Gallovidians. The relevant pas-sage ends with a reference to Cardinal Vivian's visitation to Scotland and Galloway in 1177.

An owl and a nightingale are having a debate, and the owl turns with scorn upon the songbird asking:

> . . . you never sing in Irish lands.
> Nor ever visit Scottish lands.
> Why can't the Norsemen hear your lay.
> Or even men of Galloway?
> Of singing skill those men have none.
> For any songs beneath the sun . . .

[The nightingale replies:]

> What should I do with folk to whom,
> content and pleasure never come?
> The land is poor, a barren place,
> a wilderness devoid of grace . . .

A grisly and uncanny part,
where men are wild and grim of heart.
Security and peace are rare,
and how they live they do not care.
The flesh and fish they eat are raw,
like wolves they tear it with the paw.
And wander clad in shaggy fell,
as if they'd just come out of hell.

If some good man to them would come,
— as once one came from holy Rome,
to teach them virtue's better way.
And help them shake off evil's sway —
he'd wish he'd stayed at home I swear,
he'd only waste his time up there.[38]

CONCLUSION

The defamation of Galloway and its people continued long after the deaths of Uchtred and Gilbert, but it was in their time that it reached its crescendo. Their careers do not so much explain the abuse as illuminate the clash of cultures and emotions that produced it. The charters of Uchtred provide valid points of reference against which the chroniclers' highly coloured stories can be compared. Unfortunately there is no such sober authority for the character and career of Gilbert. In such a prejudiced milieu it is uncomfortable to have to depend apart from the English Exchequer rolls, upon secondary sources alone.

Between the voice of ridicule and the chilling report of Uchtred's mutilation, the personality of Gilbert tantalises the aspiring portraitist. Gilbert was closest to Fergus in his single-minded loyalty to traditional society and Gallovidian autonomy; and he was more successful. He held his half of Galloway against all comers, played the hapless king of Scots off against Henry II's ambition, and beat Henry at his own greedy game with promises he had no intention of keeping. The dry-as-dust record of Gilbert's debt to the English Exchequer crackles still with his laughter. In his time Gilbert had the last laugh; but perhaps he was perceptive enough to see his own success for what it was — a time-limited *tour de force*. He had expended his life (and his brother's) holding back for a generation only, an irresistible tide.

6

ASSIMILATION VERSUS AUTONOMY:

Roland, Alan and Thomas
(1185–1235)

Ah debonair, thou good and noble knight!
Song of Roland[1]

The three generations covered by this chapter saw a floodtide that submerged the Celtic and Anglian culture of Galloway, eroding the power of the native aristocracy and sweeping into dominance an Anglo-Norman nobility and social organisation. Uchtred had gone with that tide; but Roland and his son Alan rode it to their own advantage. Thomas, Alan's natural son, sailed against it, and was engulfed.

ROLAND

The same fantasy that painted the native Gallovidian as savage, irreligious and unchaste, romanticised Norman militarism in terms of chivalry and the knightly virtues. Both these black-white projections were equally far from multi-coloured reality. Roland, son of Uchtred has been cast by contemporaneous chroniclers and later antiquarians in the role of the gallant knight who avenged his father, reclaimed his patrimony, rescued his overlord in a tight corner, and modernised his country to its benefit. These fictions have come near to being accepted as sober history.

Roland's reaction to the news of Gilbert's death was swift and resolute, and within the year that followed he revealed himself as a more than competent military commander. Disregarding the rights of his cousin Duncan (still Henry II's hostage) he seized Gilbert's territories in what was apparently a well-prepared *coup d'état*. Benedict of Peterborough relates:

> Roland son of Uchtred . . . immediately after Gilbert's death collected to his aid a numerous host of horse and foot, and invaded Gilbert's land . . . and slew all that opposed him and reduced that land to himself. Moreover he slew all the most powerful and the richest men in Galloway and occupied their lands. And in them he built very many castles and very many fortresses, establishing his kingdom.[2]

Another account speaks of two distinct military engagements, and names two Gallovidian leaders — Gillepatrick, evidently a native nobleman, and Gillecolum, described as a freebooter, who both died defending Wigtownshire.[3] The Kennedys, powerful in Carrick, were apparently also involved in opposing Roland. An unnamed brother of Roland's was killed in the campaign. The wholesale erection of motte and bailey castles signified the installation of Roland's Anglo-Norman vassals, ready to defend their new estates against native attack and to intimidate a sullen and reluctant peasantry. Far from reclaiming his own patrimony, which was already in his possession, Roland ruthlessly annexed Duncan's while he was in enforced captivity and supposedly protected by a code of honour.

It has been suggested that William the Lyon knew of Roland's intention and turned a blind eye to his action in its early stages.[4] Certainly Roland's apparent defiance of William altered very rapidly to a habit of close cooperation between the two men. It was Henry II who was taken by surprise, and inconvenienced most by Roland's coup. Henry was bound to intervene on behalf of his hostage, Duncan son of Gilbert, the rightful heir to Gilbert's lands, of which Henry himself was overlord. Henry declared that in seizing Duncan's patrimony, Roland had disobeyed him and his justiciars. At the time of Roland's action William had been with Henry at his royal palace of Woodstock, engrossed in his own marriage negotiations, but he hurried north, the bearer of Henry's commission to subdue Roland and send him to Henry's court to answer for himself.

Roland's response was to block the roads into Galloway with felled trees, and to hold both kings at defiance. Henry gathered an army and marched north to Carlisle. His army was not a feudal host, but lightly armed Welsh troops paid for by levying a tax — scutage — in lieu of military service from Henry's English vassals from Kent to Northumberland. It was long remembered as the Great Scutage of Galloway.[5] Roland refused to accompany William to meet Henry at Carlisle, and it was not until a second embassage, reinforced by several churchmen including the Bishop of Glasgow, used their persuasive powers and offered hostages for Roland's safe conduct, that he consented to be escorted to the king. Benedict recorded the peace terms:

> And he made peace with the lord King [Henry] in this fashion, that the land which belonged to Utred Fergus's son, his father on the day that he was alive and dead should remain for him undisturbed . . . And as for the land which belonged to Duncan son of Gilbert Fergus's son, his uncle Gilbert aforesaid claimed in opposition to him, he should come to justice in the court of the lord king of England, at his summons. And Roland took an oath upon the observation of these agreements, and gave his three sons as hostages. He swore also fealty to the King of England and to his heirs, by command of the King of Scotland, against all men . . . And Joscelin, Bishop of Glasgow, promised before all upon the word of truth and the relics of the saints, that unless Roland upheld the aforesaid convention unaltered he would pronounce the sentence of excommunication upon him and upon his land.[6]

It had taken the heaviest artillery in the Bishop of Glasgow's arsenal to bring Roland to heel. His submission to Henry II was as explicit as Gilbert's had been — he put his hands between his, and became his man. Within a short time however his vassalage to the King of England was significantly modified. William the Lyon met Henry at Lincoln and did homage expressly for Scotland and Galloway, thus becoming Galloway's overlord and interposing himself between Roland and Henry. Within four years Henry had died (1189) and the feudal relationships changed again. Henry's successor Richard I, sold his overlordship to the King of Scots for the money to finance a crusade. Galloway was not named in this last transaction, but its subordination to the Scottish crown for the time being at least, became a political reality.

Roland had already seized upon an opportunity to win King William's goodwill. In 1186 Moray and Ross rose in rebellion against the king in support of a pretender to the throne, Donald MacWilliam. Roland put himself and his Gallovidians at William's disposal at Inverness:

> the King remained in the Castle called Inverness. And he sent the earls and barons with the Scots and Galwegians to subdue his enemy . . . they chose therefore about 3000 warlike youths . . . and among them was the household of Roland, Uchtred's son, and on his nod hung the decision. They . . . slew MacWilliam and carried his head away with them and presented it to the King of Scotland.[7]

The same year Roland was administering justice in the king's name in Dumfries, and seems to have become his justiciar in the south-west.[8] The favour Roland enjoyed with the king was reflected in the eventual settlement of Duncan's inheritance, which was probably arbitrated by William after Henry II's death. Roland's acquisition of Wigtownshire was confirmed. He was to be the sole lord of Galloway from the river Nith to the Rhins, and Duncan was to hold Carrick (southern Ayrshire) and subsequently received the title Earl of Carrick.

With the formidable Henry II no more, and Richard preoccupied abroad, Roland could have made a bid for Galloway's independence. English intervention would have been no obstacle, and Roland had already shown himself more than a match for William the Lyon when it came to military conflict. But Galloway was no longer the ancient realm clinging precariously to its autonomy. Its natural leaders, bar Roland, were dead; and foreign landowners were dominating its countryside. Roland was thoroughly imbued with Anglo-Norman ideas. The status of vassalage was not objectionable to him, and his eyes were on a horizon beyond Galloway's borders. The kingdom of Scotland had more to offer him than an independent principality of Galloway. By 1192 if not before it must have been plain to Roland where his overriding interests lay. His brother-in-law William de Morville was aging and without an heir. If he died without issue the vast de Morville inheritance would devolve on Roland's wife Elena and himself. Since the major part of the lands lay in Scotland it behoved Roland to accept the King of Scots as his overlord and cultivate his goodwill.

GLENLUCE

One of Roland's first enterprises as lord of Galloway had been to found a monastery, as behoved a prince who had been threatened with excommunication. The abbey of Glenluce was established therefore in 1192. It was a Cistercian community as might have been expected, and a daughter-house of Dundrennan. Very little of its fine structure remains, and even less of its documentation. A few later confirmation charters and extraneous records afford scraps of information, but nothing like material for a coherent history of the house remains. The dissolution of the monastic estate by sale in 1573–74 to the Earl of Cassillis provides the earliest full list of the abbey's properties, most of which will have belonged to the abbey from its foundation. There are 81 of them, stretching from the shores of Luce Bay northward to the Ayrshire border, a great swathe of country dividing western Galloway in two. This very large estate may have belonged to the chief Gillepatrick, who was killed in the campaign of 1185. The chronicler described him as 'one of the richest men in Galloway'.[9]

Estate ownership in Wigtownshire in the twelfth and thirteenth centuries is poorly documented and it was not until the fourteenth that the extent to which the native aristocracy had survived feudalisation became clear. It can be inferred however from an enquiry recorded in 1296 that the lords of Galloway had held a very large estate stretching from Craighlaw in Kirkowan to the obsolete parish of Longcastle, and probably the parish of Mochrum as well.[10] Roland may have taken these lands into his own hands when he annexed Wigtownshire, or they may already have belonged to Gilbert and his predecessors from earlier times.[11] Between these valuable estates in his possession and the native aristocracy entrenched in the Rhins of Galloway — the Macdowells, the Ahannays, and the Adairs, for example — Roland established a broad band of demilitarised territory by granting Glenluce to the Cistercians.

In the abbey's hands, much of the land was devoted to sheep farming (and may have suffered some depopulation as a result). Around 1320 the current prices of Glenluce wool were jotted down in the notebook of the Italian merchant Pegolotti. The abbey had developed a regular Contintental trade, exporting wool, flax, cloth and linen, and bringing home wheat flour from Ireland, wine from Aquitaine and Bordeaux, and the finest tableware and kitchen pottery from La Vendée and Charente Inferieure. Excavation which revealed some fine examples of this thirteenth-century French pottery, uncovered also a piped water system with jointed earthenware pipes and lidded junction boxes.[12]

The abbey's trading ships were not documented until the sixteenth century but they were almost certainly in use long before. The details of the monks' standard of living indicate a relaxation of the original Cistercian austerities. Wheaten bread, plentiful wine and fine tableware suggest ample meals of meat, game and vegetables which the monastic estate, its woodlands and gardens afforded. The piped water indicated a large and highly organised institution where cleanliness and a modicum of comfort were highly rated. Very little is known of the monks

Roof-boss of Glenluce Abbey showing the heraldic arms of the lords of Galloway in compliment to Roland, the abbey's founder (Historic Scotland)

themselves except that the first abbot has left an account of his observations of the moon.

Roland made a lesser grant about this time to the Augustinian priory of St Mary's Isle at Kirkcudbright, annexing to them the parish church of Eggerness near Cruggleton and a tenth of all the food, drink, tallow and wax consumed in his own household at Kirkcudbright. This is the first time that the lord of Galloway's residence in Kirkcudbright was documented. It was presumably the motte still visible at the harbour and may have been built by Roland. It may have been indicative of Roland's continued preference for eastern Galloway even once he had become master of Gilbert's castle of Cruggleton. The canons of Whithorn will not have been pleased to see the church of Eggerness, so near them, granted away to St Mary's Isle.[13]

THE DE MORVILLE INHERITANCE

William de Morville died in 1196. The Westmorland property went to another branch of the family, but the rest — the whole of Cunninghame (the northern third of Ayrshire), Lauderdale in Lothian, and some stake in estates in Northampton — were added to Roland's own patrimony of Galloway. Roland could well afford to pay the feudal death-duty (700 merks) on the de Morville lands. He thus acquired also the de Morville's hereditary office of Constable of Scotland. Roland was by now around 50, his sons fully adult, and his wealth and security almost unassailable. He set about replacing the native landowners who perished in his campaign of 1185 with Anglo-Normans, extending his father's policy of infefting Cumbrian landowners. With their cooperation and on their initiative, the first mottes of Wigtownshire were built. Wigtownshire's old nobility were undoubtedly depleted by deaths in the campaign of 1185, and some chiefs may have been ousted from their estates by incomers whom Roland infeft. It was in Kirkcudbrightshire however that the major infiltration of Anglo-Norman landowners occurred, and their many castles overshadowed the countryside.

THE MOTTES

The typical feudal charter investing a newcomer in a barony included the right to punish offenders in the baron court, and to have 'furca and fossa' — pit and gallows — with which to enforce law and order and compel submission. These instruments of punishment were directed against the peasants of the estate, the people whose forebears had tilled the same land time out of mind and belonged there. No doubt they had been accustomed to summary justice and occasional oppressions from individual lords; but to the extent that new landowners replaced the native, the small tenants who had held their land by right of their membership of the kindred will have felt a radical change. Both they and the peasantry had now to live under an alien regime and the watchful eye of a foreign lord.

The purpose of the mottes was not primarily to terrorise the peasantry but to

Marginal drawing — in a musical score — Herdmanstone MS: a trading ship (National Library of Scotland)

*A twelfth-century motte
and bailey castle—a
timber construction
within a wooden
palisade on an artificial
mound (Whithorn
Trust)*

defend the incoming lords against native landowners, whose resentment of the
incomers expressed itself from time to time in violent forays. So many mottes
within a limited area, a concentration unmatched except in the marches of Wales,
signified not the elimination of native landowners, but the challenge they represented to the incoming Anglo-Normans. It was their insecurity not their
supremacy that quartered Kirkcudbrightshire with fortifications.

The motte of Urr has already been illustrated (see p. 107). Such castles were timber buildings at first surrounded by a timber stockade. They stood on top of an
artificial mound, itself crowning a natural hill, so that the surrounding country
could be kept under surveillance. The baron or lord of the manor, his family and
men at arms lived inside the stockade. It was more like a barrack than a home. In
the centuries that followed the timber tower was replaced with stone. Some
of these simple towers were supplanted by the great castles of the thirteenth
century, reflecting the increased wealth and refinement of that time. The twelfth-
century mottes however, were rough and ready — the expedients of a military
caste whose nervousness as much as their knightly status dictated that they should
be in a perpetual state of readiness for war.

Roland granted estates to friends who thus became his vassals owing him military service. The parishes of Southwick and half of Colvend near Dalbeattie were
allotted to Thomas son of Gospatrick of Workington in Cumbria and Roger de
Maule (Masculus) who had estates in other parts of Scotland. Perhaps the first
feudal grant in Wigtownshire was at Sorbie very close to Roland's own castle of
Cruggleton. Here he granted the two parishes of St Fillans and St Michaels to his
wife Elena's cousin Ivo de Veteripont who held lands in Westmorland. Ivo
annexed the parish church of St Fillans to Dryburgh Abbey, the de Morville family's foundation, 'saving the right of the incumbent' so that the parish priest had
security for his lifetime. It was almost certainly Ivo who built the motte there. This
castle, surrounded by marshes, was almost impregnable, and its position within
three or four miles from Cruggleton indicates Roland's caution in settling a kins-

man within the outer defences of his own castle. He was evidently aware of the local animosity to his feudalising policies.[14]

The documentation of his cousin Duncan's rule in Carrick provides an instructive contrast. In addition to Gilbert's old vassal Roger de Skelbrooke, referred to in one of Duncan's charter's as 'my knight', Duncan himself appears to have granted the lands of Dalmellington to a Lincolnshire knight Thomas Colville to defend the route into Carrick from Galloway via the Glenken. Predominantly however, Duncan's court consisted of native nobility. The Kennedys were already a power in Carrick, having opposed Roland in Duncan's cause in 1185. The witnesses to Duncan's and other charters reveal the mixture of Celtic and old Anglian tradition: Gillenef Accouelton, Gilledovengi his brother, Gilcrist MacMakin, Murdac Macgillemartin, Gilleassald mac Gilleandres and Gillemernach, his brother.[15] Roger de Skelbrooke's charters were witnessed by similar, and sometimes the same people — Gilleassald mac Gilleandres appearing again as well as Gillemen mac Colman, Gilbert MacKenedi, Gilcrist Bretnach (Gilcrist the Briton), to quote some examples. The names of many of these families are to be found later as established surnames in Wigtownshire. In Carrick the native aristocracy retained both land and power. Their culture remained strong enough to absorb one or two Anglo-Norman incomers. Roger de Skelbrooke for example, married his younger daughter to a native landowner, Roderic MacGillescop. A few motte and bailey castles were built, such as Thomas Colville's at Dalmellington; but their purpose was to defend Carrick's borders rather than to cow the countryside. Duncan of Carrick's rule of his earldom shows him to have retained his father's attachment to the native culture and kindreds.

The mottes of Galloway signified the unease between its native nobility and the Anglo-Norman ruling class. The intensity of that uneasiness is most evident once the mottes have been counted. Very few of the surviving mounds that are still a feature of Galloway's countryside have been excavated, but as far as it is possible to reckon the total, at least 12 were built in Wigtownshire and over 30 in Kirkcudbrightshire.[16] The typical cropped cone earthworks that now survive across the countryside to this day write an invoice of the cost to Galloway's people of Roland's success.

Roland died in 1200. He was among the wealthiest and most powerful of an elite whose estates spanned the borders of Scotland and England and sometimes the English Channel. An alien culture and cosmopolitan outlook made them indifferent to local identity and native tradition. Remnants of the old law system of Galloway survived into the fourteenth century, but the Anglo-Norman administration and jurisdictions operated alongside and eventually supplanted them. It remains a personal point of view whether Roland's prestige can be seen enhancing the power and importance of Galloway by bringing it into the centre of Scottish politics, or whether he is perceived as throwing away what Fergus and Gilbert had struggled to preserve. By introducing the Anglo-Norman landowning class, and accepting subservience to the King of Scots, Roland laid a time fuse under the old society, advancing his own interests at Galloway's expense.

ALAN (1200–34)

As long as Roland lived, his son Alan seems to have confined his activities to Galloway and the Scottish milieu. His presence at the court of William the Lyon was several times recorded. After Roland's death in 1200 Alan's horizon changed. As lord of Galloway his main preoccupations were western and maritime. He became involved with his younger brother Thomas in the politics of the Irish Sea. Then, after his second marriage, to Margaret of Huntingdon, her very large English estates brought him into contact with King John of England, and he became involved in the king's campaigns in Ireland. After John's death in 1216, Alan's relationship with both Henry III and Alexander II of Scotland became more distant. He and his brother concentrated upon participating in the conflict between the heirs to the kingship of Man.

MARITIME POWER

Although Alan's wealth and social standing in the Normanised societies of Scotland and England exceeded even his father's, his Gallovidian blood and affections were more evident than Roland's had been. The Anglo-Norman knight and builder of castles, was replaced by the more traditional figure of the sea-warrior. Alan's love of the sea and zest for maritime warfare, marked him as a true Gallovidian. His political alignments might be essentially Anglo-Norman, but under his vital leadership the conflict of interest was in part obscured. Galloway under Alan enjoyed more independence from the Scottish crown; and its fighting men were employed in their familiar habitat, the war-galleys of the western seaboard. After Roland, Alan and his brother Thomas must have seemed to the native Gallovidians like princes after their own hearts.

In 1209 Thomas married an heiress, Isabel of Atholl and became Earl of Atholl in her right. He also owned lands in widely separate parts of his family's estates; but his inclinations were mainly sea-faring. A great deal of his time was spent cruising the western waters between Galloway, the Hebrides, Man and Ireland. In 1205 he was supplying war galleys to King John for his preparations against the French. He cooperated with Reginald Prince of Man in attacking Derry. He fought in Ireland and was rewarded by King John with an estate for the service of three knights, and here in 1214 he built a strategic stronghold at Coleraine. In all these exploits he was reflecting the inclinations and policies of his elder brother Alan, and for much of the next 15 years Alan joined him in Ireland and at sea, often dominating the western sea lanes with their ships.

Alan's large fleet almost certainly used Loch Ryan as a harbour, and Kirkcudbright also. English documents record a casualty of Alan's warfare-cum-piracy in the narrow seas. King John instructed his justiciar in Ireland to allow Alan's men in Ireland to:

> come to England and return the ship that Alan took at Kirkcudbright and allow Alan to have the merchandise in the said ship, until the owner of the vessel shall come to speak to the King about it, the King not wishing him to lose his ship.[17]

MARRIAGE

Alan's marriage with Margaret of Huntingdon, the great granddaughter of David I, and co-heiress to the Honour of Huntingdon, had brought him great social distinction.[18] Margaret's royal blood and his own wealth put him among the powerful few in England as well as the north. He was of the order of nobles whom no medieval king could afford to slight, and King John wooed his friendship and assistance. Alan supplied mercenaries for John's abortive campaign in Wales, and for the conquest of Ireland. He supported the king at Runnymede in 1215 when English barons confronted him with their discontents and exacted his ratification of their Great Charter. There was a playful exchange of gifts. John gave Alan a 'good hound' and Alan presented the king with a breeding pair of geese. The impulse to visualise the presentation ceremony is irresistible. After the Irish campaign John bestowed enormous estates upon Alan, said to be 140 knights' fees. The grant may have been a licence 'to conquer if you can' rather than conveying orderly vacant possession, and it was up to Alan to exact what tribute he could. Nevertheless there were many indications that Alan felt himself to be very much at home in Ireland, not the least perhaps, the beautiful Gaelic name he gave his youngest daughter — Derbhorgail, known to posterity by the latinised Dervorgilla. Among the known female names of Alan's family — Affrica, Gunnild, Margaret, Elena and Christiana — it stands alone with Affrica as an Irish name.[19]

Letters passing between King John and himself show that Alan had his private 'chancery' with clerks not only acting as secretaries, but able to undertake semi-diplomatic missions on his behalf. This semi-regal state, the fleet of ships, the armies supplied to King John, demonstrated Alan's power and wealth. Following family tradition, Alan founded an abbey in 1218, the Premonstratensian house of Tongland near Kirkcudbright. The fortunes of the great Cistercian Order were temporarily in decline, for they were at odds with the Pope and under interdict, and Alan turned naturally to the Premonstratensians, the alternative Order in Galloway's monastic establishment. At about the same time the cathedral at Whithorn was renovated. The crypts were added at the east end, the nave lengthened, and its north wall rebuilt during the construction of the cloisters.[20] These improvements reflect the prosperity of the time, and the growing sophistication of liturgy and ritual. Increased numbers of laity were attending services, and Whithorn was drawing more pilgrims to the shrine of St Ninian. To what extent Alan was involved in financing the work on the cathedral is not recorded.

As time went on Alan's need for a legitimate son to succeed him became increasingly urgent. He had one daughter, Elena, by his first wife, and Margaret of Huntingdon bore him two more daughters — Christiana and Dervorgilla. Another daughter, nameless to history, had died in 1213 while a hostage in the custody of Roger FitzRoger. Alan had one son, Thomas, born out of wedlock and named presumably after Alan's brother. His affection for this boy, and his anxiety to set him up with a place in the world may have motivated Alan's participation in the wars fought mainly at sea over the kingship of Man.

The war between two brothers, Reginald and Olaf, for the kingship of Man drew Alan into the seaborne warfare of the western seas, in which Thomas Earl of Atholl was already prominent. Within a few years Thomas, Alan's natural son, became involved. The Manx princes were related to Alan and his brother through the marriage of Affrica daughter of Alan's great grandfather Fergus to King Olaf of Man. On the strength of this family tie Reginald of Man had enlisted Alan's aid against his younger brother Olaf around 1220. Hostilities, mostly at sea, occupied the next decade. For some time the success of Reginald and the Gallovidian princes seemed assured. In 1225 a marriage was arranged between Alan's son Thomas and Reginald's daughter. In the event of Reginald's death Thomas would be in line for the kingship of Man on the defeat of Olaf.

By 1228 the Gallovidian princes occupied Man, and the 'Chronicle of Man' records:

Alan lord of Galloway and Thomas Earl of Atholl and King Reginald came to Man with a great army; and devastated the whole southern part of Man and despoiled the churches, and slew all the men whom they could take; and the southern part of Man was almost reduced to a desert. And after this Alan returned with his army to his own land; and he left his bailiffs in Man to render to him the taxes of the land.'[21]

Then Olaf's fortunes changed. He appealed for aid to his long neglected overlord, King Haakon of Norway. Alan boasted that the sea was not more difficult to cross to Norway than from Norway to Scotland to anyone wanting to harry, implying that his own naval forces were equal to Haakon's. Haakon was nevertheless ready enough to reassert his authority over Man and the Hebrides. He sent a fleet southward under the command of Olaf and one Uspek (probably a son or grandson of Somerled of the Isles). The ships entered the Firth of Clyde and captured Rothesay Castle, but withdrew, according to report, at Alan's approach with 150 ships. This was a diversionary retreat only, since Olaf sailed on southward to Man, where Alan's bailiffs were driven out, and Olaf was instated without a battle. In February 1229 Reginald surprised Olaf, coming from Galloway by night with five ships. There was apparently an attempt at negotiation, then a skirmish, and Reginald was killed. It seemed that his mantle might fall on the young Thomas who still had hopes of ousting Olaf and becoming King of Man. It did not happen. Alan became otherwise preoccupied. He was planning his third and last marriage — to Roesya, daughter of Hugh de Lacy, the Earl of Ulster.[22]

The alliance with Hugh de Lacy is at first sight surprising. For when King John (who had given Hugh de Lacy large territories in Ireland and the earldom of Ulster) quarrelled with him in 1210, it was Alan and and his brother Thomas who had fought against Hugh on John's behalf. As late as 1223 they were still supporting Henry III against him, and in 1224 he attacked their lands.[23] The later change of alignment suggests negotiations and an agreement which the marriage was intended to bond. Yet the marriage had disadvantages. The church had to be appeased because of the kinship between Alan's late first wife and his new bride.

There are gaps in the record here, but it is chronicled that around 1229 or slightly earlier Alan crossed to Ireland 'with a vast retinue' in order to marry Roesya de Lacy, and narrowly escaped shipwreck on the return journey. This third marriage is best explained as the act of an aging man desperate for children.

There is no evidence that Alan considered negotiating acceptance for his son Thomas as heir to Galloway or his other possessions, though he installed him in estates to ensure him a suitable livelihood. His lack of an heir upon whom his vast possessions could devolve without partition was now urgent. In Celtic societies such as Ireland and Galloway illegitimacy counted for little and Thomas might be accepted; but in the kingdoms of England and Scotland feudal law disqualified a man born out of wedlock from inheritance. The rigour of the law has been known to be set aside for great men, but the King of Scots Alexander II was a stickler in such matters, and later insisted on a strictly legal division between Alan's three legitimate daughters. The two elder ones were by this time married to the earls of Winchester and Albemarle, and their husbands' vested interest in the division of Alan's estate was a formidable obstacle to any arrangement in Thomas's favour. Some hope that Thomas might succeed at least to the lordship of Galloway must nevertheless have been gathering currency in the principality itself in Alan's lifetime. Alan's own hopes lay elsewhere, as his marriage to Roesya shows. He still had dreams of a legitimate son.

In 1233 his daughter Dervorgilla was of marriageable age; and Alan arranged a match for her with the wealthy Yorkshire baron, John Baliol of Barnard Castle. It was a marriage which was to have historical significance scarcely predictable at the time. John Baliol was a good deal older than his bride, but if later writers such as Wyntoun are to be believed, Alan did well by his youngest daughter, and the marriage was exceptionally happy. Alan's own latest marriage produced no child, and in 1234 Alan died, the last of Galloway's hereditary princes, and was buried at Dundrennan. In his lifetime he had become a legendary figure: 'that magnificent prince', one obituary called him. The *Annals of Ulster* presented him as one of the last of the Vikings — a great sea-warrior — the king of the Gallgaidhil.[24] A Norwegian source described him as: 'the greatest warrior at that time, who had a great army and many ships, and plundered about the Hebrides and Ireland, and made great warfare through the western lands.'[25]

These voices say that it was not only in a great inheritance and an advantageous marriage that Alan was fortunate, but in his exceptional energy, his courage and leadership skills, and his dynamic presence. It was fitting that the last of Galloway's princes should leave behind memories of such panache. His misfortune, and Galloway's tragedy, was that he left no undisputed heir to follow him.

THOMAS OF GALLOWAY

In the succession crisis that followed Alan's death there emerged into historical record an entity not named before — the Community of Galloway. The composition of the Community or its leaders is not recorded, but it must have included the lesser as well as the richer nobility, the secular clergy, bishop and archdeacon, and the abbots and priors, and possibly other officers of the monastic houses. This body was able to express articulate local opinion, and it was first mentioned in the context of local protest against a tripartite partition of Galloway into three blocks of private property in the hands of the legitimate heiresses (or their husbands) as if the erstwhile kingdom had no political identity, and its people no say. Far from expressing anti-Scottish or separatist feeling, the Community petitioned Alexander II to preserve the integrity of the principality by taking it into his own hands and under his own royal administration. It was a moderate and indeed, loyal request. Alexander, possibly under pressure from the heiresses' husbands, was adamant in refusing.

The power of the moderates to guide local opinion was thus undermined. Raiding broke out along Galloway's borders, a separatist party bent on military action quickly emerged, and an army was mustered. For what follows we are dependent on accounts in the 'Chronicle of Melrose', aligned firmly behind Alexander II, and the English chronicle of Matthew Paris. The 'Chronicle of Lanercost' summarised Melrose's longer account.[26] These sources represented the interests and point of view of the Scottish establishment, and their unanimous object was to minimise the seriousness of Galloway's last bid for self-determination. The rising that followed has been, and still often is, presented as stirred up by external influences, and quickly put down. How long the resistance continued, and how difficult the King of Scotland's forces found it to defeat the insurgents, is concealed by the terseness of the records.

A leading influence in the separatist party was Hugh de Lacy, Earl of Ulster, the late Alan's father-in-law. He has sometimes been regarded in this context as wholly Irish in outlook and interests. But this was scarcely true. Powerful though he undoubtedly was in Ireland, Hugh de Lacy's family estates extended from Shropshire to France.[27] He was the same cosmopolitan breed of magnate as Alan had been. Hugh was apparently prepared initially to instate either the illegitimate Thomas or Alan's legitimate nephew Patrick as lord of Galloway. Patrick was only a child, however, and Thomas rapidly assumed the leadership. Even the chroniclers hostile to his cause called him Thomas of Galloway.[28]

He was young but not untried, and the qualities most conspicuous in his later life — courage and staying power — may already have been recognisable. His parentage, his marriage to a Manx princess, and his part in his father's maritime ventures, had built up for him respect and goodwill in parts of the Hebrides, and with an opposition party in Man as well as in Ireland. Thomas's support may also have come from Carrick, though the attitude of Duncan of Carrick remains unrecorded. He was presumably not prepared to support Thomas openly.

Before these matters were put to the test, and while the Community of Galloway were yet drafting their petition to the Scottish king, the death of the Bishop of Whithorn occasioned a disputed election, which seems to have reflected the secular conflict. By the thirteenth century the canonical requirement that a bishop had to be elected by 'clergy and people' was coming to be interpreted as election by the cathedral chapter. Royal intervention was nevertheless common. From the time of David I the kings of Scots had exercised influence in the selection of the bishops of Glasgow and St Andrews;[29] and the hereditary lords of Galloway probably expected to have a say in the choice of their bishops. For all that the cathedral chapter at Whithorn were either accustomed to considerable power of decision, or were determined to exercise it in the future.

Once Alan had died in the January and the bishop in the February, the interested parties all acted normally as they saw it. The king, Alexander II assumed the authority he attributed to the lords of Galloway, and it was announced that Gilbert, the erstwhile abbot of Glenluce, was bishop elect, and had the approval of the king. The following month the prior and chapter of Whithorn elected one Odo, a canon of their community. The two candidates clearly represented the opposing parties — the authority of the king in the absence of a lord of Galloway, and local autonomy led by the cathedral chapter. It is more than probable that the chapter was supported by the Community of Galloway.

The chapter were alarmed but resolute. The Archbishop of York would have the last word in such a dispute and they hoped for his support, but in the meantime they wrote what appears to have been an open letter addressed to 'all vassals of Christ' describing how their election had been conducted:

> we entered our Chapter House immediately after the third Sunday of Lent was past, to discuss the election of a pastor; and in the presence of all who rightfully should, and would, and conveniently could be present, we unanimously . . . chose three trustworthy men of our collegiate Chapter, named Master Paulinus, Master Bricius, and Master Cristinus, our fellow canons. And they secretly and separately enquired with care the wishes of all; and when all had agreed unanimously of one accord for the said Odo, our canon . . . and after the wishes of all had been reduced to writing, we entered our Cathedral church of Whithorn; and when the document had been made public in the presence of all; we all unanimously and with one accord granted to the said Odo . . . to rule as pastor our Cathedral church. And in witness of his election we have caused faithfully to be appended the seal of our Chapter along with the seal of our Prior.[30]

Each of the 22 canons signed this letter, which indicated how keenly they felt about the issue. They had established a full consensus by the representative clergy, and had consulted the people by reading their minutes publicly in the cathedral church. No other document evokes so vividly the medieval community of canons at Whithorn conducting the business of the chapter.

The canons described Odo as 'a man literate, honourable, modest and religious'. He was packed off to York to seek consecration, and a date was fixed for it on 5th July. By May the secular dispute as to who should inherit Galloway was escalating into military conflict. The King of Scots wrote to the Archbishop of York urging that he should not consecrate Odo. The prior and canons wrote also, clinging rather desperately to their claim to the archbishop's protection:

to their reverend lord and dearest father in Christ, Walter by God's grace Archbishop of York ... your humble and devoted Prior and canons of Whithorn, due greeting and in all things honour and obedience. Hindered by the great difficulties of our church, and chiefly by reason of the war of the lord King of Scotland against Galloway, we cannot be present with you in the greater church of York for the confirmation and consecration of Master Odo, our canon and bishop elect. We have appointed Brother Gregory, our fellow canon, to act as our proctor ... and especially to appeal if need be, for the right of our church.[31]

The archbishop referred the disputed election to a commission of enquiry. That was in June. The commissioners, foreseeing a military solution of the political struggle awaited events. Meanwhile Thomas of Galloway had been joined by an unknown war-leader called Gilleruth, whom the Melrose chronicler took to be an Irishman, and described as a 'freebooter' or pirate. Although the resistance seems to have had a base in Ireland, it is probable that Gilleruth was a landowner in Carrick, where in the previous generation a Gilleroth GilMartin and his brother had attended Duncan of Carrick's court and witnessed his charters.[32] Gilleruth was a member of that sea-faring fraternity of the west to which Thomas and his father had both belonged, and he brought ships as well as men to Thomas's standard. The English chronicler portrays the separatist forces as representative of the surviving Celtic culture, and Matthew Paris tells a story nicely calculated to arouse Anglo-Norman disgust:

They made an unheard of covenant, inventing a kind of sorcery, in accord with certain abominable customs of their ancient forefathers. For all those barbarians and their leaders ... shed blood from the pre-cordial vein into a large vessel ... and they stirred and mixed the blood after it was drawn; and afterwards they offered it mixed to one another in turn and drank it as a sign that they were henceforward bound in an indissoluble, and as it were a consanguineal covenant, united in good fortune and ill, even to the sacrifice of their lives.[33]

At midsummer a Scottish force under the command of the king himself invaded Galloway and were surprised by Thomas's forces towards evening as they pitched camp. Where this was the Melrose chronicler was unable to say — only that the king had come to 'a place sufficiently fair to the eye', scarcely a distinguishing description in Galloway. The site was marshy and the king's forces were in difficulties in soft ground. The Gallovidians had the advantage until the belated arrival on the battlefield of the Earl of Ross with his host. They took the Gallovidians in the rear and inflicted heavy casualties. It was bitter retribution for the Gallovidians' defeat of the men of Ross and Moray under Roland's leadership in 1186.

The 'Chronicle of Melrose' records unctuously that Alexander 'with all his accustomed piety, offered his peace to all who came to him', and 'the Gallovidians came to his peace with ropes round their necks'. Thomas and Gilleruth were not among them. It is said that both had escaped to Ireland. Within a day or two

136

Alexander returned home, and the Melrose 'Chronicle' was careful to say so, to exculpate the king from what followed. The military command was left with Walter Comyn, Earl of Menteith with orders to 'pacify' the country. This was done with all the brutality of which an undisciplined force in enemy territory is capable. They looted the monasteries, committing outrages on the monks, and killed the prior and sacristan of Tongland in their own church. The 'Chronicle of Melrose' says that Glenluce Abbey was sacked, but his description of a monk at his last gasp being deprived by the marauders of his blanket is a story borrowed from elsewhere.[34] It is difficult to distinguish the chronicler's genuine ignorance from intentional suppression of the truth. If the chronicler of Melrose knew what really happened, what he knew was too unpalatable to the king to be written down.

It is equally difficult to decide to what extent the attack on the monasteries represented deliberate revenge upon political adversaries or the action of troops out of control. Tongland Abbey for instance was Alan's own foundation. The canons' loyalty to Alan (and his son) may have reinforced their solidarity with their sister Premonstratensian house, the priory of Whithorn. The murder of the prior and sacristan therefore looks premeditated and political. Glenluce Abbey had been the monastery in which Gilbert, the king's candidate for the bishopric had served as a monk, but he had left and sought refuge at Melrose a year before, and the chronicler did not say why. Was the sacking of Glenluce also politically motivated?

In fairness to Alexander II it should be recalled that according to Matthew Paris he wrote two years later to a papal legate who was inviting himself to Scotland against the king's will. Alexander's tone was uncompromising, not to say churlish, but it contained the warning:

> I warn thee to proceed cautiously if perchance thou shouldst enter my land, lest any evil befall thee. For untamed and wild men dwell there thirsting for human blood; and not even I myself have power to subdue them, and if they should attack you I cannot restrain them.[35]

One wonders who Alexander had in mind — the Gallovidians, now beyond all question within his kingdom, or his army who murdered the prior and sacristan of Tongland.

Once the king had scored his initial victory in Galloway the consecration of Gilbert as Bishop of Whithorn in preference to Odo was a foregone conclusion, even though hostilities were not at an end. Both Thomas and Gilleruth returned from Ireland with reinforcements, and the Earl of Mentieth's forces withdrew in disorder. Success seemed to be within Thomas's grasp. Then the new bishop hastened to intervene, and in this he joined with the abbot of Melrose and Patrick Earl of Dunbar. The 'Melrose Chronicle' represents them as motivated by friendship towards Thomas for his late father's sake; but both the new bishop and the abbot of Melrose were markedly committed to Alexander II. The bishop and abbot went to Galloway unarmed, but the earl took an army. No military engagement was recorded. The story goes that the peace-keeping forces made contact with Gilleruth and concluded a separate peace with him. He became the Earl of Dunbar's prisoner. How he was induced to desert Thomas and give up his own liberty we are not told. Thomas's part in the final submission is left vague and unsatisfactory. Supposedly he threw himself on the king's mercy without further resistance. He is thus represented as duped by a treacherous ally or else half-hearted, or downright cowardly. Towards the end of 1235 he was imprisoned for a short time in Edinburgh Castle, and then handed over as a prisoner to the custody of John Baliol.

The involvement of Galloway's clergy and monasteries in the events of 1235 was sufficiently well-documented to lend weight and authenticity to an otherwise incomplete story. The disputed episcopal election concurrent with Alexander II's military campaign against Thomas, and the violence done by the king's forces leave no doubt that a substantial section of the people, both churchmen and laity, wanted the integrity and autonomy of Galloway to be preserved. The attacks on the monasteries by the king's army, suggest the abbots and their communities had been supporting the separatist cause. The support of these abbeys, such as Tongland, gave respectability to Thomas's cause, which might otherwise have been seen as an extremist minority.

The year after the fighting the abbots of Dundrennan and Glenluce were deposed by the General Chapter of the Cistercian Order, and both were replaced by monks of Melrose.[36] The official explanation was that the abbot of Glenluce had not been canonically elected and that the abbot of the mother-house, Dundrennan, had colluded in the irregularity. It may have been a genuine and sufficient reason for their deposition. The chapter of the Cistercian Order was an international body not necessarily influenced by local politics. Nevertheless so soon after the end of hostilities and the attack on Glenluce and Tongland abbeys the deposing of these abbots looks suspicious. In the time of Fergus the loyalty of the Cistercian abbeys might be fixed beyond Galloway's borders, and might shelter his bitterest critics. By the thirteenth century they were locally rooted. Their monks were recruited from local families and their communities reflected local feeling. In the conflict over the succession in Galloway their sympathies appear to have been with Thomas.

The strength of his local support was finally proved by the subsequent treatment of Thomas himself. The Scottish king dare not have him killed, and dare not release him. The Baliols treated him well enough to survive to old age. Perhaps Dervorgilla had a kindness for her half- brother. It is certain that neither she nor John Baliol wanted to face the Gallovidians with his death on their hands. It had been in 1235 that Thomas went to Barnard Castle, the King of Scots' prisoner. He was released 61 years later, in 1296.

In 1286 the conscience of John Baliol's son had been stirred, and he had raised with Alexander III the question of releasing Thomas. The matter was discussed at the council meeting in Edinburgh on the last day of the king's life. His accidental death on the cliffs of Fife that night put off Thomas's release for another ten years. In the end it was Edward I of England who released him, apparently to appease the Community of Galloway, who were petitioning against oppressive practices in the province. The estates Thomas's father had given him were officially restored, and he was set on the road for home with a charter of liberties.[37] By some malign chance he got no further than Carlisle and was taken again into custody.[38] No more is known of him. Sixty years' imprisonment and the final alternation of hope and despair make Thomas of Galloway's personal tragedy seem more than man-size. And so it was; for it signified much more than one man's suffering.

The old principality was henceforward to be valued as no more than a block of real estate to be parcelled out in three heritable feus. This was the turning point at which the Gallovidians' identity as a people ceased to be recoverable. Their long Christian tradition, their descent from the Men of the North, their Northumbrian heritage and membership of the Celtic commonwealth of the Irish Sea — all that constituted their uniqueness — was ignored. Against conformity with a law of inheritance they did not recognise, their past distinction and currently expressed wishes counted for nothing.

7

SCEPTRE AND CROWN:

The Baliols
(1236-1356)

The glories of our blood and state
Are shadows not substantial things;
There is no armour against Fate,
Death lays his icy hand on kings.
Sceptre and crown
Must tumble down,
And in the dust be equal made
With the poor crooked scythe and spade.
James Sherley[1]

The tripartite division of Galloway between the heiresses lasted for no more than 23 years. Initially the eldest daughter, Elena, and her husband Roger de Quinci assumed possession of the old princely stronghold of Cruggleton and its surrounding estates, and they probably built the great stone castle that used to stand on the cliff-top.[2] The de Quincis, predictably enough, were unpopular and not always able to keep order, but royal authority was fairly rapidly established. There was already a royal castle at Dumfries; Roland's 'house at Kirkcudbright' was upgraded to a royal castle on a new site; and a third was built at Wigtown. Royal burghs were established at these towns. By the untimely death of Dervorgilla's elder sister Christiana without issue in 1246, the Galloway estate was divided between her and Elena, and as later disputes show, Dervorgilla received the lion's share. The Baliols thus became the most powerful magnates in Galloway.

Dervorgilla also inherited Christiana's half of their mother's lands in the Honour of Huntingdon. Her uncle John the Scot's death in 1237 had already brought her a further share of that inheritance including control of the estates of Fotheringay, and Kempston in Bedfordshire.

DERVORGILLA

In the wistful retrospect of later generations Dervorgilla personified all the refinement and romanticism of the thirteenth century. It was perhaps natural that she should become a legend. She was a woman of almost unparalleled wealth, the

The seal of Dervorgilla de Baliol attached to the Statutes of Balliol College, Oxford in 1282 (Balliol College, EL)

Lady of Galloway in her own right for her long widowhood, and after her death she was fabled for her bounteous generosity and gentle sorrow. 'A bettyr lady was ther nane in al the ile of Mare Bretagne'. This was the verdict of the poet Wyntoun, and it is part of the spell cast for her over later generations. Those who have quoted his account of her often omit to say that it was written nearly 135 years after her death.

When Dervorgilla and John Baliol married in 1233, John was about 25 years old, and she probably at least ten years younger. In the course of their life together they had eight surviving children, four sons and four daughters, all reaching adulthood, though four of them died relatively young. The Baliols of Barnard Castle had estates in Yorkshire and Picardy and were a wealthy baronial family. Dervorgilla, although well-dowered, was not the heiress in 1233 that she rapidly became as a consequence of her father's death without a legitimate male heir, and the death of other relatives. Her married life saw a steady increase of inherited wealth on both sides.

Approximate calculations suggest that the couple's annual income in 1233 including the Baliol's estates in France was something of the order of £500 and that this had almost doubled by John's death in 1268. This was a colossal fortune. It is not possible to quote an equivalent, but a general idea can be gained from the fact that 'a ten pound land' at the time—that is lands bringing in an annual rent of £10—was a highly desirable estate such as only the wealthier gentry, though not of the Baliol class, possessed.

John's life-span had been one of increasing social and political importance, more on account of his wealth perhaps than personal distinction. He had begun as a respected baron, exercising administrative authority in a number of capacities in northern England, and occasionally in Picardy. In 1251 he acted for a few years as joint-guardian to the king and queen of Scotland in their minority. As he became known for his exceptional wealth, the King of England was apt to rely on him for supplies, and he lent the king and others substantial sums of money. Dervorgilla may have acted with him in some of his charitable endowments. Chronicles claim that they were together responsible for endowing Franciscan friaries in Oxford and Dumfries; and a house of Black Friars at Wigtown in Galloway. Their concern to further commercial interests in Galloway, for example the trade of its Cistercian abbeys, was illustrated by an English document of 1266, recording that the King of England 'at the instance of John Baliol' had taken under his protection:

> The Abbot, monks and brethren of Dundrennan and their men coming to England with wool and other goods to traffic therewith, and gives them leave to buy corn and other victuals to take to Galloway for their sustenance, paying the usual customs.[4]

John died the following year. To what extent he had shared Dervorgilla's affection for Buittle and her Galloway estates is not known. Buittle Castle may have been enlarged in their time, and it is almost certain that the thirteenth-century parish church, the ruins of which still stand, was the work either of John and Dervorgilla as a couple, or of Dervorgilla on her own account. John's provision of lodgings and a weekly stipend of 8 pence a day for poor students at Oxford is said to have begun as a penance imposed, or at least suggested by the Bishop of Durham. John is alleged to have ordered his servants to set upon the bishop in the course of a dispute.[5] This charity was later developed by Dervorgilla by the foundation of Balliol College, which effectively purchased for both John and Dervorgilla a permanent place in the memory of posterity. Balliol College still has a duty to pray for the souls of John and Dervorgilla, and in 1990 a special Requiem Mass was celebrated in the college chapel to mark the seventh centenary of Dervorgilla's death.

It was she who put the college on a permanent footing by enacting the formal

Sweetheart Abbey (Historic Scotland)

statutes, thus making a home and community for Oxford students. The new college was expected to observe simple rules of conduct and religious observance, and their communal life was to be ordered by Dervorgilla's appointed proctors. Food surplus from the common table was to be distributed among poor students. The document dated 1282, was sealed at 'Botel' (Buittle Castle).

Dervorgilla is equally remembered for her foundation of Sweetheart Abbey. It was customary in her time for well-to-do widows or widowers to endow a chantry—a small side-chapel in their local church with an income for a priest to ensure that prayers should be said for the soul of their dead spouse. Dervorgilla did not endow a chantry for John Baliol—she founded an abbey. By 1270 the General Chapter of the Cistercian Order had appointed the abbots of Furness and Rievaulx to inspect 'the site on which the widow of John Baliol intends to found an abbey of monks'.[6]

By 1273 the buildings were complete or at least habitable, and the foundation charter was drawn up. It was sealed in the presence of the bishop and all the senior churchmen of the two dioceses of Whithorn and Glasgow, including the abbot of the mother-house, Dundrennan, the abbots of Glenluce, Soulseat and Tongland, the priors of Whithorn and St Mary's Isle, and a number of local landowners. The grant was made in the name of the Virgin Mary. It was endowed not simply for the soul of Dervorgilla's late husband. The preamble reads like a celebration of all the people she revered and held dear, and it was warmly and comprehensively embracing. For the charter declared that the abbey was founded, first for the souls of all the kings of Scotland — king Alexander III, his predecessors and successors. Then her ancestors:

> Fergus of Galloway, Uchtred his son, Roland her grandfather, Ellen his wife, Alan their son and the grantor's father, Margaret her mother, and all their ancestors and successors. [And only then for the departed of her own immediate family and generation:] for the souls of John Baliol the grantor's lord and late spouse, Hugh his son and hers, Cecilia her daughter, the grantor's own soul, and those of all their ancestors and successors and of all faithful Christians.[7]

The whole of Dervorgilla's world was included in the blessing thus invoked. The lands of two entire parishes — Lochkinderloch (now New Abbey) and Kirkpatrick Durham, which had belonged to Dundrennan — were given as the monastic estate and capital base. From the first the abbey was called in the Norman French, 'Douz Coeur' (Latin: 'Dulcis Cor'), Sweetheart Abbey or in the more vernacular usage the New Abbey. Writing about 1424 Wyntoun describes it:

> That is Swet-Hart
> and now the men of Gallway
> callys that sted New Abbay.

These two endowments, the college and the abbey, have preserved the memory of John Baliol and Dervorgilla for 700 years. In that time popular memory has mythologised Dervorgilla so that the terms of her grants and charters, and her character as they reveal them have been overlaid by popular legend and virtually forgotten. Dervorgilla is known almost exclusively from Wyntoun's verses. (The language has been slightly modernised):

> When the Baliol that was her lord
> That spousit her, as they record
> Ere he was laid in sepulture,
> His body she gert open tite
> And gert his hart to be tane out quite.
> That ilk hart, as men said
> She balmed it an gert be laid
> In a coffyn of evore,
> The which she gert made therfore
> Enamellit, parfitly dight,
> Lockit, and bunden with silver bricht.
>
> And always when she ga'ed to meat
> That coffyn she gert by her set,
> Richt as her lord were in presens,
>   And to it she did reverens.

Effigy of Dervorgilla at
Sweetheart Abbey
(Historic Scotland)

This astonishing story must, one tells oneself, be mythologising. The picture of an inconsolable widow keeping up such a parade of reverence and sorrow for 20 years and more, cannot be true. The account written so long afterwards must be apocryphal. Yet while the somewhat grisly dinner-time routine may have been an exaggeration, the removal and embalming of the heart may have been true. The very fact of the abbey's name — Sweetheart Abbey from the start — suggests it, and the practice of embalming the heart of the deceased was perceived as a pious act in a romantic age. To twentieth-century taste the idea is unattractive but not in Dervorgilla's time. A generation later, the hard-bitten old soldier Sir James Douglas obeyed the last wishes of an even tougher freedom-fighter, Robert I, by setting out with his embalmed heart for the Holy Land. He did not get there, but is said to have died defending it. A charmingly feminine stone effigy of Dervorgilla is to be found today at Sweetheart Abbey, clasping a casket to her breast. The statue was all part of the romanticising of course. Dervorgilla must have been nearing 50 when her husband died and she had borne at least eight children, but the nubile figure with the prettily tied sleeves portrays a young woman.

The decade following John Baliol's death was darkened for Dervorgilla by fresh bereavement. The foundation charter of Sweetheart mentions her children Hugh and Cecilia, already dead in 1273. Her two other elder sons, Alan and Alexander died within a few years. By 1278 her one surviving and youngest son John had succeeded as head of the family and lord of Barnard Castle. He married Isabella de Warenne, probably shortly after this, and had two sons, Edward and Henry. John Baliol II seems to have been a conventional thirteenth-century baron, a dutiful man, less hot tempered than his father, with none of the dash and hardihood of his Gallovidian forebears. It is some indication of his character that in 1286 he raised with the king the plight of his illegitimate uncle Thomas of Galloway, still a prisoner of the crown but in his custody at Barnard Castle.

In her widowhood Dervorgilla divided her time between her Huntingdon estates at Fotheringay and Kempston in Bedfordshire and her Gallovidian castle of Buittle. According to Wyntoun wherever she was, a daily gift of food from her table was given to the local poor. This may echo the provision for the poor students at Oxford, or her grandfather's grant to the canons of St Mary's Isle; but it is perhaps wiser to take these authentic examples as evidence of a common practice by the charitable rich of the thirteenth century. Their vast households and generous hospitality inevitably produced abundant 'left-overs', while the poor, as Piers Plowman described so piercingly, were often at their wits' end to feed their children.[8]

Surviving records also reveal Dervorgilla in the more prosaic role of a conscientious administrator and litigious business woman. During her married life the Baliols must have been served by something like a royal chancery to govern their widespread possessions. After John's death when Dervorgilla retained her parental estates of Galloway and the Honour of Huntingdon, she employed clerks, chaplains, factors and lesser gentlemen from among her vassals. Their business was to care for her household, manage her lands and finances, dispense her liberal charity and record her transactions. Yet the charters that remain are minimal, and the accounts non-existent. What is known of Dervorgilla comes from documents that passed into other hands. The Baliol papers were lost when the family lost so much else, in the conflict and calamities of the fourteenth century.

The most fateful gift that Dervorgilla had brought to the house of Baliol as a bride was neither her wealth nor her character, notable as both were, nor her descent from the petty kings of Galloway; but her mother's royal Scottish blood. It was not until Dervorgilla was an old woman that the full significance of that dower became apparent, and then it was revealed like an equivocal wish in a fairy tale, granted at her christening with all the appearance of a blessing and the operation of a curse. As late as 1273 in the foundation charter of Sweetheart Abbey, she had proudly rehearsed her father's lineage back to Fergus, King of the Gallovidians. But in 1286 King Alexander III fell to his death when his horse stumbled in the dark on the Fife coast. Scotland's king was dead, and suddenly

Ruins of the thirteenth-century parish church of Buittle, probably built by John Baliol and Dervorgilla (Crown copyright, RCAHMS)

The House of Fergus and the Scottish Succession

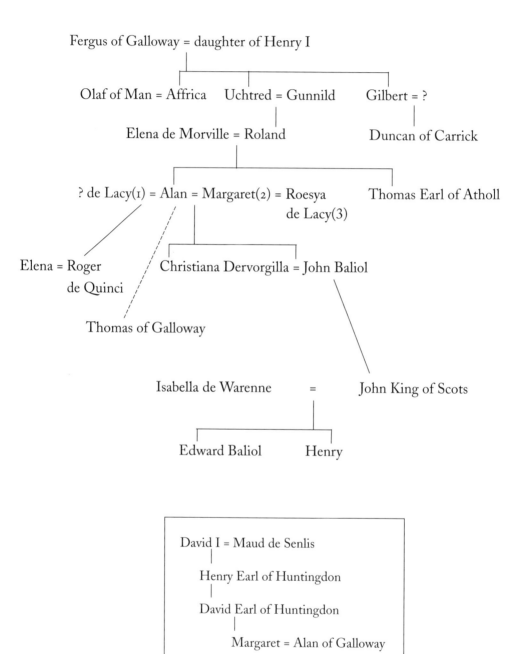

Genealogy showing Dervorgilla's descent from Fergus of Galloway and David I of Scotland

Dervorgilla's descent from King David I had relevance and immediacy for the destiny of her son John.

Alexander III had married in youth, but his first wife and her children were all dead. One daughter who had married the King of Norway, had left a baby girl, then three years old. To secure the succession more effectively Alexander had remarried a few months before, and it was to spend the night with his newly-wed wife where she lodged at Kinghorn, that the king set out against all advice on a stormy night and so met his death. One frail three-year-old Norwegian princess was then the uncrowned Queen of Scots. Those who might claim the succession in the event of her death numbered 17, none having an unquestionable right. Equally, none had a better claim than John Baliol.

JOHN KING OF SCOTS

For the next four years Scotland was ruled by three guardians in the name of the uncrowned Lady of Scotland. The concept of the Community of the Realm preserved a sense of the kingdom's identity in this interregnum, and it signified an unexpected degree of political awareness and responsibility among Scotland's bishops and nobility. It was evident that three families above all held the strongest claim to succeed in the event of the Maid of Norway's death — the Baliols, the Comyns, and the Bruces of Annandale and Carrick. In the short term it was the Bruces who showed an aggressive disregard for the law. The future King Robert I was still a child, but his grandfather, known as Robert Bruce the Competitor and his father the Earl of Carrick lost no time in attacking Galloway. It was Baliol territory, and they were declaring both a determined hostility and the intention to oppose Baliol pretensions to the succession. They stormed the castles of Buittle, Wigtown and Cruggleton and set fire to the cathedral church of Whithorn. The bishop of Whithorn contracted heavy debts to repair the episcopal estate after the raid, and in 1290 the Archbishop of York wrote on his behalf that 'he had suffered much since the death of the King of Scotland from wars in his own country so that the Archbishop had been obliged to give him work to do . . . to prevent him from starving'.[9]

Dervorgilla had been in England, and whether she ever made the journey to Buittle again is uncertain. She died in January, 1289 at Kempston. Her son John was then still only one candidate among many who might succeed to the Scottish throne in the relatively unlikely contingency that the little queen should die before reaching the age to have children. The following September that forlorn child died on reaching Orkney, on her way to her inauguration. The guardians and the majority of the aristocracy were anxious to proceed lawfully, so as to avert bloodshed in the choice of her successor. In addition to the three claimants already mentioned there were 14 others. It was for this reason that a request was made to Edward I of England to arbitrate. Edward was a respected jurist, and in the eyes of many including his own, had some title to overlordship in Scotland.[10]

Edward accepted the task of arbitration and took control of Scotland's royal castles to deter any claimant tempted to take the law into his own hands. He initiated historical researches, and held a full-scale public enquiry with all the formality of a court of law. The process took time, but in 1292 John Baliol was declared to have the strongest right, and was enthroned and crowned at Scone.

So far all was well. After an interregnum Scotland once more had a king and with the minimum of public disorder. A civil war that could so easily have been the outcome was apparently averted. On his coronation day it must have seemed to John Baliol that his Gallovidian forbears stood ranked behind him, invisible witnesses to a consummation beyond their hopes. Fergus had striven to make good his claim to be King of the Gallovidians; Uchtred had betrayed, and Gilbert had defended Galloway's autonomy. Roland sacrificed it to personal ambition, Alan — carelessly magnificent — went his own way, yet by his second marriage endowed Dervorgilla with her Scottish royal descent. Now by the irony of chance or fate John Baliol, her heir, was King of Scots, Galloway's erstwhile enemy and suzerain.

The Bruces remained dissatisfied, but the weight of aristocratic and ecclesiastical opinion was for peace and a return to normality. King John began his reign with that advantage. Perhaps he had few others. He was not by education or ancestry a true Scot. He had been born in Picardy, brought up between Yorkshire and Buittle. As the fourth son of a baron he had not been reared to exercise political power. There were hints that he had contemplated taking the vows of an Augustinian canon.[11] In favourable circumstances such a man might have made an adequate king. But John Baliol's circumstances were anything but favourable. From first to last he was confronted by the hostility and contempt of Edward I, whose bullying he had not the nerves to withstand. Edward might have been expected to retire from a direct interest in Scottish affairs once he had completed the work of arbitration, and leave the new king to find his feet. Instead he exerted constant interference and pressure.

Edward's outstanding abilities, his knowledge of law, and exceptional powers of organisation both as a statesman and a soldier, made him a crushing adversary. His will to dominate bulldozed all opposition. His understanding of human psychology was less well developed. Like many of his contemporaries raised in the cosmopolitan aristocratic tradition, he knew nothing of the sense of nationhood then breeding at grass-roots in Scotland and elsewhere. Edward and his Angevin forebears had been accustomed to rule England, Normandy, Anjou and any other province of France they could lay hold of. They had conquered Ireland. Edward had defeated the Welsh princes with great cruelty and — perhaps without intended mockery — had presented them with his own son to be their prince. Why should he not assert his theoretical rights of suzerainty over Scotland? He was never able to understand the resentment his disregard for the identity of a people aroused.

By Edward's constant intervention in Scottish affairs to the humiliation of King John, the Scots were provoked by July 1295 into taking direct power out of John's hands, and vesting it in a Council. It was the Council that concluded a treaty with France and declared war on England. Edward's response was to march into Scotland with an army. John took the field against them in March 1296, and again in April when the Scottish army was unequivocally defeated. It was July however, before King John finally submitted to Edward's overriding military power. Edward demanded renewed homage from John, couched in grovelling terms. John Baliol had borne much, and had showed he was no coward, but if he had had the spirit of his Gallovidian ancestors he would have refused to take that oath. As it was he took it, and within days, in the month of August 1296, abdicated his kingship into Edward's hands.

Edward moved immediately to take over Scotland and rule directly. In the late summer of 1296 he made a royal progress through eastern Scotland from south to north, exacting homage from all churchmen and landholders of any substance. Magnates and country lairds alike made the journey in parties to the king's presence at Berwick to do homage. Others were sworn by the sheriffs at local administrative centres. Even the prioress of the nunnery of Lincluden took the oath. A long roll of names exists today in the English Public Record Office which the Scots are wont to call the Ragman Roll.

Edward believed the Scottish problem was settled. He appointed the Earl de Warenne to govern the country, entrusted the royal castles, including Buittle and Cruggleton, to his lieutenants, and confined John Baliol and his son Edward in honorable captivity in England. The following summer he felt secure enough to embark for Flanders. But he had misjudged the situation. For then in 1297 and long after, John Baliol was still their king in the eyes of the Scots, and his enforced abdication could not change that. However forcefully imposed, Edward's action remained in their sight unlawful. Almost simultaneously rebellion broke out in Aberdeenshire, the Western Highlands and Galloway, demanding the restoration of King John. In Ayrshire William Wallace began to make surprise attacks on English office-bearers. In May the young Robert Bruce was leading a revolt in Carrick; by the summer the province of Moray was in arms, and in September, by the generalship of Wallace, an English army had been destroyed in the battle of Stirling Bridge.

In 1300 Edward himself led an army into Galloway, occupied Kirkcudbright Castle, and subsequently camped with his army at Twynholm and Gatehouse of Fleet. The Bishop of Whithorn attempted to mediate, but was not heeded. The chronicle of William Rishanger depicts the military ransacking the town and its neighbourhood for supplies of food and fodder, and loading provisions onto ships and wagons to supply the army. The yield was insufficient, but it probably included much of the stores the civilian population were relying on for the ensuing winter. A foraging party penetrated westward to the banks of the Cree, and made contact with a Gallovidian force at the river crossing. There was a brush between the two, and the following day Edward sent cavalry and archers to the spot. A sharp engagement followed during which the English knights were lured across the river. They suffered some losses and the Gallovidians withdrew into the hills.[12] That campaign ended with the summer and a nine months' truce was negotiated.

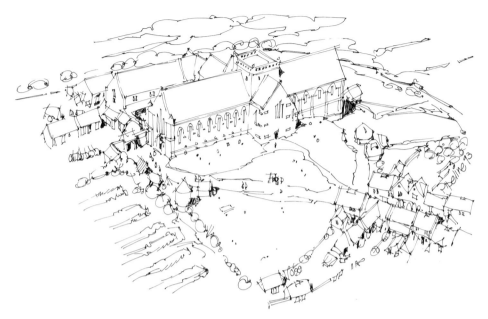

Reconstruction drawing by Dave Pollock of Whithorn cathedral about 1300. Some pilgrims continued to journey to St Ninian's shrine despite the wars, among them Edward I's son, the Prince of Wales

While Edward was yet in Galloway, Archbishop Winchelsey, the Archbishop of Canterbury, journeyed thither with a letter from the Pope, urging that John Baliol should be released from imprisonment. A compromise was reached by which Baliol was transferred to the custody of the Pope and allowed to live in one of the papal residences in France. On leaving England John was searched, presumably on Edward's orders, and the crown and sceptre with which he had been invested with kingship were removed from his luggage and lodged with the English Exchequer.

In 1302 John Baliol was released from papal custody, and installed by Philip IV of France, who still recognised him as the King of Scots, in the Baliols' ancestral chateau at Bailleul-en-Vimeu. The following year there were rumours that he was to be restored to the Scottish throne with French assistance, and Robert Bruce hastened to embrace Edward's cause lest he should lose the earldom of Carrick if John returned. In the event no move was made to restore Baliol, but it was two years later before Edward's repeated attacks began to subdue Scotland as a whole. By 1304 submissions came to him from all parts of the country, and the following spring William Wallace, whose guerilla tactics and battle strategy had constituted the main strength of Scottish resistance, was captured. He was taken to London, tried and hanged.

Fortune's wheel had turned under Edward's hand, Galloway was held down in his control and the Scottish kingdom faced final defeat. With John Baliol abroad, the remaining claimants to the Scottish succession of first importance were Robert de Brus and John Comyn of Badenoch, John Baliol's brother-in-law. If Bruce had any serious ambitions to defeat Edward, he had to be king and command all the support and resources kingship would give him. John Comyn stood in his way, immoveably loyal to King John. Bruce's desperate act in murdering Comyn in the church of the Grey Friars, at Dumfries in 1306 is well known. In the eyes of contemporaries it was not merely treacherous but sacrilegious, and laid Bruce and the whole kingdom under papal interdict. However Robert was hastily crowned at Scone;[13] and for the next few years the new king lived the life of a freedom-fighter in the hills of Carrick, often in hiding, hunted by Edward I's army.

Bruce's long guerilla campaign against the English forces occupying southern Scotland made Galloway debatable ground over which the opposing military forces fought for control. The English held Galloway's castles and exacted food and support from the people to their own cost. Bruce's guerillas descended from the hills of Carrick, equally in need of provender, and not only carried off stored corn and cattle, but fired homesteads and enforced services and recruits, bringing upon their families punitive action by the other side. Landowners and peasantry alike suffered constant threat to their food supplies, fear for their homes, and the conflicting moral pressures of civil war — divided loyalties, suspicion within the family and the community, and the presence of spies.

The effect of the war on the people was expressed by Edward I's peremptory dispatches of 1306 to England and Ireland commanding that more men and food supplies be sent to the depots at Skinburness (in Cumbria) and Kirkcudbright 'with the utmost haste'. Control over the south-western sea ports changed hands and sea-transport was subject to delay in bad weather. Local resources were being exhausted.[14] A declaration made in 1306 in southern English ports forbade anyone 'from taking corn, beasts or any other victuals' through that port to Gascony (which had recently come into Edward's possession) because 'the land of Scotland [in this context Galloway and Dumfriesshire] is wasted, destroyed and denuded' and supplies were needed by the king's army there.[15]

About this time Edward had sent an army to Galloway against Robert de Brus. He had received information from 'Sir John St John, Sir Donegal Makdouel, Sir Dougall de FitzCan and others of the greater men there . . . that he and his accomplices are burning and plundering and compelling the inhabitants to rebel'.[16] Robert's younger brothers Thomas and Alexander, were captured and handed over by the Gallovidians to be hanged in Carlisle, their heads set upon the city gate. The following spring Robert was reported to be operating in the hills along the Carrick border, and English forces penetrated the wild country around Glentrool in search of him. They were surprised in a natural ambush, and repulsed with heavy losses. But the deaths of Robert's two brothers had yet to be avenged, and his brother Edward returned from Ireland in 1308 and inflicted on Galloway a savage punitive campaign. Nobles and peasantry alike suffered, and many were killed. Sir Dungal Macdoual and his kin were driven out. In a pitched battle near the river Dee, Aymer St John and Ingram de Umfravill, a relative of the Baliols, led the local defence against Edward Bruce. Sometime around 1312 and 1313

Robert I appointed his brother Edward lord of Galloway, scarcely a conciliatory move.[17]

Edward Bruce's ravaging was not the only source of destruction. It came from both sides. The Abbot and convent of Sweetheart Abbey petitioned Edward I the same year for compensation for the damage done to their house 'by his Welshmen when last in Dumfries'. They claimed £5000-worth of damage had been done by burning granges and destroying goods, and asked to be recompensed for 'eight and a half sacks of good, teazed wool taken ... for the King's use ... out of the grange of Holm Cultram [in Kirkgunzeon] where it had been stored for fear of the Scots'.[18] Dundrennan Abbey made similar claims. Land values fell. Huew de Champaigne inherited valuable lands in Wigtownshire. He petitioned that he should be asked to pay feudal death duties on the property according to present values, 'and not the old valuation before the Scottish war, as they [the lands] have been so wasted thereby'.[19]

Meanwhile in 1307 King Edward had instructed his justiciar of the forests beyond Trent to allow the men of Galloway to feed their flocks in Inglewood Forest in Cumbria 'whither they had come to take refuge for fear of Robert de Brus and his accomplices'. The ruin of the countryside at home had driven refugees from their cottages to live rough in the woods.[20]

The peasantry, as always, took the worst of it, but the changing hands of estates by confiscation and escheat over the next few years spells out the suffering of the lairds and barons. The agility with which the local nobility and gentry changed sides in the war has often been derided, but the chivalric ideal of loyalty to a military cause or political leader was less compelling than the priority most family men attached to the survival of their wives and children. For the great ones with estates in more than one country, the loss of their Galloway lands meant a reduction of income only. But for the generality of Gallovidian landowners their local estate was their home and their family's livelihood, without which not only were their heirs deprived of future inheritance, but the present provision for their wives and children had gone.

Any native war leader like Dungal Macdoual was also aware that a fight to the death against impossible odds would involve, not the expenditure of battle fodder of a different class and ethnic origin, but his own kinsmen. 'Fill up the rampart with your English dead' pictures the prodigal sacrifice of a professional infantry that distinguished the wars in France of the Edwards and Henry V. Native Gallovidians were fierce fighters; they were prepared to be used as mercenaries against the Welsh and the Irish. But just as their war technology was less effective than the English cooperation between mounted knights and bowmen on foot, their commanders obeyed an instinctively tribal ethic that lives to fight another day. They had been accustomed to rate booty above glory, and present advantage before conquest. Both natives and Anglo-Normans lost estates in the war, or felt compelled to change their allegiance as the power struggle between Baliol and Bruce, Scottish and English forces, ebbed and flowed. The English records are full of instances.

Some landowners were driven away altogether. As early as 1292 a Lady Cecilia Lambe, then in Galloway, was granted safe-conduct to go to England 'as she was coming there to dwell with her men and her goods'. Other landed families soon followed in her wake as a consequence of war. When Sir Dungal Macdoual lost his lands near Kirkcudbright, he petitioned Edward I for an estate in Ireland 'until he should recover his own . . . lost in the King's service'.[21] Eventually Edward II granted him a manor in Temple Coulton in Yorkshire 'for the residence and support of his wife and children'. Sir Eustace Maxwell, dispossessed by the Bruces, was promised a manor of similar value, but in the end received an annuity. The English king was compelled to help out his dispossessed allies if he was to retain their services. Sir John Mareschal's widow Maydousa, was granted a pension. His son petitioned that the family's lands (probably Toskerton and Kirkmadrine) should be returned to him. David Mareschal was compensated with the ward of Berwick Castle to provide him with an income of 40 shillings a year, and Richard Mareschal was granted a lump sum of £20 to support his wife, children and himself 'until the next Parliament' because the Bruces had taken his land.[22] Gilbert McCulloch had to make do with a royal allowance of 12 pence a day.[23] These examples are by no means exhaustive.

Edward of England died in July 1307 at Burgh-over-Sands in Cumbria, still at the head of his army. His son Edward II carried on the war; but his father's charismatic leadership and indomitable will to conquer had gone. The Bruces gained control of Galloway towards 1313, when Dumfries Castle finally fell into their hands, and the theatre of war moved northward to the neighbourhood of Stirling. Hostilities came to a climax the next year with the pitched battle and resounding Scottish victory at Bannockburn. That same year John Baliol died in France. For Galloway Robert I's triumph signified defeat. Its landowners who had cooperated with the English out of loyalty to Baliol were dispossessed and replaced by Bruce supporters.

RESPITE AND REFLECTIONS

Edward I's meticulously kept records and those of his successors are the main sources from which the story of the war years can be gleaned. The astonishing volume of business conducted, especially by Edward I, threw a search-light on Gallovidian society, revealing its structure as never before. Without this evidence the extent to which Anglo-Norman landlords had monopolised the province under the lords Roland and Alan, must have been exaggerated, and the tenacity of the native families in positions of landownership and power underrated. As hostilities progressed, the Anglo-Normans who could, were either forced to withdraw or were glad enough to retire from the war zone. While it sometimes seems from the evidence that the native aristocracy bore the brunt of the war, it was also true that as a class they gained power in the long term. Their strength may have to some extent prolonged the conflict, for to the native Gallovidian John Baliol (and his son Edward after him) were both rightful kings of Scots and their 'special lord' by descent from the old princely house.

The survival of the native kindreds, resembling the kindreds of Wales, is illustrated by the list of the chief men of the kindred of Afren who submitted to Edward I after the rising of 1298.[24] They were: Gillenerf McGilherf, Neel McEthe, Gillecrist McEthe, Dungal McGillerevas, Adam McGilleconil, Gillespic McEuri, Cuthbert McEuri, Kalman McKelli, Michael his brother, Hoen McEthe, Cuthbert his brother, Achmachath McGilmocha, Michael McGilmocha. The names alone indicate both their Celtic origin and their family relationships.[25] The document relates that having aided John Baliol in his 'fole emprise' (his crazy undertaking) and hearing that Edward had been about to lead an army into Galloway to chastise them, they had confessed their fault on behalf of the whole kindred and sworn on the saints to support Edward against Baliol. That was an oath they found it in their consciences to break.

By the fourteenth century the formalities of appointing the chief of the kindred had passed to the King of Scots. Earlier, authority will have belonged to the lord of Galloway. A Scottish document of the period refers to the chief of the kindred of the Cannons, Michel McGeith. Gilbert McGillolane 'was chief [*capitanus*] of the McClellans'. His ancestor Cane McGillolane had witnessed the charter of Sweetheart Abbey back in 1273. John McKenedi, chief of the kindred of Muntircasdow in Carrick, was also listed. The name of the Kennedys' homestead, Ballemuntircasdow was gaelicised; but Guiltree, an estate also in their hands, continued to correspond directly with the Welsh 'gweli-dref', meaning the cradle homestead of the kin.

The native families of Galloway recorded at this period included the McCullochs, the Macdouals, the McNeills, the Accoultons, the Askolocs, the Acarsons, the Ahannays, and the Edgars or Adairs, names which survive almost unchanged today.[26] The kindred of Afren (the McGhies), the Cannons and McClellans were concentrated in the Glenken, the McGhies in the parish of Balmaghie at the southern extremity of the district, the McClellans in what was to become the parish of Balmaclellan. The numbers within these kindreds cannot be guessed, but the Gallovidians ability to put mercenaries at the disposal of their allies suggests considerable numbers. For example in 1170 Alan of Galloway had been asked for 2000 'of his most active Gallovidians' by King John of England for his Irish campaign; and in 1304-5 Edward I commanded Gibon McCan and Duncan Macdoual to bring him 2000 foot soldiers, 'the chosen men of Galloway'[27]. The fact that 2000 were asked for is not proof that 2000 were forthcoming, but the expectation was significant.

By contrast the landowning families of Norman stock can be identified by their territorial names. These derived either from the estates of their Continental forebears, such as the Champaignes, the Mundwells (de Mundville), and the Morvilles (de Morville), or from their lands in Galloway. John of Gevelestone (Gelston), Thomas of Bombie, Thomas of Erbigland (Arbigland) and John de Meynreht (Monreith), for example, all swore fealty to Edward I in 1296. Galloway society consisted on the one hand of Anglo-Norman barons served by a Celtic peasantry in varying degrees of bondage, and the older British kindreds. Their rank and file, bonnet lairds, warriors and seafarers may have retained within their own culture the status of an elite. Some of the poorer sort may have been free peasants; but an under-class of bondman not recognised as belonging to the kindred, nor counted among their warriors, probably existed. In a Normanised milieu, men with the right to bear arms were by definition free men, for villeins and serfs were disqualified by law from carrying weapons. The lowest stratum in both societies had few rights, but for most of the working population there must have been an untold difference between the peasant under a lord of foreign origin and the clansman who could claim he was related to his chief by blood.

These social diversities explain the native tenacity in supporting Alan's successors, the Baliol line. A feudal baron's position depended on the king's goodwill, and if he broke his oath of fealty he could be dispossessed and disappear from the scene, as many did. A native chief could also be penalised — even be imprisoned or lose his estates; but the kindred ensured continuity. Another stabilising force in this essentially divided society was the Community of Galloway, still active and retaining a civic awareness, and ready to petition against abuse of power.

For example they were determined to rid Galloway of a practice by royal serjeants of the peace of the summary accusation and hanging of offenders in place of trial by jury. This went along with compulsory powers of the billeting of the serjeants' men and horses. This summary justice, called in Norman French 'surdits de serjeants', had been introduced into the kingdom of Scotland where it was not native, and had been abolished by Alexander III. His abolition had not been effective in Galloway where the abuse had probably been introduced under Alexander II. The Community of Galloway petitioned Edward I for immunity, and because he was anxious to propitiate them, he granted it. In conditions of civil war enforcement proved difficult, and in the reign of Robert I the declaration of immunity had to be repeated, this time, apparently at the intercession of the priory of Whithorn, for it was pronounced specifically in relation to their estate of Glenswinton in the Glenken. It appeared in Robert's charter confirming the endowments of Whithorn Priory, part of his policy of restoring peace and order to the kingdom as a whole in his latter years.

EDWARD BALIOL

In 1328 the ratification of the treaty of Edinburgh brought to a formal end the war that had been suspended by truce since 1314. Robert I was terminally ill, and anxious to leave no unfinished business. He had taken his kingdom by force rather than right, but he had ruled it well. Even in Galloway, erstwhile enemy country, he was accepted when old and ill, so that it was possible for him to make the physically taxing pilgrimage to Whithorn and the shrine of St Ninian. He died the next year in June 1329, leaving a five-year-old son. The Baliol-Bruce conflict was not over, but there had been 15 years' respite from war during which a new dramatis personae had come to the stage. Edward II of England had been deposed in

1327, and was later murdered. His son Edward III succeeded as a minor. In 1330 he assumed power and showed promise of being as formidable as his grandfather and namesake had been. Edward Baliol, the son and heir of the late King John of Scots was a middle-aged man living in Picardy, where the family estates had been restored by the French king.

As long as Robert I had lived, his strength and popularity had ruled out any attempt by Baliol to claim his father's throne. By temperament Edward Baliol was endowed with some of the fire and steel his father lacked; but John Baliol had lost his far-flung estates in the war and left his son little but debts. Edward Baliol lacked money and military backing. He could only wait, an uncongenial task for a determined man. Despite his age he was unmarried — unable to win a wife from the royal families of Europe and too proud to accept less.[28] His younger brother Henry was his only heir. In every aspect of life he was frustrated and held back. The news of Robert I's death changed everything. It brought an end to his enforced patience, and made him the focus of the barons Bruce had dispossessed. They became a cohesive and politically conscious group known as the 'disinherited'. In the summer of 1332 an expeditionary force headed by Edward and Henry Baliol set sail from France and landed in Fife. The war thus renewed lasted another 24 years.

On Dupplin Moor outside Perth, in August 1332, Baliol's army was confronted by a Scottish force which greatly outnumbered them, but in a pitched battle the 'disinherited' defeated their opponents despite the odds. Baliol made his headquarters at Perth, and in the September was crowned King of Scots at Scone. The Bruce government forces then besieged Perth, and a Gallovidian army came spontaneously to Baliol's assistance with diversionary tactics. The Baliol expeditionary force seemed all set to succeed. Edward Baliol rode westward through Ayrshire into Galloway. Then his army advanced to take control of the western march, and camped for the night at Annan. There calamity overtook them. They were surprised in the hours of darkness when most of the army was sleeping. Henry Baliol seems to have tried to cover an orderly withdrawal and was killed in the attempt. The Baliol forces scattered, abandoning baggage and equipment. Edward Baliol escaped over the English border, galloping it is said in such disarray that he rode with one boot on and the other left behind.

Baliol called on English help. In 1333 Edward III besieged Berwick, and the Scots hastening to relieve it were heavily defeated at Halidon Hill. Edward Baliol's position was nevertheless unenviable. He had had to choose either to give up his claims to the Scottish crown altogether, or accept what terms the King of England was prepared to offer him as the price of coming to his aid. Edward III's obsessive ambition to conquer France made him unwilling to contemplate the Scottish border in hostile hands, like a knife at his back. Lest David II's regents should become tools of the French, he preferred to back Baliol in a second attempt to make himself King of Scots, and his own grateful vassal. Plantagenet kings were not given to generosity towards 'out at elbows' pretenders. His terms were exorbitant: he had taken an army into Scotland, providing Baliol with money and men. Baliol should do him homage for the whole of Scotland, and should cede to England for all time Scotland's southernmost territories, from the Forth and North Sea coast to the river Cree. That is to say the seven modern counties of the three Lothians, Selkirk, Roxburghshire, Berwickshire and Dumfriesshire (including the Stewartry of Kirkcudbright).

Baliol might have had more political sense than to accept such terms. His credibility in Scotland could not in the long run survive it; but he had been made desperate by long waiting, and by the taste of success. He must have been aware too, that he had no more time. Edward III was twenty. He was more than twice that age.[29] He should have known that Scotland could not afford to give up the southern lands. Since the time of David I burghs and monasteries had been concentrated there, promoting trade, religious organisation and cultural life as nowhere else in the kingdom. The burghs of Edinburgh, Selkirk, Roxburgh, and above all Berwick nurtured the promise of a wealthier Scotland; and the abbeys of Holyrood, Melrose, Dryburgh and Jedburgh were among the most learned and distinguished of its monasteries. To modern eyes, and especially to Scottish eyes, the very idea of the cession seems an outrage. The national consciousness that rallied the Scots to Robert Bruce was still too much alive for many Scots to endure the amputation of Scottish territory. The concession was to disable Edward Baliol as surely as cutting off his right arm.

It would be a mistake nevertheless to project upon the fourteenth century the frustrated aspirations of the twentieth. The concept of Scotland as a territorial unit was still new and only partially realised. The Western Isles had only recently ceased to owe allegiance to Norway, and both the Western and Northern Highlands still tended to be a law unto themselves. Galloway was strongly separatist, and despite border warfare, shared a common past with Cumbria and north-eastern England in the ancient kingdom of Northumbria. That memory was preserved in the diocese of Whithorn's adherence to the ecclesiastical Province of York. There were still many landowning families like Baliol's own, whose estates stretched from Scotland to England and from England to France. To them the newly articulate awareness of national identity must have seemed like an inexplicable mutant from nowhere. They can scarcely be blamed if they misjudged its vitality.

In 1334 Edward III marched into Scotland, and during the ensuing winter sent out savage raiding parties in all directions. The attack was so swift and so severe that few records of the devastation survive. A short statement that the town lands of Kirkcudbright — no doubt among many others — were derelict and yielded nothing implied a hungry winter.[30] Resistance was effectively forestalled, and by 1335 the ceded territories were in English hands. Sheriffs were installed at Berwick, Roxburgh and Dumfries, and the castles of the south were garrisoned by English troops. The guardians of the child David II sent him to France for safety, and prepared to face a prolonged war. Neither side can have foreseen how long it would last. Over the next 20 years three bodies claimed authority in

Scotland: the supporters of David II — the 'Bruce establishment' — holding the Clyde valley, Ayrshire and parts of the north; the English administration of the ceded counties; and Baliol's military and civil government, based for some years at Perth, but thereafter peripatetic.

This tripartite alignment is partly obscured by Edward Baliol's dependence on the English administration for supplies and military support, and his acting at times as Commander-in-chief of the English army. It would be an over-simplification to regard the war as simply between the English and the Scots. It was at once more complex and more painful.

One of Baliol's necessary responses to that complexity was constant travelling. He regularly traversed the triangle from Perth to Carlisle and on to Newcastle. He held his own Parliaments in Edinburgh (1335) and Perth (1341 and 1342). On several occasions he attended the English Parliament at Westminster and Edward III's court at Fulham in Middlesex. On some of these journeys he had the company of William of Aldebrough, a Yorkshireman whom he described as his valet (meaning approximately his equerry). Even with this companionship, it was a restless, homeless, comfortless existence. Worse perhaps, because it was humiliating, was Baliol's increasing dependence on Edward III for money. The English records refer quite crudely to his wages, and where there were not funds for Baliol to pay his way, the English king paid his debts. There is no evidence whether Baliol found this bitter, or if he tried to shut his eyes to it.

Edward III's devastation of southern Scotland was avenged in 1337 by a punitive raid by the Bruce army from Teviotdale across the country to Dumfries and into Galloway. So the people who had suffered before suffered again. Baliol seems at the time to have been in Perth. In the south-west Sir Eustace Maxwell and Dungal Macdoual, leading a defending force, were defeated and made their personal peace with the Bruce side. They and Michael Macgethe rejoined Baliol two years later and Dungal Macdoual established himself in the strategic stronghold on Hestan Island, provisioned from south of Solway.[31]

Hestan is a little eye of an island lying slightly west of the Urr estuary and partially sheltering Auchencairn Bay from the sea. On a clear day the mountains of the Lake District spread out behind it and the accessibility of the English coast is plain. Rarely now a few sheep are grazed on the island, driven there across a perilous causeway from the shore at low tide. The island is roughly 276 m by 480 m across, its coastline rocky, its green centre level. A derelict cottage reminds the occasional picnic party that it was once inhabited. The squared wall footings of the fourteenth-century peel were photographed about 1956. In the fourteenth century Hestan had belonged to Dundrennan Abbey, and it must have been with the goodwill of the monastery, enforced or otherwise, that the peel was built and occupied by Dungal Macdoual. Some writers have regarded its occupation as constituting a refuge from threatening forces on the shore, but this cannot have been so. It would be impossible to hold Hestan if the mainland were hostile.

While an island homestead must always have a measure of natural defence, and was traditional in Galloway, its strategic purpose must have been to intercept ship-

Hestan Island, the site of Baliol's stronghold. Seen from the shore near Auchencairn with the mountains of the Lake District behind (Hugh Thompson, EL)

ping approaching the natural haven of the Urr estuary or the anchorage at Palnackie, the creek at Glenshinnoch and the moorings of Auchencairn Bay. The bay offers only shallow and perilous moorings today. Solway has silted significantly in the last few hundred years, and in Edward Baliol's time the landing-places within reach of the island were of more use than is easily imagined now. Even around 1800 these were viable smuggling ports.[32]

In 1341 David II, now 17, returned to Scotland and his government was sufficiently in control of Ayrshire and Wigtownshire to create the earldom of Wigtown for Malcolm Fleming the following year. Edward III returned from France more than anxious to suspend hostilities in Scotland. Both sides seemed to have reached stalemate and in 1343 a three-year truce was concluded. On the resumption of war in 1346 David II's supporters were able to exert enough pressure on Dungal Macdoual to bring him to David's allegiance. He was therefore promptly attacked on Hestan by an English landing party that:

> numbering 80 men of Coupland and Allerdale without a knight or squire, entered upon the sea near Workington and sailed to the peel of Estholme [Hestan Island] in Galloway and took none other than Sir Donkel Makduel, a knight of great renown amongst the Scots, and with him his two sons and 30 squires and sergands of the country and his servants, and all the goods found within the peel, and dispatched them to England without disturbance and gave

the said peel to fire and flame. And then the said Donkel was lodged in the Tower of London.[33]

That autumn David II implemented a promise to the French and invaded northern England. In a battle at Neville's Cross near Durham he was wounded by a deeply lodged arrow, and taken prisoner. For him and for Scotland it was a disaster as much financial as military, since the king was not released until attempts had been made to pay a ransom Scotland in its war-weary and impoverished condition could not afford. With David a prisoner, the prospect for the Baliol cause seemed brighter and Edward III readier to give support. He installed Edward Baliol in Caerlaverock Castle, and gave him virtually royal powers.

Yet Baliol's situation had changed radically for the worse. Edward III's interest in his cause was to ebb away in his preoccupation with France. Baliol moved from stronghold to stronghold but he could no longer be said to be ruling Scotland. He held no more Parliaments in Edinburgh or Perth, nor could he arouse support anywhere beyond Galloway's borders.

David II's imprisonment and the loss of many Scottish leaders at Neville's Cross left the Scottish government in the hands of the king's nephew and heir, Robert the Steward. He was older than David and less able — incapable of asserting authority over the Scottish nobility, or of controlling local administration or national finance. Yet this was of comparatively little advantage to Baliol. Both sides were exhausted by the long war, and in 1348 the first outbreak of the Black Death struck their forces mutually, and brought hostilities for the time being to a standstill.

Baliol's days showed all the contradictions of a civil war situation. They were both hazardous and sufficiently ordered for him to promulgate several charters which are extant. Each was made in the name of 'Edward King of Scots and lord of Galloway'. The gist of the first is preserved in a papal confirmation of a charter dated by Baliol in 1347 at Buittle. It conferred upon Sweetheart Abbey, presumably to relieve its problems due to the war, half the income of Buittle parish church and the right to present its vicar. The charter was sealed in the presence of Patrick the Archdeacon, Giles Abbot of Dundrennan, Bede Abbot of Glenluce, Walter Abbot of Tongland, William de Kars, Prior of St Mary's Isle, the bishop's clerk, and the rector of Gelston.[34]

The Bishop of Whithorn had written specifying how the income of the church was to be divided. The Bishop of Glasgow was silent. In letters dispatched from Hestan Island Baliol declared him 'our rebel and enemy'.[35] The abbots who witnessed the charter indicated how the church in Galloway supported Baliol. So did the native aristocracy. The witnesses had included: Sir Dougal Macdoual, Sir Matthew McClellan, Gilbert son of Gilbert McClellan, and Cuthbert Macilguum. In 1348 Baliol was on Hestan, being provisioned as Macdoual had been from England, and Edward III described him as 'being in the utmost danger'. He nevertheless promulgated one or two charters from there sealed with an elegant Privy Seal.

The Privy Seal of Edward Baliol of 1343, bearing the arms of the lords of Galloway. Compare with the roof boss at Glenluce Abbey on p. 125 (Durham Cathedral Library)

Baliol moved into his castle of Burned Island in the Glenken, as the poet Wyntoun described many years later:

> Bot in Karryk John Kennedy
> Warrayid Gallway sturdaly
> He and Alane Stewart tha twa
> Oft did Gallways mekill wa.
> Yhit the Ballol al that quhill
> In Gallwa wes at the Brynt-yle.[36]

Wyntoun, writing when national feeling had hardened against Baliol's memory, seems to imply that he had been skulking in the safety of an island while the Bruce forces prosecuted the war. He was perhaps unaware that the castle on Burned Island commanded the lower Glenken, effectively blocking his enemies' access to Galloway from the north. The Glenken is a narrow valley slotted through by a partially navigable river and an ancient road.[37] The river Ken rises in the rough hills that divide Galloway from Ayrshire and descends to lush and well-wooded country where it loses itself in a long inland loch north of the modern town of Castle Douglas. Out of the southernmost end of Loch Ken the river flows south, joining the Dee, and taking a final western sweep to the old port of Kirkcudbright.

The Glenken route crossed the old Roman road running east-west and continued traceably due south to Auchencairn Bay and Hestan island. Baliol was intent on defending this corridor from the mountains of Carrick to the coast. In any confrontation between the English and Gallovidian forces occupying Galloway and the Scots holding Ayrshire, its defence was critical.

From the year 1348 onwards Baliol systematically transferred his own demesne estates in the Glenken to William de Aldebrough. At Hestan in that year he granted him the lands of Balmaghie; and in a second document erected the estate into a free barony with full baronial jurisdiction 'in order to maintain order and keep down robbers'. Both the breakdown of law and order and the disturbed political situation in the district are evoked by these words. In 1354 Baliol granted Aldebrough more lands in the Glenken, the barony of Kells on the west of the river Ken, with his castle of Burned Island and the reversions of the baronies of Crossmicheal, in the south of the Glenken, and Kidsdale in Wigtownshire. The grant was *blenche ferme* 'for a rose in the season of roses', and it was witnessed at Buittle by the local nobility most affected by the transaction: Sir Matthew Maclellan and his son, Sir Patrick McCulloch, Sir Roger de Mowbray, Gilbert McCulloch, and John de Rerrick. Sir Dungal Macdoual was conspicuously absent, probably still a prisoner.[38] The effect was to put Aldebrough in a vice-regal position as unacknowledged lord of Galloway. Baliol himself continued to occupy the castle and estate of Buittle.

The acceptance of Aldebrough by the local aristocracy is indicated by the witness list; and two documents may help to explain it. In an undated petition Dougal Macdoual, Sir Dungal's brother, asked Edward III that as his brother and his own son had been killed in the king's service, his brother who had been in prison for four years should be released.[39] Edward III refused the petition but by 1353 Sir Dungal Macdoual was once more in Galloway. In the same year the Scottish army under William Douglas launched a vigorous attack on Galloway and Macdoual once more led the local defence. The casualties among the native nobility in the course of the war may have significantly depleted their fighting force.

The war seemed to drag on and Baliol's journeys continued. He had attended the Westminster Parliament in 1348. He was in Hexham and Newcastle in 1351, and Westminster again in 1352. As the years passed the exhaustion of these journeys became a growing physical burden. In response to a summons to Westminster in 1354 he sent William de Aldebrough in his place. He remained at Buittle, and even hunted in Inglewood; he was coming to admit he was old and tired.

The next year the King of France, still at war with England, confiscated the Baliol lands in Picardy. He regarded Edward Baliol as the English king's vassal and ally. The blow was unhappily timed, and the emotional impact on Baliol may have been the breaking point. His Picardy lands were the oldest of his ancestral possessions, towards which perhaps in defeat his thoughts had been turning. In January 1356, after more than 20 years' struggle, he was ready to acknowledge he was beaten. An English document dated from Roxburgh accords him his title

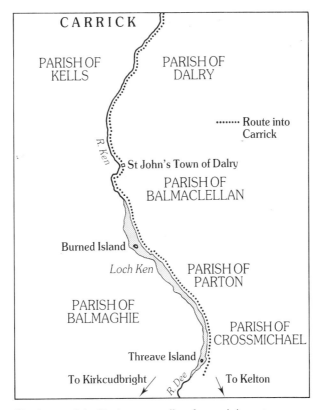

Sketch-map of the Glenken — a valley of strategic importance

'Edward King of Scots' and relates that he ceded to Edward III his lands of Galloway. The next month he went through the ritual of wearing his golden crown, taking it off and handing it to Edward III with a handful of Scottish soil. Thus, for a pension, and in the absence of any heirs of his own, for he had never married — he resigned all pretensions to the Scottish crown to the English king. Rather unexpectedly the English records explain that it was 'on account of his great age and feebleness and his inability to continue the great labours he had to sustain'. Even through the stiff indifference of the words, Baliol's weariness can be heard.[40]

Robert I had been praised by his contemporaries for having 'cheerfully endured all manner of toil, fatigue, hardship and hazard' in his struggle for the crown.[41] As much could have been said of Edward Baliol; but memories in Scotland, if not in Galloway, were too bitter to accord him justice. In the present generation it has been said Baliol had the mettle to be a king, but it seems that 700 years had to pass before such an assessment was possible.[42] His struggle for power began bravely. He had come to his own, claiming his father's crown and the rights of the disinherited lords. He ended the catspaw of Plantagenet imperialism, and sold Scotland for a pension at the last.

The Gallovidians shared his own disillusion. Edward Baliol had been in their eyes the rightful king, and their 'special lord', but they do not seem to have romanticised him in retrospect. They wanted no more adventures with predatory English kings. Galloway had no future henceforward but within the kingdom of Scots. Yet integration seemed far away. The Scots felt betrayed by the Gallovidians' support of Baliol; and the Gallovidians could not forget that it was the Scots who had burned their homes and killed their sons, and left them short of food winter after winter. Of all the damage done by the war, the pestilence and the famine, that mutual rancour seemed to be the wound that would be hardest to heal.

Illuminated MS: English archers training (British Library)

8

INTEGRATION:

The Pilgrims' Way
(1356–1513)

Than sad he: 'Sir, I consel yow
To Sancte Niniane yet ye awou,
In gud intent and hart meke
Ye faste his faste, and hyme seke . . .
For as a lantern he wes lycht,
That in myrknes giffis men sycht'.

Legend of St Ninian[1]

Towards the end of the fourteenth century the Cumbrian abbey of Holm Cultram leased away their profitable sheep walks in Kirkgunzeon and adjoining parishes. They had held them for over 200 years, managing them with successive groups of monks from Holm, one of whom had served the parish church of Kirkgunzeon. Now however they were finding their task increasingly difficult if not dangerous, on account of a new local hostility arising from the wars; for as they said in a petition to the Pope: 'Englishmen cannot dwell in Scotland'.[2]

Edward Baliol's withdrawal had not ended the wars between the Scots and the English. David II was ransomed from captivity in 1357; but sporadic warfare continued, and some of the strategic strongholds of southern Scotland such as Berwick and Lochmaben castles remained in English hands — Lochmaben until 1384, and Berwick much longer. The military action moved eastward, away from Galloway. A second epidemic of plague scourged Dumfries and its environs in 1362, and less serious outbreaks continued at intervals. Aldebrough and Baliol's few remaining English supporters departed, and Galloway, stricken and exhausted, was no longer disposed to cooperate with the English.

THE DOUGLASES

Intent upon establishing effective control in the south-west, David II granted the lands between the Nith and the Cree to Archibald, Earl of Douglas in 1369. The Douglases were among his wealthiest and most powerful supporters, and he extended the scope of the grant three years later when Archibald purchased the earldom of Wigtown from Thomas Fleming. The king made Douglas lord of Galloway. Galloway thereby became unquestionably Scottish in name, though it continued to be effectively hived off from royal administration. The Douglases ruled the province with the semi-regal jurisdiction then normally conferred by a 'regality'.[3] Whether they had the legal right to do so was never clear, as David II's grant is not extant. The matter became one of the many causes of friction between the crown and the Douglases during their 80-odd years of rule.

The war and the epidemic of 1362 had left the countryside impoverished and partially depopulated. The hunting reserve in the Glenken changed hands more than once, and the Glenken ceased to be a rural deanery.[4] Reconstruction and repair was very slow. The Douglases left little more documentation than the Baliols had done, for similar reasons. Their excessive power and the mounting hostility between the Douglases and the Scottish royal house brought them to ruin in 1455. James II bombarded Threave Castle and annexed their Galloway estates to the crown in the general forfeiture of the Douglas lands. Their domestic and estate papers apparently perished in the fire and panic of their downfall. In consequence most of the documentation for 80 years of Galloway's history is missing.

A few precious documents survive. A rental of the demesne estate of Buittle when under the control of the Douglases of Dalkeith and Morton — covers the years 1376–8 and gives a useful glimpse of the farming and financial transactions of the peasantry and bonnet lairds, and a hint of a reduced acreage in cultivation.[5] The dearth of records otherwise has been remedied somewhat in the last 40 years by papal correspondence transcribed from the Vatican archives. Vignettes of a ruined countryside and semi-derelict towns have come to light, and a rather more idiosyncratic portrait of the third Earl of Douglas, Archibald the Grim.

He was illegitimate; but this had not prevented his purchase of the earldom. As lord of Galloway, he built for himself the great tower house and stronghold of Threave on an island in the river Dee, guarding the entrance to the Glenken and the flood plain of the river at Balmaghie. Archibald figures in papal correspondence as a magnate of great wealth and power, as the 'most devoted and eldest son of the Pope in Scotland'.[6] He knew how to win this accolade. In 1378 he petitioned for papal authority to build a poor hospital in the vicinity of the ancient monastic site at Dercungal or Holywood in Nithsdale:

Whereas in the realm of Scotland on the borders between it and England, and in the territory of the Earl of Douglas and Mar, there are places anciently dedicated to the service of Christ's poor, as poor hospitals, and lazar houses and the like, which were endowed by their founders, and are now rendered uninhabitable by wars, the said Earl purposes to restore the same to usefulness, and to maintain them and cultivate their lands and to defend them against the enemies of the realm, for the poor pilgrims who frequently visit the monastery [Holywood], encountering great difficulty because of the depopulation along the borders between England and Scotland.[7]

Threave Castle, as it was in 1812. This was the stronghold built by Archibald the Grim. He died there in 1400 (EL)

In 1389 Archibald embarked on a much more ambitious endowment within a mile of the same site at Lincluden. The nunnery founded in the twelfth century had suffered severely during the wars, and always small, it was now reduced to a handful of nuns eking out an impoverished existence. It was a splendid opportunity for Archibald to show his benevolence, and so he did. For he endowed a collegiate church, a new and fashionable form of ecclesiastical community, with resident canons serving surrounding parishes. The poor hospital a mile away was to be incorporated into the foundation. The old nunnery was of course an obstacle to this lavish endowment, and had to be swept away. Archibald therefore petitioned the Pope in the following terms:

> these women [the nuns] have now taken to leading dissolute and scandalous lives, allowing the beautiful monastic buildings to fall into disrepair and ruin through neglect, while they dress their daughters, born in incest, in sumptuous clothes with gold ornaments and pearls. The number of nuns including the prioress is reduced to four and they neglect the observance of the day and night offices, devoting their time to the spinning of wool . . . The local neighbours, who are very evil men, repair to the monastery in order to defend themselves from the enemies of Scotland, being situated on the borders, or to a house about a mile distant from it, where they hold a market and even commit incest.[8]

The earl petitioned that the nuns should be transferred 'to some other nunnery'. They had no defence against his ruthless slander, and so were hustled out

of history in disgrace. The two records just quoted illustrate the derelict condition of the countryside and the collapse of law and order as much as they reflect
upon the character of Archibald the Grim. He died in 1400, and although he had
undoubtedly boosted the morale of eastern Galloway by the endowments at
Lincluden and Holywood, it was not until after his death that the bishops of
Whithorn (mainly absentees since the mid-fourteenth century) once more took
up permanent residence in Galloway, and the repair of churches and towns made
progress.

The earls of Douglas who succeeded Archibald were somewhat faceless — rich,
powerful and for the most part vicious. Only six of them (and a Countess) were
actually lords of Galloway. Five out of nine met violent deaths: the second and
fourth in battle; the sixth, seventh, and eighth were murdered. Of the remainder,
the fifth was imprisoned by James I for plotting and the ninth was dispossessed
for treason. Those earls who ruled Galloway at all, apart from Archibald the Grim,
appear to have done so as absentees.

The frequent changes in the lord of Galloway these figures entailed may explain
the slow progress made towards the reconstruction of Galloway society under
their rule. In 1393 Soulseat Abbey was described in a letter of Pope Clement VII
as 'in a ruinous and collapsed condition on account of wars in those parts'.[9] In 1408
a letter to the Pope from the Bishop of Whithorn which was quoted in the Pope's
reply, referred to several empty and derelict houses in the main street of the cathedral town of Whithorn. In another of the same date the cathedral itself was
described:

> the structure of the church of Whithorn in which the body of the blessed Ninian
> is enshrined, and to which people are wont to resort in great multitudes because
> of the miracles that God . . . frequently performs there . . . is unsound, mean and
> old, beyond what is fitting for such a church.[10]

As late as 1428 comes a haunting description of a deserted village, its parish
church falling into disrepair. The rector of St John's Town of Dalry in the
Glenken, John Beton, took the only means available to him to raise public funds
for the repair of his church. He petitioned the Pope to allow indulgences to people
contributing to a reparation fund. His petition described the church:

> which is situated in the woods, far from the habitation of other Christian faith-
> ful and among fierce men ill-versed in the faith, is on account of its antiquity so
> badly collapsed in its structures, roof, and other buildings that unless it is speed-
> ily succoured . . . it may suffer ruin and fall to the ground.[11]

The longest term of constant and conscientious government was provided by
Margaret, Countess of Douglas and Duchesse de Touraine, the widow of the
fourth earl, between 1426 and 1449. She was the daughter of Robert III and elder
sister of James I, who made her lady of Galloway in her widowhood in 1426. The
grant was 'for life' but it was not 'in regality'; and so long as Margaret ruled
Galloway and James I Scotland, her charters were referred to him for confirma-

Ruins of Lincluden Collegiate church established by Archibald the Grim, Earl of Douglas (EL)

tion, and the province was brought more directly under the crown. It is perhaps significant that the papal letters just quoted dated from her time. Her path as ruler of Galloway had been smoothed in the preceding 20 years by the rehabilitation of the bishopric of Whithorn after the appointment of Bishop Eliseus in 1406.

THE BISHOPS OF WHITHORN

One of the most serious casualties of the wars had been the effect on the bishops of Whithorn, whose allegiance to the archbishops of York became a source of embarrassment both to the bishops personally and to the Gallovidian church. The late fourteenth century saw the growth in Scotland of a strong nationalistic feeling, reflected in the literature of the time, and especially in the historical writings of Wyntoun, Fordun and others.[12] In this atmosphere the need to integrate Galloway into Scottish culture placed the bishops of Whithorn in an acute dilemma. If Englishmen could not dwell in Scotland (and Galloway was by now unquestionably part of Scotland) what was to be the standing of bishops deriving their authority from the Province of York?

The problem was compounded so long as the rest of the Scottish church supported the Pope in Avignon, while the archbishop of York and the English episcopacy recognised the pontiff in Rome. So long as Scotland owed loyalty to one Pope and England to the other, it was inevitably the bishopric of Whithorn that took the strain. The result was that several bishops of Whithorn became absentees. Edward Baliol's bishop, Michael Mackenlagh died in 1358, and it is doubtful whether his successor, Bishop Thomas Macdowel, or his, Bishop Adam de Lanark, ever exercised their office at Whithorn or resided in Galloway. In 1388 Bishop Oswald of Whithorn, whose appointment had the sanction of Pope Urban VII (in Rome) fled across the English border and sought the protection of King Richard II because he was 'in danger of his life'.[13] Oswald finished his days as a supernumerary suffragen at York, while Bishop Thomas de Rossy, a polemicist for Avignon, also held office as Bishop of Whithorn until 1406. For 18 years (1388–1406) two bishops claimed the see of Whithorn. What effective service either was able to render the diocese is not known. The neglected state of the cathedral and town of Whithorn, and the parish church of Dalry, speak for themselves.

Bishop Eliseus was elected in 1406, and two of his petitions to the Pope in Avignon have already been quoted. Another referred to the absence of a bishop's residence in Whithorn. It was evident that the bishop was confronted by difficulties, including the hostility of the prior of Whithorn who would not offer him one of the derelict houses in the town within his gift. Eliseus moved into the old Bishop's Palace at Clary in Penninghame, and got to work. He was resident, active and determined to put the diocese in order.

MARGARET OF TOURAINE

By the time Margaret of Touraine became lady of Galloway in 1426 the papal schism was at an end, and at the same time the impossibility of Whithorn's continued adherence to York was tacitly recognised. So it was on an incoming tide that Margaret of Touraine took the helm, and she seems to have done her best to steer the province towards recovery. Most of her extant charters are preserved in royal confirmations enacted by her brother James I.[14] Her patronage of the lesser nobility conformed with James's own policies. At the same time they show a strong attachment to family loyalties and interests, for example by the confidence and power Margaret vested in William Douglas of Leswalt 'her esquire' and Sheriff of Wigtown. He was a somewhat obscure member of the Douglas family, but a Douglas nonetheless. Margaret also granted the lands of Kirkennan which had been part of the old barony of Buittle to her own kinsman, Alexander Stewart of Girthon; and confirmed the ancient endowment of Glenluce Abbey.

It is inevitable that comparisons should be drawn between Margaret of Touraine and Dervorgilla de Baliol. Margaret ruled Galloway for 23 years, Dervorgilla for 21, but there their similarity ends. Margaret did not command anything like Dervorgilla's wealth. Nor had she the devotion of local people, the legacy of her ancestors the native princes. Her position was always over-shadowed by the earls of Douglas, so that it was worth no aspiring chronicler's while to idealise her. The romantic aura that surrounds Dervorgilla's name did not gather round Margaret's. It is tempting to say that she had scarcely been noticed by Scottish chroniclers. Her grand-daughter and namesake, Margaret Douglas, had the mis-

Margaret of Touraine's seal, discovered during the excavation of Threave Castle, 1974–8 (Historic Scotland)

fortune to be married off before she was 12 to her cousin the eighth Earl of Douglas, and after his death to his brother, the ninth. By some obscure law of compensation, evidently, she has been endowed by posterity with the title of Fair Maid of Galloway and a reputation for beauty. She was the last of the direct line of the Black Douglases, but the extent of her inheritance and her jurisdiction over the province is undocumented.[15]

Margaret of Touraine was a contemporary of Joan of Arc and Dame Julian of Norwich thus implying further comparisons, which are perhaps doubly unfair. But these visionaries throw into relief an ordinary woman, a dutiful royal lady called upon to take great responsibilities and managing reasonably well in an age of violence and vice. In the service of Galloway she seems to have outshone most of her more affluent male kinsmen. Her sole endowments were a chapel within the cathedral church of Whithorn and one in the collegiate church of Lincluden. At Lincluden the elegant tomb blazoned with heraldic arms with true Douglas ostentation, contains her bones. The arms imply that the tomb was intended also to enshrine her husband who was killed and buried in France, and it may have been built at his command. The chapel however was hers, and she endowed a chaplain to pray for her husband's soul with lands 'purchased with her own silver and gold'.[16] Her seal was recovered from Threave Castle, when the site was excavated in 1974–8 (see page 173).[17] These remains and a handful of charters, are all that is known of her. The names of her successive men of business survive: Sir John Betoun the Rector of Dalry and Archdeacon of Whithorn was her 'familiar clerk'. Sir Gilbert Caven who held the parish churches of Kirkbean and Kirkinner was her chaplain, and tutor to her first-born, Archibald. Her secretary was Sir Gilbert Park. These men must have contributed significantly to her administration and estate management; and it reflects Margaret's own limited influence beyond Galloway's borders, that none of them was rewarded with a bishopric.

When these scraps of evidence have been put together, Margaret of Touraine is revealed as a steadfast and somewhat tragic figure. She lived in a family atmosphere of corruption and lawlessness. The almost incestuous power struggle between the Stewart kings and the earls of Douglas which characterised her lifetime, placed her, a Stewart by birth and a Douglas by marriage, at the centre of a particularly brutal drama. Her role was to carry on business as usual against a back-drop of violent death. Her husband, son and son-in-law were all killed in one battle. Her brother King James I, to whom she was loyal, eventually imprisoned her surviving son, the fifth earl. Later he died of plague. King James himself was murdered (1437), and Margaret's two grandsons done to death at a banquet in Edinburgh (1440). Mercifully, perhaps it was not until after her death that one nephew, the eighth earl, was stabbed to death by another nephew, James II.

In 1439 famine and plague hit Dumfries and was almost certain to have affected the countryside to the west. The disaster was chronicled in the Scottish vernacular:

the samyn tyme thar was in Scotland a gret dirth for the boll of quweit was at xl schillings and verraly the derthe was as gret that thar diet [died] a passinge [great number] of peple for hunger. And als the land ill, the waime [stomach] ill was so violent, that thai diet ma that yer than evir diet ouder in pestilens or yet in only uthir seiknes in Scotland. And that samyn yer the pestilens come into Scotland and began at Drumfres, and it was callit the pestilens bot mercy, for thai that tuke it nain ever recoverit, bot thai deit within xxiv houris.[18]

The chronicler stressed the famine came first but he may have been confused if he was not in Dumfries at the time. In a subsistence economy famine was usually a consequence of epidemic if the sickness reduced manpower at seedtime or harvest. How severely Galloway was affected is not recorded, but the setback may

*Tomb of Margaret
Duchesse de Touraine at
Lincluden (EL)*

have been one of the factors that made recovery from the fourteenth-century wars and devastation so slow.

In 1448 the sporadic border warfare between the English and the Scots swung westward, and the English burned Dumfries. This may have given the seventh earl a pretext to put pressure on Margaret, now elderly, to surrender the lordship of Galloway to him, although it had been granted to her for life. She was certainly in her sixties by then and perhaps more. She had married before 1400 — the *Scots Peerage* says before 1390.[18] Neither she nor her son the fifth earl had received any revenue from the Duchy of Touraine, and her petition for a widow's portion was now refused. The next year she gave up her dominion of Galloway. She died in 1450. Five years later the great bombard (one of Scotland's first pieces of artillery) was trained on Threave Castle, and the estates of the earls of Douglas were annexed to the crown. Their rule of Galloway was at an end.

The end of Douglas rule brought Galloway once more under royal control. The king's justice was dispensed and royal customs collected. Within a generation the royal assize, which came all too rarely to the south-west to enforce law and order, was supplemented by the itinerant courts of the Lords of Council and the Lords

Auditors of Causes and Complaints. Breaches of the peace, family feuding, and civil debt were alike brought before them. The penalties exacted were not harsh, though they extended to imprisonment and distraint of goods for serious and repeated offences.[19] The erstwhile demesne estates of the Douglases when lords of Galloway were administered by successive local magnates in the king's name. Though policy varied and standards occasionally slipped, there was a serious attempt at fair treatment for the small 'kindly' (customary) tenants, and cases of hardship were accommodated. For example, a tenant's rent was remitted because he had many sons, and the Chamberlain recorded that he had visited the house and seen the boys. Ascending the social scale, the widowed Lady Monypenny, in severe financial difficulties, was allowed to surrender temporarily leases she could not pay for.[20] How this relatively benign regime compared with the Douglas administration is not known.

THE DOUGLASES: A POSTSCRIPT

In 1473 a grant by Roger, Prior of Whithorn was confirmed by the crown. It conveyed an annuity to one of the canons of Whithorn, William Douglas 'for his pure life, his good counsel, and his honorable service'. The annuity consisted of the rents from the priory's estates, which were the erstwhile demesne lands of Cruggleton Castle and associated lands, amounting to 40 merks, equivalent to the annual income of the prior.[21] What had Canon William (whose vows included poverty) done to explain this generous endowment of worldly goods? Documents of 1447 and 1450 reveal that he was then himself prior of Whithorn.[22] In 1450 indeed, the eighth Earl of Douglas had successfully petitioned the Pope on his behalf that he and his successors should be privileged to wear the white mitre without gems. The priors of Whithorn must have coveted this quasi-episcopal dignity, at any rate ever since 1398 when it had been granted to the abbots of Dundrennan.[23]

Evidently William Douglas as prior had enjoyed some distinction, but by 1473 he had reverted to the status of an ordinary canon, with compensation for loss of office. It could be said that according to his own standards William had furthered the interests of the priory. Not only had he acquired the right to wear the mitre for all the priors coming after him, he had obtained confirmation of the prior's position as superior of the burgh of Whithorn.[24] He had moreover fought the good fight against the Abbot of Dundrennan in a dispute over the lands of Bysbie.[25]

His deposition was explained in 1466. The Pope wrote to the Bishop of Whithorn, the Abbot of Soulseat and the Archdeacon of Galloway, the three chief authorities in the diocese of Whithorn apart from the prior himself. The letter commanded them to enquire into accusations made against Prior William by the Provost of the Collegiate Church of St Bothans, Fergus Macdowell. Macdowell was of course a Gallovidian, and had been a canon of Soulseat, the mother-house of the priory of Whithorn. He was keenly interested in Whithorn's affairs. He was also secretary to King James III, and so equal to challenging Prior

Mitred figure from the margins of the Herdmanstone MS (National Library of Scotland)

William. His allegations were that the prior 'has committed fornication with his married sister-in-law, has committed simony [bribery], and had delapidated and committed to his own damnable uses a number of precious movable and immoveable goods belonging to the priorship'. The Pope directed that if Fergus accused the prior before the bishop, abbot and archdeacon, they should deprive him of office.

Evidently they did so. What their enquiry had uncovered is not recorded, but in 1467 the Pope granted plenary remission (which implied guilt on at least some of the charges) for both William and his brother canon and presumably his natural brother, Simon Douglas.[26] Fergus Macdowell may have held the office of prior for a short time, but the document of 1473 shows Prior Roger in office, thanking ex-prior William for his services and apparently compensating him. The fact remained that he had been deprived. The deprivation of the rank of prior and the compensation seem contradictory, to say nothing of the white-washing tribute to William's 'pure life, good counsel, and honorable service'.

The conclusion may be drawn at this point that William Douglas was no obscure member of the Douglas family, but nothing definite can be discovered as to his identity until papal correspondence of some 20 years earlier is consulted. In 1437 a petition was made to the Pope on behalf of a young canon of the Premonstratensian Order at Candida Casa 'being in his probationary year and only twenty years old, that he should be elected to abbatial dignities' — dignities such as being prior of the distinguished monastery he had just entered as a novice![27] This was William Douglas, and dispensation was sought on grounds of his illegitimacy as 'the son of a great and noble unmarried Duke and a married woman'. If William was born in 1417 he must have been the son of the fifth Earl of Douglas (Margaret of Touraine's son) who was of course also the second earl to be Duc de Touraine. The fourth earl had been married before 1400. That is as far as it is possible to unravel the threads of this abuse of power and religious office. William Douglas's exalted office and privileges are explained. Nearly 20 years after the downfall of the ninth Earl of Douglas, his illegitimate kinsman still had sufficient bargaining power to procure for himself a senior churchman's income for life, despite apparent misconduct.[28]

The hushing up of William Douglas's case can be ascribed to the bishop and chapter itself in the interests of the priory. Nobody wanted to advertise that the Prior of Whithorn of over 20 years' standing had been corrupt and possibly unchaste, especially at a time when Whithorn was increasingly esteemed as a holy place by an enlarging public. It was nevertheless a symptom of low morale and disillusion which had struck the priory in William Douglas's youth, that another canon, William Crafurde petitioned the Pope in 1432. His plea was that several years before he had left the priory without permission and had gone to France 'as a vagabond and apostate for about three years and used arms in various engagements in which many were killed'. The young canon was apparently conscious that the use of arms was incompatible with his vows, and pleaded that 'he wishes to return home and serve God in the monastery as far as human frailty permits'.[29]

William Crafurde's story wins a deal more sympathy than the apparently complacent abuses of William Douglas.

It would have taken more than one scandal and William Crafurde's escapade in a worldly age to diminish Whithorn's reputation as a holy place. Whithorn had already been the destination of pilgrims for nearly a thousand years. The successive calamities of the fourteenth century must have diminished numbers, and the pilgrim traffic of that period is mainly unrecorded. Through the worst years of war, epidemic and food scarcity, nevertheless, stories of varying authority tell of royal pilgrims; and from their patronage it may be assumed that other people went also. At the height of Edward I's occupation of Galloway in 1300, a dispatch to the king explains the Prince of Wales's absence from headquarters with 'My lord your son had gone to St Ringan's on pilgrimage'.[30] Robert Bruce's pilgrimage in his last year of life (1328) has already been related; and there was a story that David II was eventually relieved after years of pain from the arrowhead lodged in his flesh years before at the battle of Neville's Cross. This operation was performed, miraculously it is claimed, at Whithorn where he had gone for healing.[31]

ST NINIAN

As life gradually returned to normal after the worst of the Anglo-Scottish wars, the reputation of Whithorn as a cult centre rose to a climax. The Knights of St John established hostels (called hospitals without any implication of treatment, merely hospitality) for pilgrims along the main routes. Some of these are documented and some traceable at bridges and cross-roads from the place-name 'Spital'. An affluently endowed Chapel of St Ninian was established on the route through Ayrshire in the parish of Colmonell near the castle of Ardstinchar where in 1467 funds were needed for the repair of its buildings, and 'the better supply of its books, chalices, and other ecclesiastical ornaments'. Indulgences were offered to subscribers.[32] The village of Myrton in Glasserton was elevated to the status of a free burgh in 1504 'for the convenience of lieges and pilgrims making pilgrimage to St Ninian at Whithorn'.[33]

The chapel at the harbour at the Isle of Whithorn where pilgrims arriving by sea began the last stage of their journey, had been built in the thirteenth century, perhaps on older foundations. Shrines to local saints punctuated the road northward from the Mull, at this period in the care of the Knights of St John. The port and burgh of Wigtown, the last stopping place on the road grew prosperous not only from its sea-borne trade, but from the pilgrims who flocked there in the summer season for lodgings and refreshment on the way. The prosperity of Whithorn itself, and its noisy, crowded streets throbbing with life, is difficult to imagine by anyone visiting that small, quiet town today.

The medieval devotion for the saints derived from the perception that the human body is, in biblical terms, the living temple of the Lord, and that the power of the Holy Spirit is invested in the bodies of holy men and women even after death. The transmission of that power (the medieval word was 'virtue') by touch is as old as the Gospel itself. It was a short step from this to the cult of relics. The resurrection of the departed might find expression, if he or she were truly holy, in the power of his physical remains, or in his simple personal possessions, to convey both psychological and physical health to anyone who touched them. It was only human that in the first generation of Christians anything belonging to Jesus should be treasured — even fragments of the cross. The heroic witness of so many Christians in the early days of Roman persecution built up the concept of the saint and martyr already inspired by the death of apostles and above all St Peter. By the time the Christian church reached Britain, many congregations both in the Mediterranean world and at home centred upon no more than a consecrated burial ground with a 'special tomb' in which an honoured and well-loved church leader was buried. It became the custom to make an aperture in such a tomb where the faithful could insert a hand and touch the relics.

Ailred of Rievaulx puts the point clearly in his Life of St Ninian written in the twelfth century:

> When the most blessed Ninian had been translated into the Heavens, the faith-
> ful people who had loved him in life, frequented with the greatest devotion that
> which seemed to them all that was left of him, namely his most holy relics . . .
> But now this is the end of this book, though not the end of the miracles of St
> Ninian which do not cease to shine forth even into our own times.[34]

The honouring of relics was based on a mystical association of the human body with the Holy Spirit, and an affectionate interpretation of human inter-dependence. Galloway's lesser saints were honoured on many rural sites — wells and springs, hospital crofts, and wayside shrines, and the small thatched parish churches by the shore: St Andrew at Kirkandrews of Senwick and Borgue, St Medan and St Madrun at Kirkmaiden and Kirkmadrine in the Machars and the Rhins, St Cuthbert at Kirkcudbright, and St Malo (Machutus) in the burgh of Wigtown. Over all such lesser lights the figure of St Ninian was dominant — a bright star radiating the light of the Christian faith, which is the life of men. A charming medieval Latin hymn to St Ninian hails him as 'gemma confessorum' — the jewel of all believers, the rose of holiness, and the world's bright lamp.[35] Pilgrims came from a wide catchment area from Scotland, England, Ireland, Man and France. All through the summer they came, but especially after the harvest to celebrate the Feast of St Ninian on 16th September.

All manner of men and women flocked to Whithorn as pilgrims from royalty and nobility, bishops and abbots, to burgesses and peasants, as well as the pedlars, beggars and buskers who were out to exploit them. For many a pilgrimage was a spree, a prolonged day out, the medieval equivalent of the modern holiday. It was a last hope for the maimed and chronic sick, an exaltation of the spirit for the devout, and an act of expiation for the guilty. The courts of justice had the option to require convicted homicides to go on foot to one of the four 'heid sancts of Scotland', of whom one was St Ninian.[36] This recognition of St Ninian by the courts of Scotland represented a notable step forward in the integration of Galloway. The benefits of royal patronage were added.

In 1462 repairs to the cathedral church were once more necessary and King James III, his mother and the prior joined together and sponsored a building fund. They petitioned the Pope that indulgences should be allowed:

> to pilgrims visiting on Palm Sunday, Easter, the Feast of the Nativity of St John the Baptist [Midsummer], Lammas [1st August], and St Ninian's Day [16th September] the church [that is, Whithorn cathedral] to which we and other Christians even in sundry realms and lordships, bear singular devotion.[37]

James III and his consort made pilgrimage to Whithorn, more than once, but their son James IV formed the habit of almost annual, and sometimes more frequent pilgrimages to Whithorn. His regular visits made him a major architect of Galloway's integration into Scotland.

JAMES IV

James was one of the lesser Renaissance princes of Europe but one of the most engaging. He built himself an elegant palace at Linlithgow and another at Holyrood. He imported crimson velvet for his doublets and satin for his queen's dresses. He enjoyed hunting, hawking and jousting. In an Arthurian tournament he played the part of the 'Wylde Knight'. He loved music, and applied himself with zest to languages and the developing sciences. He combined a patently sincere devoutness with an exuberantly pleasure-loving temperament. He always had time to hear a story, a song or watch a juggling act. He had a soft heart for a hard-luck tale. To his old nurse, Alice Turing he could show touching warmth and gratitude. Soon after his accession he granted her and her son James an estate outside Edinburgh:

> for the great constancy, attention, and unwearying care of the king . . . in nursing and bringing him up and watching over his person in his very tender years, and on account of his warm love and very tender affection the king bears her and the aforesaid James.[38]

The shadow-side of so much charm and talent can be glimpsed, not only in James's questionable alignment in the affair of his father's death, and his rather frequent amorous adventures. James appointed his illegitimate son Alexander Stewart to the Archbishopric of St Andrews. The boy was elected at the age of 11, and took up his charge — the highest office in the Scottish church — at 17. In the same year he was given the highest civil office in the state — that of Chancellor.[39] Such abuses were, of course, common enough in the Europe of the time, but they should not be glossed over if a balance is to be kept in our inevitable enthusiasm for James IV.

As a statesman James negotiated peace with England, and sealed it by marrying Margaret Tudor; and only Henry VIII's determined aggression induced him to break it. Those years of peace made possible the reduction of Border raids and local feuding that had become habitual as the result of war. In Galloway it is possible to trace the gradual restoring of the rule of law, and to recognise increasing success, both in the burghs and countryside. The king worked to pacify and unite his kingdom, which he had inherited in a state of civil war. He travelled about his realm as no monarch had done before or since, and knew how to make himself popular.

James's patronage of the arts extended to the new technology. The first printing press in Scotland opened in Edinburgh in 1507 under his royal patent. Its first book, the monumental *Breviary of Aberdeen*, represented a major work of revision and coordination by Bishop Elphinstone of Aberdeen to provide an up-to-date and essentially Scottish order of service. It was to replace the prayer book according to the Sarum use which had served Scotland for centuries. (Galloway had clung to the old York use, and the Western Isles to the service-book of Trondheim.) The new breviary was to unite the church in Scotland. Its Calendar of Saints, with lections narrating the saints' lives based on local legendaries, dropped some of the obscurer local saints, but gave prominence to national ones such as St Columba, St Kentigern and St Ninian. He was accorded the highest honours, with the full nine lections and his Office printed in red signifying a red letter day.[40]

The Lord Treasurer's account, which gives details of the disposal of James IV's casual spending money, has kept alive a portrait of James at his most relaxed, on his pilgrimages to Whithorn. It traces the routes he took — and they were almost always different, via Ayr, or Biggar or Kirkcudbright, for example. Within Galloway's borders the king often stayed at the religious houses: at Glenluce Abbey, the friary at Wigtown or the priory at Whithorn. A favourite stopping place on the way was Tongland Abbey, where the abbot, John Damian was a man after his own heart, given to quasi-scientific experiment, and keenly interested in the possibility of aviation. His most notorious experiment was an attempt to fly from the top of Stirling Castle, as a result of which he sustained some injury and much popular derision.

The most trivial details of the royal journeys are recorded: a coin thrown to the 'dumb cheld that kepit the yet', or the reckoning for 'the aill drunk by the King's hors'. A more substantial gift was handed to 'ane Inglisman that St Ninian kythit a miracle for', and there was a hand-out for the man who carried St Ninian's bell. Between Edinburgh and Biggar in 1508 the royal party was joined by four Italian minstrels who accompanied the king to Whithorn and back again, putting the king's household to a deal of trouble to procure horses for them at every stage.[41]

James became well-known to all classes of people both at Whithorn and in Wigtown, where at the friary he often spent the last night on the way. The witness lists of his few charters made locally show him rubbing shoulders with the parish clergy and landowners, and the burgesses and business people in the towns. These regular informal contacts with his gay, accessible presence could not fail to soften old animosities and attach Gallovidians to the crown. His regular visits brought prosperity, and added to the devotees who poured in each summer to worship at St Ninian's shrine. This was the time when many Scottish churches were dedicated to St Ninian. Chapels and altars in his honour were founded within the cathedrals and collegiate churches in many parts of Scotland. An altar was dedicated to St Ninian in the high kirk of Bruges in Flanders; and a portrait was incorporated in an altarpiece in Copenhagen.[42] Hand-painted *Books of Hours* were produced on the Continent for Scottish great ladies, and were ornamented with miniatures of the saint. A special Mass and other liturgical works were written for him.[43]

After a thousand years, the last major relic of St Ninian — an arm bone — was threatened with disintegration. James IV had it encased in silver, and it was thus preserved for another 300 years, first at Whithorn, and after the Reformation in France, where it was eventually lost in the turmoil of the revolution of 1789.[44] The honours paid to Galloway's own best loved saint by the Scottish church and crown must have contributed towards the reconciliation of Galloway and Scotland. It cannot have failed to blur painful boundaries, the legacy of centuries of hostility, while building up Galloway's prosperity and resurgent pride.

The climax of each royal pilgrimage was a procession through the streets and into the cathedral church, lit by innumerable candles. The bishop with his gilded crosier, accompanied by the mitred prior, led the royal party, then followed the white-clad canons and the chanting choir, and after them nobles, gentry, burgesses and a host of pilgrims. Inside the cathedral the king was led through the outer kirk to the High Altar, to the Lady Chapel, to the Rood Altar and into the crypt. There the tomb and relics — the shrine — was lit by wax candles that were never allowed to fail. In that light the majesty of Scotland was to be seen a suppliant pilgrim, on his knees before Galloway's most ancient bishop and most honoured saint.

It would be false to present this as a happy ending. It was rather a point of rest in an unending story. Had James IV not died in the prime of life at Flodden, and had not half Scotland's natural leaders died with him, the promise of his reign might have come nearer to fulfilment. Instead, Scotland slipped back into weakness under a minority. The growing prosperity fell away, and Galloway and the Borders lapsed into another century of raiding and blood feud.

The Anglo-Norman social revolution had suppressed Galloway's distinctive Brittonic heritage, but it survived in devotion to St Ninian. Without any sleight of hand or claim to the miraculous, that devotion played a significant part in bringing Galloway and Scotland together as one. But the Scottish Reformation outlawed the saints. Pilgrims no longer thronged Whithorn's streets each summer. St Ninian's shrine was swept away, the nave of the old cathedral was used as a reformed parish church, and the rest allowed to fall into decay. To Galloway the Reformation brought conflict between puritan extremism and a bigoted, intolerant establishment. The seventeenth century was darkened by the shooting of tenant farmers on their own doorstones for their faith. The self-same tenantry tortured old women on charges of witchcraft. The folklore recalling that time is

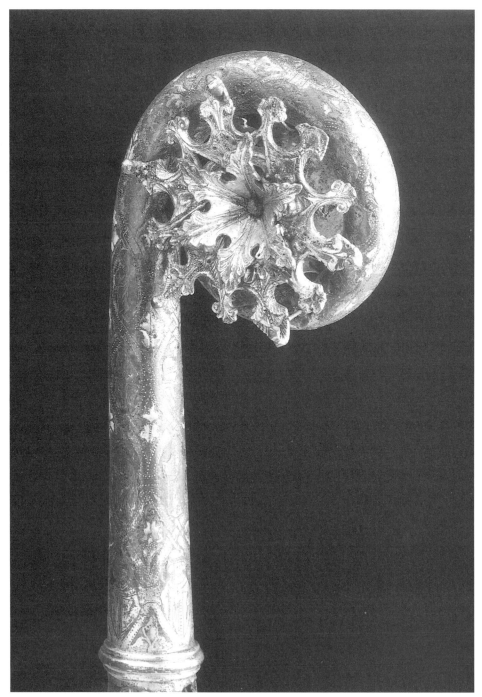

A bronze-gilt bishop's crosier, symbol of care and reconciliation. Found in a grave at Whithorn in the excavation of 1962 (Royal Scottish Museum)

characterised by a guilt-ridden obsession with evil. At the same time extreme protestantism averted its eyes from the unreformed past as papist and too shameful to remember.

By the time that sectarianism had begun to be shamed out of existence, it seemed as if Galloway's pre-Reformation past had been obliterated, even from the hearts and memories of its own people. It has taken time and pains since then to recover Galloway's early Christian and medieval history, and to reveal its uniqueness as a sparkling facet of Scottish identity. Many scholars have joined in the work: historians, place-names people and archaeologists, both professional and amateur, and their number is growing. In recent years the chink of the spade upon bedrock, and the soft scrape-scrape of the archaeologist's leaf, patiently investigating the ancient site of Candida Casa at Whithorn have awakened new appreciation and widened the circle of interested people. It is to be hoped that they, and readers of this book, may find their present enriched as they rediscover the past.

NOTES

PROLOGUE

1 R D Oram and G P Stell (eds): *Galloway: Land and Lordship*. Edinburgh. 1991. (Daphne Brooke: 'Gallgaidhil and Galloway'. pp. 97–116).
2 A L F Rivet and Colin Smith: *The Place-Names of Roman Britain*. London. 1979.
3 Ibid. Glenlochar is almost certainly a rather late Gaelic name — 'gleann luachrach' (valley of the rushes). I am grateful to W F Cormack for the suggestion that Carlingwark Loch may be identified with Loctrebe.
4 Rachel Bromwich: *The Welsh Triads*. 2nd edn. Cardiff. 1978.
5 W J Watson: *History of the Celtic Place-Names of Scotland*. Edinburgh. 1926.

CHAPTER I

1 F H Hoare: *The Western Fathers*. 1960. London, p. 12. (Preface to the 'Life of St Martin'.)
2 Charles Thomas: 'Whithorn's Christian Beginnings'. First Whithorn Lecture. 1992. Professor Thomas first suggested the alternative translation of *sinum*, which implies not a memorial to the dead, but the record of an event.
3 *Gildas* (quoted in Dumville).
4 David Dumville and Michael Lapidge (eds): *Gildas: New Approaches*. Cambridge. 1984.
5 At Llanerfyl in Wales.
6 Rosemary Cramp: 'Early Northumbrian Sculpture'. Jarrow Lecture, 1965.
7 Bede: *History of the English Church and People*. Trans. Leo Sherley-Price. Revised R E Latham, 1955. Penguin Classics.
8 'The Miracles of Bishop Ninian' ('Miracula Nynie Episcopi') trans. by Winifred MacQueen (in John MacQueen: *St Nynia*. Edinburgh. 1991).
9 Ailred of Rievaulx: 'Life of St Ninian'. Trans. Winifred MacQueen. In *St Nynia* above.
10 John MacQueen: *St Nynia*.
11 'Miracula', pp. 10–11.
12 'Miracula', chap. 2.
13 P C Bartrum (ed.): *Early Welsh Genealogical Tracts*. 1966. Cardiff.
14 N K Chadwick: 'St Ninian: A Preliminary Study of Sources'. *TDGNHAS*. 1950.
15 P A Wilson: 'St Ninian and Candida Casa: The literary evidence from Ireland. *TDGNHAS*. 1964.

16 Peter Hill correspondence.

17 Peter Hill: *Whithorn 3* and *4*.

18 Kenneth Jackson: *The Gododdin: the Oldest Scottish Poem*. Edinburgh. 1969.

19 A Haggarty and G Haggarty: 'Rispain Camp'. *TDGNHAS*. 1983.

20 'Life of St Martin' (Hoare).

21 N K Chadwick: 'St Ninian: A Preliminary Study of Sources'. *TDGNHAS*. 1950.

22 E G Bowen: *Saints, Seaways, and Settlements*. Cardiff. 1977.

23 P A Wilson: 'St Ninian and Candida Casa' above, and 'St Ninian: Irish Evidence Further Examined'. *TDGNHAS*. 1969, pp. 140–59.

24 MacQueen: '*St Nynia*' p. 13.

25 A strongly argued case for an opposing view to my own is expressed by Alan Macquarrie: 'The Date of St Ninian's Mission. A Reappraisal'. *Records of the Church History Society*. 23. 1987. pp. 1–25.

26 Kenneth Cameron: 'Eccles in English Place-Names' (in M W Barley and R C P Hansen (eds) *Christianity in Early Britain*. 1968. Leicester); and G W S Barrow: 'The Childhood of Christianity'. *Scottish Studies*. 1983.

27 A A M Duncan: *Scotland: The Making of the Kingdom*. 1975. Edinburgh. pp. 39–40.

28 'the king's barons held it proved that on the day King Alexander caused the chapel to be dedicated' he conferred upon the chaplaincy and upon the landholders on his demesne of Stirling, certain specified rights. (1137–40). Lawrie: *Early Scottish Charters*. 1905.

29 Jocelin of Furness: 'Vita Sancti Kentigerni' (in A P Forbes, *Historians of Scotland*: *The Lives of St Ninian and St Kentigern*. London. 1874.

30 Jocelin of Furness, p. 50.

31 G Macdonald: *The Roman Wall in Scotland*. Oxford. 1934.

32 *Mabinogion:* trans. Jeffrey Gantz, 1976. Penguin Classics, p. 155.

33 The trouble between Ninian and Peibio may not have been personal but may reflect rivalry between the Christian centres, Cadder and Eccles, or between the churches of Strathclyde and the Pictish church at a later period.

34 Mill of Bannoc and Utred Bannoc 1215 (Cambuskenneth Reg), Uchter Bannoc 1261 (Dumfermline Reg), Wester Bannoc 1373–4 (Regesta Magni Sigilli Scottorum — Register of the Great Seal) i 789, and Ochterbannoke 1373–4 RMS i 464).

35 A W Wade-Evans (ed. and trans.) Llifris: 'Life of St Cadog'. *Vitae Sanctorum Brittaniae*. Cardiff. 1944. pp. 24–141.

36 J N G and A Ritchie: *Edinburgh and S E Scotland* (Regional Archaeologies). HMSO 1973. London. (I am grateful to Peter Hill for calling my attention to this.)

37 The commemoration of St Ninian in the upper Clyde valley cannot yet be sufficiently authenticated as earlier than the twelfth or thirteenth century.

38 The argument for St Ninian's mission is given more fully in Daphne Brooke: 'St Ninian and the Southern Picts: Speculations as to Topography and Personnel'. *TDGNHAS*. 1989.

39 The medieval church of Kirkintilloch was dedicated to St Ninian, but whether before the twelfth century is not clear. The place-name was Caerpentulach in the ninth century (Nennius).

40 I should like to thank Professor Charles Thomas who informed me of this by correspondence. He had had it verbatim from the late Marquess of Linlithgow. Mr R McD Seligman (Factor of the Linlithgow estate) very kindly confirmed in writing the existence of the estate map showing Nyniwells Field.

41 The Brockie MS discovered at Ratisbon included what purports to have been the litany of the Culdees of Dunkeld. Although a sixteenth-century compilation, it has perhaps been undervalued, as it appears to contain genuinely early material. See David McRoberts: 'Catalogue of Scottish Medieval Liturgical Books and Fragments'. *Innes Review.* 1953.

42 Research into the cults of local saints in Galloway, Fife and Forfar promises to establish contacts between the Pictish church and Candida Casa prior to the eighth century.

43 Ailred of Rievaulx: 'Life of St Ninian' (trans. Winifred MacQueen).

CHAPTER 2

1 Holy Bible (authorised version) 'Song of Solomon', 2. p. 11–13.

2 A tree-ring date of a timber in one of the Northumbrian buildings is AD 681. The Northumbrian annexation should probably be dated between AD 650 and 670.

3 Bede: *History of the English Church and People*, trans. Leo Sherley-Price and revised R E Latham) 1955. Penguin Classics, p. 127.

4 Michael Alexander (ed.): *Earliest English Poems*. 3rd edn 1991. Penguin Classics. The 'Dream of the Rood' was composed to celebrate the finding of a fragment of the true cross by Pope Sergius I in AD 701. Ceolfrith of Jarrow was in Rome at the time. Part of the poem is inscribed in runes on the Ruthwell Cross.

5 Illustrated on the cover.

6 Lloyd Lane: *The Archaeology of Late Celtic Britain and Ireland*. London. 1975. pp. 33–6.

7 Bede, p. 331.

8 Ibid., p. 304.

9 David Farmer: *Oxford Dictionary of Saints*. 2nd edn. Oxford. 1987. p. 11.

10 Ralegh Radford: 'The Crosses of Hoddam', *TDGNHAS*. 1954.

11 Edward Kylie: 'The English Correspondence of Bishop Boniface'. 1911.

12 A P Forbes: *Kalenders of Scotland*. Edinburgh. 1873.

13 Richard of Hexham: 'History of the Church of Hexham'. Surtees Soc.

14 Peter Hill: *Whithorn 3* and *4*.

15 Eddius Stephanus: 'Life of St Wilfred'. *The Age of Bede*. D H Farmer (ed.), Penguin Classics. 1965.

16 John MacQueen: *St Nynia*. 2nd edn. 1990, pp. 41–2.

17 'Miracula', Chap. 7.

18 Peter Hill: *Whithorn 2*.

19 'Miracula', Chap. 10.

20 Ibid.

21 W M Metcalfe (ed.): *The Legends of St Ninian and St Machar*. Paisley. 1904.

22 J Cameron Peddie: *The Forgotten Talent*. 1961. London and Glasgow.

23 Rex Gardner: 'Miracles of Healing in Anglo-Celtic Northumbria'. *British Medical Journal*, vol. 287. December 1985.

24 A C Lawrie: *Early Scottish Charters prior to 1153*. 1905. Glasgow.

25 Rev. James Bulloch: 'A Whithorn Miracle' (Antiquaria Addenda). *TDGNHAS*. 1953. p. 191.

26 'The Arbuthnot Missal'. (*Proceedings of the Society of Antiquaries for Scotland*, vol. xxvi, 1891–92. p. 89.)

27 Bede, p. 243.
28 'Life of St Wilfred'.
29 I am grateful to Mr R R Stratton, the Assistant Librarian, Worcester Cathedral Library, for identifying the statue in the chantry. I have drawn on D H Farmer: *Oxford Dictionary of Saints* (1987, Oxford) for the life of St Egwin.
30 Daphne Brooke: 'The Northumbrian Settlements in Galloway and Carrick'. *Proceedings of the Society of Antiquaries of Scotland*, 121. 1991.
31 A L Rivet and Colin Smith: *The Place-Names of Roman Britain*. 1979. London. pp. 394–5.
32 At the British Museum. Illustrated in I M Stead: *Celtic Art*. 1985. BM. The find-spot has usually been called Torrs, but a more recent boundary change puts the site on the lands of Ernespie in the parish of Crossmichael. I owe this information to my friend Alistair Penman.
33 W F Manning: *Iron Work in Iron Age Britain*. Brittania. 1973.
34 Reginald of Durham: 'Libellus de Admirandis Beati Cuthberti Virtutibus'. Surtees Soc. 1835.
35 Exchequer Rolls of Scotland (eds) J Stuart and others. Edinburgh 1878–1908, vol. vi.
36 D Whitlock (ed.) *Anglo-Saxon Chronicle*. Revised trans. 1961. London.
37 Kenneth Sisam: 'Cynwulf and his Poetry'. Proceedings of the British Academy. 1932; and David Dumville: 'Textual Archaeology and Northumbrian History subsequent to Bede' (in D M Metcalfe (ed.) 'Coinage in Ninth-Century Northumbria'. *British Archaeological Report*, 180. 1987).
38 Peter Hill: *Whithorn 4*.

CHAPTER 3

1 T Arnold (ed.): 'Symeonis Monachi Opera Omnia', (Rolls Series No. 76). 1882–5.
2 A P Smyth: *Warlords and Holy Men*. 1984. London, p. 191. See also P Holm: 'The Slave Trade of Dublin'. *Peritia*, 5. Journal of the Medieval Academy of Ireland. 1986; and Barbara Crawford: *Scandinavian Scotland*. 1987. Leicester.
3 Peter Hill: *Whithorn 3* and *4*. The year 844 was a year of crisis in the kingdom of Northumbria proper.
4 A P Smyth: *Warlords and Holy Men*. 1984. London.
5 A O Anderson: *Early Sources of Scottish History AD 500–1296*. 1908, reprinted Stamford, 1990.
6 Ibid.
7 The early forms of Glenapp ('Glenop' and variants) appear in RMS ii App. 2.826 and 1242 and unpublished papers at the Scottish Public Record Office (GD 25 i 21; GD 25 i 25; and GD i 59).
8 Lachtalpin is documented in *Regesta Regum Scottorum* ii (see 37 below), the Register of the Great Seal of Scotland (RMS), and the Exchequer Rolls of Scotland (ER).
9 Daphne Brooke: 'Gallgaidhil and Galloway' (Oram and Stell (eds): *Galloway: Land and Lordship*) 1992. Edinburgh.
10 Peter Hill: *Whithorn 4*. The marigold pattern appears in Irish and Visigothic art. E G Bowen: *Saints, Seaways, and Settlements*. 2nd edn. 1976, p. 130.
11 Peter Hill: *Whithorn 4*.
12 Asser: *Life of King Alfred*. Penguin Classics. 1983, p. 83.

13 This was the 'Liber Vitae Ecclesiae Dunelmensis I'. Surtees Soc. No. 156. Durham. 1923.

14 Symeon of Durham.

15 Daphne Brooke: 'Northumbrian Settlements in Galloway and Carrick'. *PSAS*. 1991.

16 The Norse place-names along the Galloway coast have been tentatively dated between 880 and 920 (Gillian Fellows-Jensen: 'Scandinavians in Dumfriesshire and Galloway: the Place-name Evidence': Oram and Stell (eds): *Galloway: Land and Lordship*. 1991, p. 80.

17 J Stuart and others (eds): *Exchequer Rolls of Scotland*. 1878–1908. Edinburgh.

18 Ibid.

19 Joseph Bain (ed.): *Calendar of Documents relating to Scotland*. 1881–8. Edinburgh, vol. ii.

20 Derek Craig: 'Pre-Norman Sculpture in Galloway: Some Territorial Implications' (in *Galloway: Land and Lordship*. 1991). Dr Craig very helpfully allowed me to see his PhD thesis while in preparation.

21 Reginald of Durham: 'Libellus Beati Cuthberti'. Surtees Soc.

22 W F Cormack: *Barhobble Interim Reports*. 1987–90.

23 Daphne Brooke: 'The Deanery of Desnes Cro and the Church of Edingham'. *TDGNHAS*. 1989.

24 The place-name forms of Bysbie come from CDS ii and CPL x. The bishop's petition to the Pope is quoted in 'Papal Letters 1394–1419'. *SHS*. 1976, p. 174.

25 W G Collingwood: 'The Early Crosses of Galloway'. Reprint Series No. 1: produced by the Dumfriesshire and Galloway Natural History and Antiquarian Society and the Whithorn Trust, p. 217.

26 K H Jackson: 'Sources for a Life of St Kentigern', (ed.) Nora Chadwick: *Studies in the Early British Church*. Cambridge. 1958.

27 Relations between the royal houses of Strathclyde, the Scots, and even the leaders of their enemies in the contest for Northumbria — the Hiberno-Norse of York, were complex, and extended to repeated intermarriage. For detailed accounts see: Alfred P Smyth: *Warlords and Holy Men*, 1984, and William Kapelle: *The Norman Conquest of the North*, 1979. London.

28 Richard Oram: 'The Lordship of Galloway 1000–1250'. PhD thesis. 1991. St Andrews University.

29 Daphne Brooke: '"Kirk" — Compound Place-Names in Galloway and Carrick'. *TDGNHAS*. 1983, p. 64. I owe my explanation of 'Manhincon' to the late Professor Kenneth Jackson, who was kind enough to give me his assessment of the original form *'Manhingion' in correspondence.

30 G W S Barrow: *Kingship and Unity, Scotland c. 1000–1306*. 1981. London. pp. 11–12.

31 Leslie Alcock: 'Some Reflections on Early Welsh Society and Economy'. *Welsh History Review*, 2. 1963.

32 John MacQueen: *St Nynia*. pp. 45–47.

33 Notitia of the history of the See of Glasgow and of the Inquisition by David Prince of Cumbria AD 1124 (*Registrum Episcopatum Glasguensis*. Bannatyne and Maitland Clubs. 1875).

34 Daphne Brooke: 'Gallgaidhil and Galloway'. The text was written in 1985. Since then my stance on the 'Gallgaidhil' or the Hiberno-Norse has modified somewhat in the light of the Whithorn Excavation as reported by Dave Pollock: *Whithorn 5*, and my own research into church dedications.

35 Kenneth Jackson: *Language and History in Early Britain*. Edinburgh. 1953.

36 Barbara Crawford: *Scandinavian Scotland.* Leicester, 1987. pp. 100–103.
37 G W S Barrow: *Regesta Regum Scottorum* vol. 2. Edinburgh, 1971. pp. 213–14.
38 Unpublished papers in the Scottish Record Office: Reg Vat 322.
39 The sole authority for Gallovidians in Malcolm III's war-host was Ailred of Rievaulx, writing 50 to 60 years later (Anderson: *Annals*). An incident in the same year (1097) in which Magnus Barelegs invested Man and exacted timber as tribute from the Gallovidians (Anderson: *Early Sources*) supports the possibility that the main force of their fighting men were away from home.
40 Peter Hill: correspondence.

CHAPTER 4

1   Robert Henryson: *The Testament of Cresseid and Other Poems* (selected by Hugh MacDiarmid). Penguin Classics. 1973.
2   A C Lawrie (ed.): *Early Scottish Charters before 1153.* Glasgow. 1905.
3   Ibid.
4   A O Anderson: *Early Sources,* pp. 96 and 228.
5   A C Lawrie.
6   W Dugdale: *Monasticon Anglicanum.* 6 vols. 1846.
7   Richard D Oram: 'The Lordship of Galloway *c.* 1000–1250'. PhD thesis. St Andrews. 1988.
8   Daphne Brooke: 'Fergus of Galloway: Miscellaneous Notes for a Revised Portrait'. *TDGNHAS.* LXVI. 1993.
9   *Foedera, Conventiones, Litterae et Cuiuscunque Generis Acta Publica.* (ed.) T Rymer. Record Commission edition 1815–69. London, vol. i. pp. 107–8.
10 Maud de Senlis was heiress of the Earl Waltheof of Northumbria, and as widow of Simon de Senlis she had possession of the Honour of Huntingdon. (David I did not always respect the rights of her son by Simon de Senlis.)
11 Ailred of Rievaulx who wrote a eulogy of David was specially concerned to exculpate him for the atrocities, and so blamed the Gallovidians.
12 Richard of Hexham (A O Anderson: *Scottish Annals from English Chroniclers*. London. 1908. Republished 1991. Stamford). Northern English writers often called the Gallovidians 'Picts' at this period. It does not seem to have had any ethnic significance.
13 Ibid.
14 William Kapelle: *The Norman Conquest in the North.* Oxford. 1979.
15 G W S Barrow: *Kingship and Unity (Scotland 1000–1306).* London. 1981, p. 38.
16 Anderson: *Annals.*
17 Ailred de Rievaulx: ('De Standardo'), Anderson: *Annals.*
18 Richard of Hexham: Anderson: *Annals*, p. 200.
19 Ailred de Rievaulx: Anderson: *Annals*, p. 202.
20 Roger de Howden: 'Chronica (732–1201)'. W Stubbs (ed.) *Rolls Series.* No. 51. 1868–71.
21 Peter Hill: correspondence.
22 Keith Stringer in the Buchan Lecture 'Lordship, Prestige and Piety: the monastic endowments of the Lords of Galloway circa 1140–1234'. Kirkcudbright. 1992.
23 *Chronicle of Melrose* (facsimile edition), (eds) A O Anderson and others. Edinburgh. 1936.
24 F M Powicke (ed.) Walter Daniel: *Life of Ailred of Rievaulx.* Oxford. 1950.

25 For an alternative view see J G Scott: 'The Origins of Dundrennan and Soulseat Abbeys'. *TDGNHAS*. LXIII. 1988.

26 CDS ii.

27 H J Lawlor (ed.): *St Bernard de Clairvaux: Life of St Malachy*. SPCK. 1920.

28 The Rev. Norbert Backmund: 'The Premonstratensian Order in Scotland'. *Innes Review*. 1953.

29 R C Reid (ed.): *Wigtownshire Charters* (1960) SHS. Edinburgh, pp. xix–xx.

30 D H Farmer: *Oxford Dictionary of Saints*. Oxford. 1987.

31 St Bernard's pursuit of William Fitzherbert was consistent with his implacable victimisation of Peter Abelard.

32 *The Life of Ailred of Rievaulx by Walter Daniel*. F M Powicke (ed.) Nelson's Medieval Texts. 1950.

33 *Chronicle of Melrose* (see A O Anderson: *Early Sources of Scottish History*. London. 1922. Republished Stamford. 1990.

34 *A Scottish Chronicle known as the Chronicle of Holyrood* (ed.) M O Anderson. SHS 1938.

35 G W S Barrow: *The Anglo-Norman Era in Scottish History*. Oxford. 1981. Chap. 2.

36 Barrow: *Kingship and Unity*, p. 38.

37 John of Worcester: Anderson: *Annals*.

38 Jordan de Fantosme: 'Chronique de la Guerre entre les Anglois et les Ecossais' (written before 1183). Anderson: *Annals*.

39 Guillaume le Clerc: Fergus of Galloway (trans.) D D R Owen. Discussed in Chap. 5 below.

40 *Life of Ailred*.

CHAPTER 5

1 Gerald of Wales: *The Journey through Wales, Description of Wales*, ed. Lewis Thorpe. Penguin Classics. 1978, p. 261. Gerald was Welsh by blood, Norman by education. He was writing about 1190.

2 *Regesta Regum I: The Acts of Malcolm IV* (ed.) G W S Barrow. Edinburgh. 1960. p. 253.

3 Gilbert's son Duncan later referred to his own vassal Roger de Scalebroc and a charter by Roger himself refers to Gilbert as 'my lord' (Liber Melrose).

4 Roland is called Lochlann in several early charters. Lochlann is a Norse name, meaning 'stranger'.

5 Catfach was an obscure saint culted in Wales: Molly Miller: *Saints of Gwynedd*. Woodbridge, 1979. p. 32.

6 R C Reid: 'Wigtownshire Charters'. *SHS* 1960, xix–xx n.

7 F Grainger and W G Collingwood: *The Register and Records of Holm Cultram Abbey*. Kendal. 1921. no. 133.

8 *Regesta Regum II: The Acts of William I*, ed. G W S Barrow. Edinburgh. 1960. p. 474.

9 Robert Edgar: *An Introduction to the History of Dumfries*. Dumfries. 1915, republished 1986, pp. 91–2.

10 *Register of Holm Cultram*.

11 D E Easson and I B Cowan: *Medieval Religious Houses of Scotland*. London. 1976. p. 143.

12 The church appeared to be in the hands of a curate when annexed to Holyrood. (see Brooke: 'The Church of Edingham').

13 A O Anderson: *Scottish Annals from English Chroniclers AD 500–1286.* 1908 (republished 1991) p. 253.

14 Roger de Howden: Anderson: *Annals*, p. 256.

15 Benedict of Peterborough: Anderson: *Annals*, p. 256.

16 William de Newburgh: Anderson: *Annals*, p. 257. William calls Gilbert the elder, but the charters make clear that this was not so.

17 Benedict of Peterborough: Anderson: *Annals*, p. 257.

18 I am grateful to my friend Mr Bill Blythe of Blowplain, Balmaclellan, for this information.

19 Benedict of Peterborough: Anderson: *Annals*, p. 257.

20 Anderson: *Early Sources*, p. 260.

21 Snorri Sturluson: 'Heimskringla' (P. Foote (ed.): *Sagas of the Norse Kings*. London. 1961).

22 Anderson: *Early Sources*, p.35 on. I am grateful to Dr Barbara Crawford for calling my attention to this.

23 Benedict of Peterborough: Anderson: *Annals*, p. 263.

24 Ibid, p. 287.

25 Anderson: *Annals*, p. 268. Benedict ends this passage: 'having made his peace he then went home and commanded that all foreigners who had any holding in Galloway through the King of Scotland to go into exile' on pain of capital sentence. This reads like a repetition of the 1174 account.

26 The Cardinal's mission is described in Anderson: *Annals*, p. 269 and *Early Sources*, p. 296. The founding of the Premonstratensian Priory at Whithorn is discussed by Norbert Backhouse: 'The Premonstratensian Order in Scotland'. *Innes Review*, iv. 1953, and Richard Oram: 'In Obedience and Reverence: Whithorn and York *c.* 1128–1250'. *Innes Review*, vol. xlii, no. 2. 1991. The Premonstratensian obituary naming Fergus of Galloway as co-founder with Bishop Christian cannot be reconciled with the date 1177. Fergus died in 1161.

27 Peter Hill: correspondence.

28 Reginald of Durham: 'Vita Godrici Eremitae'. Surtees Soc. 1848.

29 *The Register of Holm Cultram*, charter no. 140.

30 Benedict of Peterborough: Anderson: *Annals*, pp. 286 and 287.

31 Chretien de Troyes: 'Roman de Percival' in *Arthurian Romances*, trans. D D R Owen.

32 Ibid., p. 6285.

33 D D R Owen (trans. and intro.): *Fergus of Galloway*. London. 1991. See also Domenica Legge: 'Some Notes on the Roman de Fergus'. *TDGNHAS*. 1950.

34 Miss Legge suggested that the author was William 'the beloved and familiar clerk' of Alan of Galloway who was sent on a mission to Henry III in 1220. It is just possible that an elderly emissary of 1220 had written the romance in his youth, but the chronology proposed here makes it unlikely.

35 Cruggleton Castle has since crumbled into the sea. One arch remains.

36 There are jibes at the rough clothes of the Welsh in Percival. The parallel with the description of the clothes and armour worn by the Gallovidians in 'Fergus of Galloway' is close.

37 CDS i, no. 2176.

38 'The Owl and the Nightingale', trans. Brian Stone. Penguin Classics. 1971, pp. 213 and 216.

CHAPTER 6

1   *Song of Roland* (trans.) Dorothy L Sayers. Penguin Classics. 1937.
2   Benedict of Peterborough: Anderson: *Annals*, p. 288.
3   'Chronicle of Melrose': Anderson: *Early Sources*, p. 310.
4   A A M Duncan: *Scotland: The Making of the Kingdom*. Edinburgh. 1975, p. 183.
5   'The Great Roll of the Pipe for the 32nd year of Henry II AD 1185–86'. (ed.) J H Round: *Pipe Roll Society*, vol. xxxvi. 1914.
6   Anderson: *Annals*, p. 290. There is no record that Duncan appeared before an English court.
7   Anderson: *Annals*, p. 290.
8   RRS ii, p. 45.
9   The princes of Nithsdale included a Gillepatrick, but his territory could not be confused with Gilbert's.
10 CDS ii, no. 824.
11 The MacCullochs retained estates in the neighbourhood centering upon Myreton as late as the fifteenth century.
12 Stewart Cruden: 'Glenluce Abbey'. *TDGNHAS*. 1951–2.
13 *Regesta Regum II*, p. 293.
14 Ivo de Veteripont held the patronage of the two parish churches of Sorbie between 1185 and 1200 which he granted to Dryburgh Abbey. The motte is described in I F Macleod: 'The Old Place of Sorbie'. *Studies in Grey Galloway 1*. 1969.
15 'Liber Sancte Marie de Melros': Bannatyne Club. 1837.
16 Grant G Simpson and Bruce Simpson: 'Charter Evidence and Distribution of Mottes in Scotland' (in K Stringer (ed.) *Essays on the Nobility of Medieval Scotland*. 1985); and C J Tabraham: 'Norman Settlement in Galloway' (David Breeze (ed.) *Studies in Scottish Antiquity*. Edinburgh. 1984.
17 CDS i, no. 617.
18 The Honour of Huntingdon was the very large estate in the English Midlands which passed in a direct line to Dervorgilla's mother from King David I.
19 George Black: *Surnames of Scotland*. New York. 1946. p. 10.
20 Peter Hill: correspondence.
21 'Chronicle of Man'. Anderson: *Early Sources*, pp. 465–6.
22 K Stringer: 'A New Wife for Alan of Galloway'. *TDGNHAS*. 1972.
23 A J Otway-Ruthven: *History of Medieval Ireland*. London. 1965.
24 W M Hennessy and B MacCarthy: (eds) Annals of Ulster. Dublin 1887–93.
25 G W Dasent: (ed.) 'Haakon's Saga'. Rolls Series. 1894.
26 'Chronicle of Lanercost' and Matthew Paris: *Chronica Majora*: most relevant passages appear in Anderson: *Annals*. The Lanercost chronicler could not resist a dig at the Gallovidians: 'this rough nation eager for wrong-doing'.
27 Robin Frame: *Political Development of the British Isles*. Oxford. 1990.
28 It is confusing that chroniclers sometimes referred to his uncle Thomas, Earl of Atholl, as Thomas of Galloway.
29 Richard Oram: 'In Obedience and Reverence: Whithorn *c.* 1128–*c.* 1250', *Innes Review*, vol. xlii, no 2. 1991. Oram visualises a period when the Kings of England may have exercised this power over Whithorn.
30 Anderson: *Annals*, p. 347.
31 Anderson: *Annals*, p. 348.

32 Black's *Surnames*, p. 309.

33 Matthew Paris: Anderson: *Annals*, pp. 341–2. There is also a reference to this blood pact in Gerald of Wales: *Topography of Ireland*, trans. John O'Meara. Penguin Classics. 1951.

34 This story appears in an account of the sack of Holm Cultram Abbey by the Scots in 1216 (Anderson: *Early Sources*, p. 408).

35 Matthew Paris: Anderson: *Annals*, pp. 343–4.

36 'Chronicle of Melrose': Anderson: *Early Sources*, pp. 500–501.

37 CDS, v.

38 Richard Oram: 'The Lordship of Galloway'. Doctorial thesis, St Andrews University. 1990.

CHAPTER 7

1   *An Anthology of Seventeenth Century Verse* (ed.) John Hayward. London. 1948.

2   CDS ii, no. 616.

3   Geoffrey Stell: 'The Baliol Family and the Great Cause of 1291–2' (in K Stringer (ed.) *Essays on the Nobility of Scotland*). Edinburgh. 1985.

4   CDS i, no. 2414.

5   W Huysshe: *Dervorgilla Lady of Galloway*. Edinburgh. 1913.

6   Ian B Cowan and David Easson: *Medieval Religious Houses of Scotland*. 2nd edn. Edinburgh. 1976.

7   *Calendar of the Laing Charters 854–1837* (ed.) J Anderson. Edinburgh. 1899, p.46.

8   William Langland: *Piers the Plowman*, trans. J F Goodridge. Penguin Classics. 1959. Appendix B: 'the poor in their hovels, overburdened with children, rackrented by landlords. For whatever they save from spinning they spend on rent, or on milk and oatmeal to fill the bellies of their children' etc., p. 260.

9   Register of Archbishop John le Romeyn. Surtees Soc. 128, vol. ii.

10 From the time of the English King Athelstan, Scots kings had sworn fealty when the occasion demanded.

11 R C Reid: 'Edward Baliol': *TDGNHAS*. 1956–7.

12 Edward was handicapped by the lack of troops accustomed to hill fighting. He subsequently employed Welsh forces in Galloway. It was sad how the Celtic peoples — the Welsh, the Irish, the Gallovidians and the Men of Moray — allowed themselves to be used as mercenaries against one another.

13 With a gold circlet hurriedly made for the occasion (CDS ii, no. 1914).

14 CDS iv; and 'Chronica by William Rishanger' (ed.) T H Riley. Rolls Series. 1865.

15 Close Rolls 1296–1302, p. 522.

16 CDS iii, no. 15.

17 Edward Bruce was said to have burned a castle 'on an island in the river Dee' which may have been Burned Island, previously Arsbotl.

18 CDS iii, no. 69.

19 CDS ii, no. 1984.

20 CDS iii, no. 14.

21 CDS iii, no. 83; CDS iii, no. 501; CDS iv, no. 1815; CDS iv, nos. 1360 and 1380.

22 CDS iii, no. 404.

23 CDS iii, no. 1390.

24 G W S Barrow: *Kingship and Unity: Scotland 1000–1306*. London. 1982, pp. 11–12.

25 Names starting with the initial 'a' mainly derived from the Brittonic patronymic corresponding to the Welsh 'ap'.

26 Another document refers to the heads of the kindred (in Welsh 'pencenedl') in Norman French as 'chevetyns des linages'.

27 J Stevenson: *Documents Illustrative of the History of Scotland 1286–1306*. Edinburgh. 1870.

28 Negotiations for a marriage with a de Valois failed to materialise.

29 Baliol was old enough in 1296 to be attached to the Prince of Wales household. He was probably between 12 and 14. That would have made his birth at the latest in 1284. He was at least 72 in 1356.

30 CDS iii, no. 911.

31 C A Ralegh Radford: 'Baliol's Manor House on Hestan Island'. *TDGNHAS*. 1932.

32 The Solway appears to have silted quite dramatically between the sixteenth and early nineteenth centuries. See Sinclair: *Old Statistical Account*. 1793.

33 'Animolle Chronicle' (see Radford).

34 H Bliss: *Calendars of Entries in Papal Registers for Great Britain and Ireland*. 1893, vol. iii.

35 Reid: *Edward Baliol*, p. 63.

36 'Original Chronicle of Andrew Wyntoun'. Scottish Text Society. 1903–14.

37 Daphne Brooke: 'The Glenken 1275–1456'. *TDGNHAS*. 1984.

38 Unpublished document in the Scottish Record Office: RH i i.

39 CDS iv, no. 1462.

40 CDS iii, no. 1591; Rot Scot, i p. 800.

41 Declaration of Arbroath.

42 Ranald Nicholson: Edward III and the Scots. Oxford. 1965.

CHAPTER 8

1 W M Metcalfe (ed.): *The Legends of St Ninian and St Machor*. Paisley. 1904.

2 'Calender of Entries in Papal Registers' (Papal Petitions) i. Edinburgh, p. 576.

3 The king's officers had no authority in a Regality. The lord had his own Officers of State, and his courts had jurisdiction over all cases except treason.

4 Daphne Brooke: 'The Glenken 1275–1456'. *TDGNHAS*. 1984.

5 'Registrum Honoris de Morton' (Bannatyne Club), p. 155.

6 *Calendar of Supplications to Rome 1418–22*, (eds) E R Lindsay and A I Cameron. Edinburgh. 1934.

7 *Calendar of Papal Letters to Scotland of Clement VII of Avignon 1378–94*, (eds) C Burns and A I Dunlop. SHS. 1976.

8 Ibid.

9 Ibid.

10 Ibid.

11 'CSSR 1423–28', (ed.) Annie I Dunlop. Edinburgh. 1956.

12 Johannis de Fordun: *Chronica Gentis Scottorum* (ed.) W F Skene and others (Historians of Scotland). Edinburgh. 1872. Wyntoun: *Oryginal Cronykil of Scotland* (ed.) D Laing. 1872–9. Walter Bower: *Scotichronicon* (ed.) F J H Skene. Historians of Scotland. Edinburgh 1880. J Barbour: *The Brus*. 1375. Scottish Text Society. 1894.

13 Gordon Donaldson: 'The Bishops and Priors of Whithorn'. *TDGNHAS*. 1950.

14 For example: *Registrum Magnum Sigilli*, (eds) J M Thomson and others. Edinburgh. 1882–1914. vol. ii, pp. 12, 86, 87, 133, 255; Wigtownshire Charters (ed.) R C Reid. SHS. Edinburgh. 1960, pp. no. 37; and unpublished papers in the Scottish Record Office: RH6 i. 296; and G10.

15 Sir Balfour Paul: *The Scots Peerage*. Edinburgh. 1904–14. Paul says this lady 'succeeded' in 1444. Not much is known about her. She was apparently heiress to extensive estates in Galloway.

16 *Exchequer Rolls of Scotland* (eds) J Stuart and others. Edinburgh. 1878–1908, vol. viii.

17 George Good and Christopher Tabraham: 'Excavations at Threave Castle'. *Medieval Archaeology*, vol. xxv. 1989.

18 *Bower Cronicle II*, p. 514. See also John Ritchie: 'The Plague in Dumfries'. *TDGNHAS*. 1939.

19 *Acts of the Lords Auditors of Causes and Complaints*, (ed.) T Thomson. Edinburgh. 1839; and *Acts of the Lords of Council in Civil Causes*, (eds) T Thomson and others. Edinburgh. 1839–1918.

20 ER, ix.

21 CPL, vol. ix and xii.

22 CPL, ix and CPL, x.

23 I B Cowan and D I Easson: *Medieval Religious Houses of Scotland*. Edinburgh.1976.

24 RMS, ii. no. 383.

25 CPL, xii.

26 CSSR, 1428–32.

27 CSSR, 1433–47, (ed.) A I Dunlop and David Maclauchlan. Edinburgh. 1933.

28 James IV allowed the erstwhile ninth Earl of Douglas a handsome pension until his death in 1491.

29 CSSR, 1428–32, p. 259.

30 See *Calendar of Documents relating to Scotland* (ed.) J Bain. Edinburgh. 1881, vol. ii. 'Ringan' is a Gaelic form of Ninian, popular at this time.

31 J Major: *History of Greater Britain*. SHS. 1892. The original source was Bower's *Scotichronicon*.

32 CPL, xii.

33 RMS, ii.

34 Ailred of Rievaulx: 'Vita Sancti Niniani' (ed.) A P Forbes: *Lives of St Ninian and St Kentigern*. Historians of Scotland. 1874.

35 'Ave gemma confessorum' quoted in Francis Bond: Dedications and Patron Saints of English Churches. Oxford. 1914.

36 Denis Mackay: 'The Four Heid Pilgrimages of Scotland'. *Innes Review*, xix. 1968.

37 CPL, xii.

38 RMS, ii.

39 Leslie Macfarlane: *William Elphinstone and the Kingdom of Scotland 1413–1514*. Aberdeen. 1985.

40 Norman Macdougall: *James IV*. Edinburgh. 1989.

41 *Accounts of the Lord Treasurer of Scotland 1877–1916*, (eds) T Dickson and J Balfour Paul. Edinburgh.

42 G Hay: 'A Scottish Altarpeice in Copenhagen'. *Innes Review*, vii. 1956.

43 Daphne Brooke: 'The Medieval Cult of St Ninian'. Friends of the Whithorn Trust. 1991.

44 R M Chadwick SJ: 'The Arm of St Ninian'. *TDGNHAS*, 1940–4.

FURTHER READING

This is a list to guide anyone starting out to enlarge his or her knowledge of Roman, early Christian and medieval Galloway. Owing to the scarcity of specialist books, much has to be gathered from general studies of Scotland as a whole; and these are anyway indispensable for a proper understanding of the lesser realm. Many more detailed works, some of them articles in learned journals, are referred to in the notes.

EARLY CHRISTIAN PERIOD (AD 450–850)

Leslie Alcock: *Arthur's Britain*. 1971. Pelican Books. Harmondsworth.

E G Bowen: *Saints, Seaways and Settlements in the Celtic Lands*. 2nd edn 1977. University of Wales Press. Cardiff.

Shepherd Frere: *Brittania: History of Roman Britain*. 3rd edn 1987. Guild Publishing. London.

Peter Hill: *Whithorn and St Ninian*, Whithorn Trust. 1997.

A L F Rivet and Colin Smith: *Place-names of Roman Britain*. 1981. Batsford. London.

Charles Thomas: *Christianity in Roman Britain to AD 500*. 1981. Batsford. London.

W J Watson: *History of the Celtic Place-Names of Scotland*. 1926. 1986 impression, Irish Academic Press. Dublin.

THE EARLY MIDDLE AGES (850–1100)

A O Anderson: *Early Sources of Scottish History AD 500–1286*. 1991 edition. Paul Watkins. Stamford.

A O Anderson: *Scottish Annals in English Chronicles AD 500–1286*. Reprinted 1991. Paul Watkins. Stamford.

Barbara Crawford: *Scandinavian Scotland*. 1987. Leicester University Press.

P McNeill and R Nicholson: Historical Atlas of Scotland *c*. 400–1600. 1975. Atlas Committee of the Conference of Scottish Medievalists. St Andrews.

Alfred P Smyth: *Warlords and Holy Men*. 1984. Edward Arnold. London.

GENERAL: THE HIGH MIDDLE AGES (1100–1513)

George Black: *Surnames of Scotland*. 1945. New York Public Library.

G W S Barrow: *Kingship and Unity*. Scotland 1000–1306. 1981. Edward Arnold. London; *The Kingdom of Scots*. 1975. Edward Arnold. London; *The Anglo-Norman Era in Scotland*. 1980. Oxford University Press; : *Robert Bruce and the Community of the Realm of Scotland*. 1976. Edinburgh University Press.

A A M Duncan: *Scotland: the Making of the Kingdom*. 1975. Oliver and Boyd. Edinburgh.

Alexander Grant: *Scotland: Independence and Nationhood: Scotland 1306–1469*. 1984. Edward Arnold. London.

William E Kapelle: *The Norman Conquest of the North*. 1979. London and University of South Carolina.

Leslie J Macfarlane: *William Elphinstone and the Kingdom of Scotland*. 1985. Aberdeen University Press.

Ranald Nicholson: *Scotland: The Later Middle Ages*. 1974. Mercat Press. Edinburgh; *Edward III and the Scots*. 1965. Oxford University Press.

Norman H Reid: *Scotland in the Reign of Alexander III* (Collected Essays by members of the Conference of Scottish Medieval Research). Edinburgh 1990.

Norman MacDougall: *James III*. 1991. John Donald. Edinburgh; *James IV*. 1989. John Donald. Edinburgh.

Christine McGladdery: *James II*. 1990. John Donald. Edinburgh.

WORKS SPECIFICALLY ON GALLOWAY

There is a body of antiquarian literature which is interesting and strong on local knowledge, but historically it needs to be read with caution. Most of these books were written before many of the sources now in use were available or properly understood. Most assume a hypothetical conquest and rule of Galloway in the early Middle Ages by the Scandinavian Vikings or the Hiberno-Norse called the Gall-gaidhil. A new perspective, based upon primary documentary sources and professional critical techniques has emerged over the past 30 years. Very important is the short collection of studies: *Galloway: Land and Lordship*, eds Richard Oram and Geoffrey Stell. Published in 1991 by the Society of Northern Studies. Edinburgh; and the archaeological reports on the Whithorn Excavation by Peter Hill: *Whithorn: 3*, and *4*, and by Dave Pollock: *Whithorn 5*.

The following specialist studies are also valuable:

W G Collingwood: *The Early Crosses of Galloway*. 1925 (reprinted 1988) Dumfriesshire and Galloway Natural History and Antiquarian Society and the Whithorn Trust. Dumfries.

W Huysshe: *Dervorgilla de Balliol, Lady of Galloway*. 1913. David Douglas. Edinburgh.

John MacQueen: *St Nynia* (2nd edn 1990). Polygon. Edinburgh. This literary and linguistic study represents a different perspective from the historical essay in Chapter 1. Professor MacQueen's second edition contains indispensable translations by Winifred MacQueen of the eighth-century Latin poem the 'Miracles of Nynia the Bishop', and the twelfth-century 'Life of St Ninian' by Ailred of Rievaulx.

D D R Owen: *Fergus of Galloway: Knight of King Arthur*. (Translation of the Norman-French Roman de Fergus). 1991. Everyman. London.

Alistair Penman: *Some Stewartry Sketches*, 2nd edn, 1987. Castle Douglas; More Stewartry Sketches. 2nd edn. 1988; *Some Customs, Folklore, and Superstitions of Galloway*. 1992; all published by Alistair Penman.

R C Reid: *Wigtownshire Charters*. Scottish History Society. 1960 (especially the Introduction) T and A Constable. Edinburgh.

Geoffrey Stell: *Exploring Scotland's Heritage: Dumfries and Galloway*. 1986. HMSO. Edinburgh.

Alan Temperley: *Tales of Galloway*. 1979. Mainstream Publishing. Edinburgh.

Numerous articles in the *Transactions of the Dumfries and Galloway Natural History and Antiquarian Society* (*TDGNHAS*) over the past decade are important, and make rewarding reading. Some older volumes of these *Transactions* contain much that is interesting and useful, especially Atholl Murray's article on 'Crown Lands in Galloway' (1958–9); many articles by the late R C Reid mainly about the feudalisation of Galloway; and the whole 'Whithorn Volume' of 1950. In addition there are some indispensable antiquarian works:

Rev. C A Dick: *Highways and Byways in Galloway and Carrick*. 1916. Macmillan. London.

Robert Edgar: *An Introduction to the History of Dumfries*. 1746 (republished 1915 and 1986). J Maxwell & Sons. Dumfries.

The New Statistical Account of 1845 for Dumfriesshire, Kirkcudbright, and Wigtown. 1845. William Blackwood and Sons. Edinburgh.

Sir John Sinclair: *Statistical Account of Scotland 1791–99*. Republished 1983 with the Kirkcudbrightshire and Wigtownshire returns bound up together in vol. 5. 1983. EP Publishing. East Ardesley, Wakefield.

Andrew Symson: 'A Large Description of Galloway'. 1684 (available as an appendix to W Mackenzie: *History of Galloway*. 1846. Dumfries.)

D R Torrance: *The Maclellans in Galloway*. 1993. Scottish Genealogical Society. Edinburgh.

R. Trotter: *Galloway Gossip*. 1877. Robert Trotter. Chappington, Northumbria.

Two good short monographs of a previous generation are by A H Christie on *Dundrennan Abbey*. 1914. Fraser. Glasgow; and J. Robison: *Kirkcudbright*. 1926. Useful but not wholly reliable is Sir Ernest Maxwell: *Place-Names of Galloway*.

1930. Jackson and Wylie. Glasgow, special edition 1991. GC Books. Wigtown. His other works have the charm of local knowledge and love of place.

Works of value to the historiographer and anyone interested in an earlier interpretation of Galloway's history include:
P H M'Kerlie: *The Lands and their Owners in Galloway.* 3 vols, 1870–9. William Paterson. Edinburgh.
W W Skene: *Celtic Scotland.* 3 vols, 1876.

INDEX